MEDIEVAL MILITARY COMBAT

MEDIEVAL MILITARY COMBAT

Battle Tactics and Fighting Techniques
of the Wars of the Roses

TOM LEWIS

CASEMATE
Oxford & Philadelphia

Published in Great Britain and the United States of America in 2021 by
CASEMATE PUBLISHERS
The Old Music Hall, 106–108 Cowley Road, Oxford OX4 1JE, UK
and
1950 Lawrence Road, Havertown, PA 19083, USA

Copyright 2021 © Tom Lewis

Hardcover Edition: ISBN 978-1-61200-887-5
Digital Edition: ISBN 978-1-61200-888-2

A CIP record for this book is available from the British Library

All rights reserved. No part of this book may be reproduced or transmitted in any form or by any means, electronic or mechanical including photocopying, recording or by any information storage and retrieval system, without permission from the publisher in writing.

Printed and bound in the United Kingdom by TJ Books

For a complete list of Casemate titles, please contact:

CASEMATE PUBLISHERS (UK)
Telephone (01865) 241249
Email: casemate-uk@casematepublishers.co.uk
www.casematepublishers.co.uk

CASEMATE PUBLISHERS (US)
Telephone (610) 853-9131
Fax (610) 853-9146
Email: casemate@casematepublishers.com
www.casematepublishers.com

Front cover image: A re-enactment at the Tewkesbury Medieval Festival. (Antony Stanley/Wikimedia Commons)

Contents

Acknowledgements		vii
Introduction: A Medieval Mystery		1
1	The Wars of the Roses	5
2	The Genesis of Infantry Combat	11
3	The Black Hole of Knowledge Regarding Medieval Combat	21
4	Misunderstanding Medieval Tactics, Armour and Weapons Through Modern Books and Movies	45
5	Armour in the Medieval Period	53
6	The Longbow's Place in Medieval Battle	67
7	The Fight of the Poleaxe Soldier	79
8	How were Medieval Battles Actually Fought?	91
9	Towton as an Example of Medieval Battle	137
10	The Myth of Fatalities in Medieval Battle	161
Conclusion: A New Theory of Medieval Battle		187
Appendix 1: Accounts of the Battle of Towton		193
Appendix 2: Percussive Weapons of the Leeds Armouries Database		199
Appendix 3: Re-enactor Analysis		203
Endnotes		207
Bibliography		229
Index		241

To Keith and Vicki

Acknowledgements

My thanks to Dr Peter Williams for his perceptive comments and fearless advice. I owe much to Peter's encyclopaedic knowledge of battlefields and military history.

Thanks to Chris Allen for his critique in the early stages.

Ric Fallu's forensic eye was most welcome indeed, as were his thoughts on wood techniques in weapons.

Much appreciation to Dr Lloyd Browne, and his comments reflecting the enormous breadth of his reading.

Clinton Bock's honest views were most appreciated.

As always, Ron Lewis's and Kaylene Anderson's comments have been gratefully received.

Sections of this work, discussing modern battlefield behaviour, have appeared in the same author's *Lethality in Combat*. Thanks to Big Sky Publishing for their assent in reproducing them.

Introduction

A Medieval Mystery

Over the past 500 years, there has been a steady measure of analysis of the battles of the Wars of the Roses, in 15th-century Britain. A growth in films and television shows depicting medieval-style battle, including the hugely popular *Game of Thrones*, has brought a new understanding of armour and ancient weapons – although often a flawed one – into the lounges of the world.

There has been some sterling work done in analysing the many battles fought between the two great houses of the time: York and Lancaster. Thanks to the work of such scholars as Andrew Boardman and Robert Hardy, something is known of where and when battles were fought, to a reasonable degree how they were supplied, and the end results. Archaeologists such as Tim Sutherland, Anne Curry and Glenn Foard have revealed the reality of battlefield burial, but also opened up mysteries, for numbers of dead seem to be missing.

Hardy's works especially have opened up the field of the longbow, a weapon that, given the right timing and circumstances, proved a most significant factor on the battlefield – not just in Britain but when the British forayed into Europe – for 300 years. Due to the significant achievements of historians such as Tobias Capwell, it is known how the soldier of the day was armoured against injury, and therefore to some extent how well he could survive as a fighting man on the battlefield.

What is not known is exactly how these battles were fought at a unit and personal level. The basic tactics and dispositions are understood: there were almost always three groups – known as 'battles' – which formed a great line; each of the three was commanded by as capable a captain as was available, with the most prominent, often a King of England, in the centre.

Longbowmen were almost always present. Armoured men-at-arms rode to the fight, but then dismounted and their horses were led to the rear. This was because otherwise the bowmen would shoot the horses down. That is not to say that cavalry were never used, as a sudden surprise shock force to overwhelm foot soldiers before they could react, or being especially useful chasing down the losing side as they fled.

With the plated men to a good degree impervious to arrow fire, the two lines would close. Then they would fight, hand-to-hand, using edged, penetrating and percussive weapons: hammerheads and sharp blades, together with points designed to pierce. Maces, mauls, poleaxes, spears and bills were all backed up by swords and daggers. However, the procedure for carrying out that fighting is not fully understood; it is here that modern authors have glossed over the detail.

It might be that the soldiers fought in a single line. It could also be that they were just two struggling masses, with the best fighters seeking to be the most forward. But this work argues as a hypothesis that the most logical and likely arrangement was two or three lines, with men replacing those in the front line as those soldiers became tired. It will be explored in this work whether the front line stepped back, and how were they commanded to do so. It will also be analysed how the second line went forward to take their place without confusion or the enemy taking advantage. In the press of battle, an apparently minor withdrawal, followed by confusion, could hearten the enemy to seize the moment.

The most damaging and significant weapon of choice for the plated man-at-arms appears to have been the poleaxe. The reasons this weapon appeared on the battlefield will be analysed: was it so superior to the sword or the hand-axe? The use of the mace will be explored too, and that of the bill – a sort of blade on the end of a spear.

The use of the poleaxe seems to have been little studied. But it featured largely, as archaeological and pictorial evidence suggests, with its bladed edge able to be alternated with the percussive hammer on the other side. The spike at the end of the poleaxe indicates it was not only used in an overhand swing, but also as a jabbing and thrusting weapon. The amount of space a soldier needed on either side to avoid hitting his neighbours with his swings will be examined. Exactly how he decided – presumably in a flash during the fight – to rotate its shaft in his hands and use the hammer rather than the axe will also be explored.

The effectiveness of the poleaxe is not fully understood. If two equally skilled soldiers, similarly protected with good plate, took on each other, how long would they have to fight before one gained the upper hand? And presumably the men did not fight in single combat – would three band together, perhaps to take on another group?

Another 'staff weapon' – that is, a pole with a blade – was also present. This was the bill, a development of the agricultural method of pulling fruit from trees. The bill had an edge and a hook, and was useful for stabbing and to a limited extent cutting. Its length meant it was less useful in a sweeping cut, but more practical against people whom a soldier wanted to pull over; it was thus of some use against horsemen to haul them out of the saddle. Soldiers also used spears of a sort; not the lances with which horsed soldiers were armed, but a smaller, simpler spear with a wooden shaft and a metal head.

What of men with swords? Logical analysis and re-enactment – two of the processes used in this book to achieve its findings – suggest that swordsmen were a much lesser factor against blades and points. But the man armed with an edged weapon still had a significant weapon in his hand. How it was used in a melee – the general confused hacking and stabbing that battles usually became – will be examined.

How the bowmen earned their keep while all of this was happening will also be assessed. It is presumed that they did not simply stand and observe matters. Did they function as a sort of light infantry? But if they did, what successes and failures did they have? Lastly, the true nature of the rout at the end of a battle will be assessed. Was it a massacre, as many claim, a riding down of the panicked and fleeing rabble of what had once been an army?

The nature of medieval battlefield recording means that it is not possible to offer a definite answer to any of these questions. Reports of battles were not really interested in such matters: they were more concerned with who won or lost, or sometimes how well 'My Lord of This' had fared – if he had commissioned such an account, we can imagine with what superlatives he would have been described. He would undoubtedly have been the bravest, if not the strongest and the tallest on the field!

Until the coming of the musket and the development of its companion weapon, the pike, this was the scene on many battlefields. It is with answering the questions above, mainly through analysis and reasoning, that this book is concerned, thereby revealing how battles in the Wars of the Roses may have been fought. In its conclusion it reaches five statements, and in doing so sheds new light on medieval military combat.

CHAPTER I

The Wars of the Roses

The Wars of the Roses were one of the most destructive internal conflicts in Britain's history. They basically revolved around who should have command of the kingdom: the House of York or the House of Lancaster. Fought over the years 1455–85, the Wars of the Roses – although only named so years afterwards – were in reality a series of rebellions followed by battles, some indecisive but others instrumental in deciding which faction would rule. Revenge killings often then took place. A period of uneasy peace usually followed, until a dispute attracted sides once more, and then argument would again boil over into armed conflict.

The Wars arose out of argument as to which descendants of King Edward III, of the House of Plantagenet, should rule the kingdom. The Plantagenets had ruled since 1154, with their most famous monarch being Richard I – 'the Lionheart' – but hundreds of years later their Henry VI was a weak ruler had who married Margaret of Anjou, a scheming French princess. The Queen and her Court friends were known as Lancastrians, from Henry of Lancaster's surname. The nobles who opposed the Queen's group were led by Richard, Duke of York – Henry's cousin – also descended from Edward III. They were known as Yorkists.

The various tensions and arguments had arisen from a number of causes, amongst them succession to the throne, the illnesses of Henry – which often seemed like madness – and competition for power. The first battle of St Albans, fought in May 1455 22 miles (35km) north of London, was one of the first major clash between the factions. Richard, Duke of York, and his allies the earls of Salisbury and Warwick from the Neville family, defeated an army commanded by the Duke of Somerset, Edmund Beaufort, who died on the field. King Henry VI was captured, and a subsequent parliament appointed Richard of York as Lord Protector.

Successive battles broke out through the following decades. These fights were often quite small affairs, with armies generally numbering in the low thousands. The struggle tended to be ignored by the general population of the country, who had no real interest in which faction ruled the land. Peasants, however, were often conscripted under the levy system of the time, whereby they were compelled to serve under their local lord. Nevertheless, the local men often did have quite a loyalty to their lord, for he was the source of law and order in their area. Following battles, such levied forces were usually released to return home.

There was no standing English army at the time. The leading figures on both sides commanded local forces with the assistance of the garrisons of their own castles or lands. The cavalry soldiers – who when dismounted become heavy infantry – were made up of men-at-arms: professional soldiers who had trained for combat. To this was added the mass of the troops: levied forces from the local peasantry. To identity their forces on the field, most of these soldiers generally wore a prominent sleeve badge or some such device. Richard Neville, for example, the 16th Earl of Warwick – nicknamed 'the Kingmaker' – used the device of a bear and a ragged staff, while Richard III utilised a white boar.

The Wars of the Roses contain some of the most instructive clashes of the medieval period for those interested in studying how the art of battle was developed. They have three unique characteristics.

First, they were deliberate planned battles. Both sides decided to thrash out their differences. In this way they are very different from a battle resulting from, for example, an English *chevauchée* through France; that is, a raiding progression. The battle of Crecy (1346) is a typical example of the latter. There, the English force was brought to bay by pursuing French cavalry, and almost forced to stand and fight.

Second, both sides contained soldiers who could afford the latest equipment, such as the best armour. These, therefore, were the ultimate warriors of the age, almost archetypal. The battles of the Wars of the

Roses were the medieval equivalent of the German King Tiger tank battling it out with the US Army's M26 Pershing during World War II.

Third, the two sides fighting each other in the Wars of the Roses were extremely highly motivated. It was literally a case of win or die. Executions, particularly of the defeated leaders or any captured personnel who were defined as 'rebels', was the norm. The leader brought to the battle his followers, whose lives were bound up with his good fortune. The soldiers on the two sides would consequently fight to their best.

So here were the best and fittest of the day battling it out. These were professional, well-trained men. There is evidence that medieval commanders were practiced in, and had an interest in, the art of war, and this included the use of missile weapons. One particularly prevalent planning manual, for example, was Vegetius's *Epitome of Military Science*.[1] Vegetius was the first Christian Roman to write on military affairs, and his work became, and remained for centuries, the military bible of Europe,[2] an analysis deriving from the late Roman Empire period. The *Epitome of Military Science* was reprinted and studied widely across the technically accomplished parts of the world – that is, those areas that had printing methodologies and the practice of literacy. Vegetius was so popular, one researcher has found, that over 300 copies have been located; King Edward I owned a copy, and folding, pocket-sized versions were made for use on the battlefield.[3]

Armed might is known to have been an established part of English society. Violent crime was always present, and all over the country there were men living 'outside the law'. Robbery on the highways was common, and travellers were routinely armed with a sword. Ian Mortimer describes solo travellers as a 'walking liability … the principal reason why you might think twice about travelling by road is the danger of attack'.[4] Murder rates were extremely high compared to today. In the mid-1400s they were the highest ever recorded, at 73 deaths per 100,000 of the population annually; in 2010, by comparison, they stood at five deaths per year.[5]

Military might ruled England for hundreds of years, and many men lived by the sword. The invasion of 1066 brought with it the establishment of 'the march', or countrywide lines of Norman castles, and a system of subjugation of the populace by local garrisons with strongholds impervious to assault by anything but specialised sieges. The Marcher Lords – knights of the manor – and all of the trappings of feudal society were governed by soldiers who took armed violence as a very necessary way of life, to be studied; its techniques practiced and often used.

It is logical enough to say that medieval battles were not simply two groups of opposed thinkers turning up to a battlefield site and setting about each other. The junior and senior commanders of the Wars of the Roses fully understood the strategic, tactical and logistical demands of their military situation. There are plenty of accounts of the time which show that battles took place, that soldiers in quantity turned up to fight them and that, logically, they had enough supplies to allow them to travel to the battlefield. What is unknown is how those battles were tactically sustained; how accurate were the numbers of those present, and of those who died; and how battles ended – for, as will be shown, there is room for considerable doubt there too.

Some of what is under discussion here must be surmised; for example, that the sergeants who organised the soldiers in the ranks knew how to control their men on the march – otherwise the soldiers would have arrived both piecemeal and hungry. The sergeants must have also known how to control their men in battle – otherwise battles would have been characterised by mass desertion. What we don't know precisely is how those medieval soldiers were controlled, but modern scholarship is working towards a new understanding. They were not, it is emphasised, the professional soldiers of the Roman legions, but nevertheless they had to fight in a reasonably organised way.

Once a conflict was joined, with both sides either thinking they had a good chance of success or being in a situation where they had to fight to survive, there were routines to be followed. Vegetius instructs in the use of missile weapons, particularly in the case of provoking the enemy to fight:

> The light troops, archers and slingers, provoked the opposition, going in front of the line. If they managed to put the enemy to flight, they pursued. If they came under pressure from the other side's resolve or numbers, they returned to their own men and took up position behind them.[6]

Men generally took their own weapons to battle. They were divided, in very general terms which will be broken down into detail later, into three groups: - billmen' – a generic term describing those who took along a bladed hook weapon on a pole; bowmen, for most men were capable with the longbow; and men-at-arms – plate armour-clad poleaxe - or mace-carrying professional soldiers. This work focuses on the role of the latter of the three groups: the heavy infantry, the most capable forces in the battles of the Wars of the Roses. The combat elements of the force were always followed by a tail formed of the logistics elements: cooks, carters, armourers, farriers and more, plus an element of 'camp followers' – family partners, prostitutes, beggars and so on.

This book focuses primarily on the battle between the two sides at Towton, the biggest action of the Wars of the Roses, chiefly because in terms of combat it is one of the most typical examples of late medieval infantry fighting. When campaigning in Europe (England regarded Normandy as its own property), the English primarily employed the longbow, while the French clung to the outclassed crossbow. While cavalry were often used – Crecy, for example, saw the French cavalry charges cut down by the longbow – infantry combat was more often seen, for example at Poitiers (1356) and Agincourt (1415). The analysis made in this work is therefore useful for understanding any infantry combat where armour and edged and percussive weapons were employed. The way in which these soldiers actually fought has not been studied in precise detail.

The battles between the forces of York and Lancaster were often marked by extreme bitterness, and consequently violence, on both sides. The winning faction would customarily label those defeated as rebels, and executions usually followed, especially amongst the leading figures. Such reprisals led to brooding resentment, which boiled over into a desire for revenge when the next conflict came along.

Although the Yorkists won 65 per cent of the battles, the Lancastrians were the eventual victors at the battle of Bosworth, with the first Tudor monarch, Henry VII, defeating Richard III, who died in combat. Henry cleverly married Elizabeth of York, within months, thus combining the two Houses. He also blended two of the symbols of the sides, the red rose of Lancaster and the white rose of York, into the Tudor Rose. His son

Henry VIII and his children – Edward VI, Mary I and Elizabeth I – were to carry the Tudor reign forward for nearly a hundred years.

The battles of the Wars of the Roses

Date	Name	Victor
22 May 1455	1st St Albans	York
23 September 1459	Blore Heath	York
12 October 1459	Ludford Bridge	Lancaster
10 July 1460	Northampton	York
30 December 1460	Wakefield	Lancaster
2 February 1461	Mortimer's Cross	York
17 February 1461	2nd St Albans	Lancaster
28 March 1461	Ferrybridge	York
29 March 1461	Towton	York
25 April 1464	Hedgeley Moor	York
15 May 1464	Hexham	York
26 July 1469	Edgecote	Lancaster
12 March 1470	Losecote Field	York
14 April 1471	Barnet	York
4 May 1471	Tewkesbury	York
22 August 1485	Bosworth	Lancaster
16 June 1487	Stoke	Lancaster

(Total battles 17; York victories 11; Lancaster victories 6)

CHAPTER 2

The Genesis of Infantry Combat

Pictures of plate-armour-clad soldiers deserve careful inspection. Imagine such a man in action in a medieval battle. He and his poleaxe were the ultimate battlefield combination. His armour made him impervious to attack by arrow, spear, sword or dagger. Even percussive weapons such as a mace or the fearsome poleaxe could be warded off by good plate.

Humans are a very aggressive species. If they weren't, with their soft skins, inability to run very fast and lack of offensive inbuilt weapons such as tusks, they would not have lasted very long. Their lack of skills was compensated for in the main by their superior intelligence, but they also have some additional skills which improved – perhaps prompted by intelligence – their survival prospects. These will be discussed first.

Humans have some intrinsic features that allow them to fight effectively. These include reasonable height: they can see over their physical surroundings a bit better than comparatively low-slung animals such as tigers. It was probably a learnt skill, and may indeed have been prompted by superior intelligence along the lines of, 'If I stand up I can see predators.'

Humans also have an opposable thumb. So do apes and monkeys, but they have a smaller brain. The human thumb makes its owners excellent tool-users; far better than a wolf, for example, which finds it difficult to pick up anything. Tools for combat can include percussive (bashing or pounding) and edged weapons, for example rocks and sharp sticks. These can be fashioned into a variety of types: edged weapons such as swords; pointed weapons such as thrusting spears and tridents which can be used to jab. Having a thumb and fingers, some of these weapons can become missiles, that is, those that are thrown: spears; boomerangs and so on.[1] While apes are known to throw materials, humans have perfected it with the skill of slingmen, spearmen and knife-throwers.

The thumb, palm and fingers combination also give an ability to climb, enabling humans some escape from animals which can speedily pursue but not climb. Many animals have this too, but with humans it is part of the set of advanced skills.

Even so, the human is not that well equipped for fighting. Despite the abilities described above, it would be not much of a fight between a single hungry lion and a human given a spear, club and a small tree. Miss with their weapon, or fail to climb the tree, and the human is toast; or rather, lunch. Even confined to the tree, the human will not last long if a pride of lions decide to wait him out. And a well-thrown stone or primitive spear, or a good blow with a club, will not slow down the lion much unless the human is very lucky.

What makes the human much more effective than this, however, is the brain. Far bigger by percentage of body weight than most species, the brain makes humans into tool-making and wielding creatures; it gives them insight into how to trap and how to fight, and when and where to use both for advantage. The human brain is '7.5 times bigger than the brain of a typical mammal weighing as much as we do'.[2] Apart from tool-making and using, it also gives humans highly advanced communication, which aids teamwork. A group of humans using thinking skills can, with some risk, lure, trap and kill an angry lion.

Humans are also very aggressive, and in addition to this, are familial and tribal creatures. They have fierce loyalty to family members, and beyond that, to their extended family, the tribe. Consequently, in human history, it is common to see humans fighting in packs. How this was done in simple terms is reasonably easy to understand, and furthermore supported by archaeology. Two packs fired their missile weapons at each other, and then – if not deterred by the other side's better results with their missiles – closed for combat with club and edged weapons. Some animals do this too, but only humans have the complete set of pack work; opposable thumb, upright stance and a huge brain.

It is easy to see that there would be some leaders in pack combat. Inevitably, one person would have been possessed of more opinions as to how to win than the others; and if he, say Alexander the Great (or she, with warriors like Boudica), gave voice to those opinions, and in particular if they were successful, he became the leader of the pack, at least as far as combat against other humans went. Such skills might have not been as relevant in hunting, which requires a slightly different skill-set, needing an understanding of wind and scent, animal psychology, terrain and so on, in a way different to human-versus-human aggression. Then again, team sports – rehearsal for warfare in many ways – looked for just such a leader.

So a leader in such fighting might have a few more ideas than simply have his crowd advance towards the other crowd and slug it out. Essentially, of course, that is what happened. Inevitably, given human brains, there would have been some thinking about how best to proceed. For example, if a tribe was heavily outnumbered, then it might avoid combat for the day by simply moving away.

That night, a leader might arrange some scouts to see what the enemy was up to. Observing them heavily drinking whatever the opiate of the times was – mead, grain alcohol or some sort of herb – he might take advantage of their heavy night, falling upon them with surprise early the next morning.

Combat leaders would have found that planning gave results. Rather than have their 100 attack the other 100, with both sides swinging their clubs until one side ran away, perhaps the leader would be best served by having 60 men attack from the enemy's front, with a force of 40 to attack from the side. Flanking manoeuvres were thus born.

One interesting problem is how to endure in such fighting, for as the years passed, it became more useful for soldiers to have two things: heavier weapons and some sort of protection against having their soft skins pierced or crushed. This we might call armour, although the first such protection would have been minimal, given the technologies of the time. The Greeks and Romans perfected techniques for making a type of plate armour – the latter knowing it as *lorica segmentata*, basically metal strips fastened onto leather – but with the collapse of the Roman Empire, this seems to have fallen into disuse.[3] Cloth padding was better than nothing, and indeed armour along these lines did develop extensively in the East. Metal would have been better, but for centuries could not easily be made into some sort of plate; however, leather could. The hides of animals could also be layered. So too might a shield be fashioned: a timber frame covered with more timber and/or leather.

Heavier weapons – a thicker and longer sword, for example – gave better cutting power, combined with some sort of crushing effect as it struck. But the more the soldier was encumbered with weight to carry, the more tired he became, and the less effective his fighting was as his speed became less and fatigue sapped his arms and legs.

Thousands of years ago, combat thinking also developed slowly and steadily in human groupings. The massed force became more effective than the dispersed force. Grouping soldiers together gave both protection and, if organised effectively, a better attacking force as the body of men moved with formidable power through the battlefield. It is not the intent of this work to study the many and varied developments of such thoughts. But two methodologies of group combat are instructive: that of the Greeks and the Romans.

The ancient Greek city-states, preceding the Roman Empire, fought out their battles by means of their soldier-citizens utilising their skills as hoplites. Equipped with a round shield and a stabbing spear, the soldiers were deployed into lines and columns in a pack formation known as a phalanx. This grouping of soldiers faced their enemy, who was similarly equipped, and after some engagement from missile troops, sought to virtually push their foes off the field. Each soldier's shield, slung on his left arm, protected both him and his companion on his left. Consequently, the extreme right of the phalanx was not as well protected, so often the best and most experienced troops were positioned there. Soldiers in the ranks behind the front line pushed gently forward, not so much propelling but supporting those ahead of them. Contact with the enemy featured both stabbing and pushing against their shields. The first army to break and run from the field was pursued; many prisoners were customarily taken, who could be ransomed.

The Romans fought in a formation developed further from the phalanx. Although, like the Greek unit, it changed over the hundreds of years of the Empire, it too consisted of massed soldiers fighting in supporting lines. The Roman soldier had a rectangular shield, offering fewer gaps for the enemies' pointed weapons. It was supported by the left arm. The Romans used throwing spears for initial engagements, but then relied on aggressive combat with their swords.

Rather than a solid mass of fighters, however, the Romans used ranks of soldiers with different levels of experience, to which were matched tasks. The less experienced, the *hastate*, stood at the front, just behind raw, lightly armed *velites*. Behind them were blooded troops, the *principes*, and then *triarii*, rather like experienced sergeants.

The use of the infantry legion in battle was quite complex, evolving from the maniple to the cohort over many years. The maniple was a block of 120 men in 12 files of 10 ranks. It attacked with the pilum, a short spear which could be thrust or thrown, and the gladius, the heavy sword. Groups of maniples were manoeuvred around the battlefield to best advantage.

The later cohort which developed was three times the size of the maniple, so 360 men. By the time of Julius Caesar, the legion was 10 cohorts strong. It was a mix of 3,600 heavy infantry, with lighter infantry added and a cavalry component. Four cohorts were up at the front of an attack, some sources say, with three in another line behind them and another three behind that.

The cavalry guarded the Roman army's flanks on either side. The infantry was grouped in cohorts, with reserves behind. The right wing was considered to be strongest – that was the men's fighting sword side – and therefore this attempted to get around the enemy's left flank, while the centre and left held contact. The enemy centre could then be pressed as it began to be weakened by having to defend to the side as well.[4]

There seems to have been little research carried out on how the Roman battle lines were maintained. Maybe they did not need to be replaced if the battle was short enough. The second and third lines were there in case the first line ran away, to cover a flank if the enemy made a flanking move and to fill gaps. A separate reserve was often maintained to plug gaps. For as this work will show, soldiers wearing protective gear and equipped with manual close-quarter weapons – swords, clubs, stabbing spears and the like – cannot fight indefinitely. They need replacing as they become tired. This is the central study of this book, as manual weapons and armoured soldiers reached their zenith in the late medieval period. What this book is particularly concerned with is a particular period of human pack combat: from around 1380 to 1500. For it seems there is a mystery to solve.

Armour development

It has been mentioned above how layered leather would give some protection from attack. There are four discernible periods of armour development: leather, mail, plate and Kevlar. Leather could be developed in various ways: moulded to useful body-hugging shapes; layered; based on a wooden or metal frame; and treated to give better protection. As metalworking developed, so leather armour could be combined with it to give more usability. Mail and plate then developed consecutively, as will be detailed.

The trouble with all armour, from its beginnings to the present day, is that it restricts movement. Some of this is because of its weight, which as armour improves usually means an increase. The more the soldier has to carry around, the more tired he gets. Armour would not be worn all the time, and often was carried on wagons, but then again many a commander ordered it worn often to increase familiarity, endurance and strength of the wearer. Another disadvantage is that armour slows some of the wearer's movements. With a combination of less speed, less flexibility and less visibility, he is restricted to a degree where his armour is more trouble than it is worth. Perhaps the ultimate example of this is the subject era of this work – the medieval period – where a fully suited, plate-clad soldier might oppose a bowman wearing a quilted jack, metal helmet and little else in the way of protection. The two might be compared to a stegosaurus versus a velociraptor; the armoured, triple-horned lumbering dinosaur with the spiked club tail, pitched against the speedy creature which ran on two legs and had formidable teeth. Which is it better to be in combat in terms of protection or attack effectiveness?

The problem with armour persists in the modern age. Helmets have been found to give up to a 75 per cent improvement against head injuries, and by mid-World War I both sides focused on providing better protection to their soldiers. But even with modern helmets made of Kevlar, there is a trade-off between protection and not being able to see as widely or turn one's head fast. The same applies to body armour. The modern Kevlar jacket with its inserted plates is bulky and tiring enough, but if arm and leg protection are also worn, the modern soldier – as this author found – is slowed to an enormous degree. This is not just tiring; it can also mean slowness in reaction in bringing one's weapons to bear against an attack.

The look of Roman armour is quite well known. The Empire endured for hundreds of years, and there were steady changes, but in general the Roman soldier wore torso protection of a jacket or shirt type arrangement, with strips of metal secured onto it, along with a helmet. Arm and leg protection was lesser, but has been found in archaeological digs and was shown on architectural columns. Helmets look to have been bronze and later iron.

Following the fall of the Roman Empire, the development of more skilled metalwork saw the emergence of the type of armour known as mail; sometimes erroneously called 'chain mail'. This is a tautology, for the structure of mail was in itself a series of metal loops in a chain, linked to another chain to encompass the limb or torso. It was flexible yet strong, and was a major leap forward in protection for the soldier. Good mail can resist a sword cut – a thrust lesser so – and gives good protection against arrows fired from short bows such as those used by the Muslim forces in the Crusades engaged upon by the kingdoms of Western Europe from AD 1095–1291.

The development of the horsed soldier proceeded at a similar pace to that of his more humble companion the infantryman, who walked everywhere. Perhaps the nadir of the horsed cavalry was the domination of the Crusades by the man-at-arms on that medieval tank of the battlefield, the big Western European horse carrying a shield-protected, lance-wielding armoured horseman. Backing up his spear with a big sword, here was the ultimate shock trooper. Few lines could stand against such a thunderbolt of energy, and Richard the Lionheart's troops smashing into the lines of Infidels – as the Crusaders termed their enemies – must have been a sight to see, and a heart-stopping moment to experience.

The unhorsed armoured man, however, was still a component of the battlefield. Essentially this is because infantry are always the ultimate decider: only infantry can take and hold ground, whether it is the Romans taking Gaul or the Soviets storming Hitler's Berlin in 1945. One side of infantry taking the objective is always the decider, while cavalry (and later air forces) come and go, and navies fight from the sea for domination of the land.

But if the lanced charge was a battle-decider, so too did the English order of battle become unhorsed through its own development: the longbow-wielding archer. While the Crusader horseman was the decider of many a Middle Eastern battlefield, back at home the same soldier could become unhorsed both individually and as a battlefield cohort through the development of the longbow. Although their big horses, occasionally carrying some metal protection, could absorb the impact of the short bow and its fired arrow, the tremendous kinetic shock of the longbow shaft was a major factor in changing the cavalryman back to mounted infantry at best.

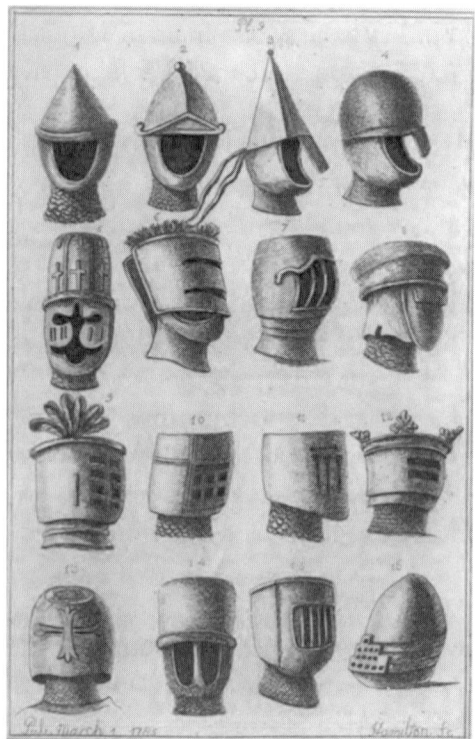

Illustrations of the helmet, from open face to bascinet. (Grose)

Taking a horsed rider into a battlefield within the British Isles, where bowmen were a factor, could become a dangerous course of action. Bowmen might be encountered in strength or in small numbers, but either could be deadly. Where bowmen stood and loosed, there too would be the undoing of the cavalry shock troops. The horse simply could not withstand the tremendous shock of the longbow shaft. Armour pieces were tried, but the entire horse could not be armoured. Time and again it meant that riders had to dismount, ensure their helmets were in place and walk forward into the arrow storm, trusting to their shields and armour, and to closing the enemy soon enough so that the enemy bowmen could not fire for fear of hitting their own. The battle of Stirling Bridge in 1297, for example, saw cavalry negated to the wings, where they might have made a difference save for the large numbers of bowmen and infantry. The first could hold off horsed troops, and the second then attack or retreat to settle the fight. If that battle had been fought 100 years previously in the Crusades, the light bow of the Infidels would not have been a deciding factor. Horsed troops would have been used decisively to smash enemy lines.

So on foot, with cavalry at the rear, attacking someone wearing armour demanded different consideration than the techniques used without it, for example in sword-to-sword combat. If a slash or thrust was largely rendered ineffective (save for the percussive effect) by the armour, then how best to attack? Heavier swords were one answer, and the development of the sword into a weapon that sometimes could be wielded two-handed for extra power has been well documented. This leads us to an examination of the ultimate age of armour and the only weapons capable of dealing with it – the poleaxe and its derivatives, to which a later chapter will be devoted.

The physical effects on infantry fighting against armoured troops

The development of armour had the effect of not only protecting soldiers, but also of lengthening battles. A well-protected man could trade blows for longer. Conversely, as armour got heavier – and these aspects will be discussed in more detail later – to a maximum of around 50 kilograms, and developed in its coverage across the body, it also dictated a converse degrading of a soldier's ability to fight. We might picture this in stages to best understand the concept. Eventually, armour versus weapons reached what in modern terms would be termed a 'tipping point'. As armour got heavier and heavier, and more impervious to weapons, at the same time it would have rendered its wearer unable to move with useful speed. It would reach a point where its wearer was unable to fight.

At this point, the whole concept of wearing armour on the battlefield would have been negated. There would have been no point in having such a soldier present, for he was of no use. It is as if a modern heavy tank, for example the Abrams, reached a point well over its present 60 Imperial tons of being completely impervious to any sort of weapon, but also so slow that it never caught up with a moving battle, or could not turn quickly enough to avoid enemy contact.

The medieval battle almost reached that point in the Wars of the Roses. The man-at-arms was of two basic types: first, the plated wielder of whatever weapons would take down his opponent, who was also plated. This weapon seems from several accounts to have been the poleaxe. The second type of infantry soldier was in two classes: the billman, more lightly armoured and less offensively equipped, specifically with a slashed weapon capable of hooking an opponent and hopefully pulling him to the ground; and the bowman, also offensively equipped, but with a missile weapon – the longbow. All three types wore secondary weapons, usually the sword, but also types of dagger, usually designed to penetrate the gaps between armour plates.

What is of primary interest to this work, however, is how the plated soldier fought. For the problem referred to above had reached its zenith: if the armoured soldier was protected but slow, how did he get around the problem of the weight and difficulties presented by the armour being almost enough to render him useless? He could not fight for long periods of time. So if that was the case, how exactly did the units of men fight in terms of being replaced as they became tired?

That the units of soldiers needed replacing, or swapping around, is proposed in much greater detail later, for this is a central aspect of this book. The usual fighting time for a fully plate armoured fighter with a fully enclosing helmet, using percussive or edged weapons, seems to be around 14 minutes. There are variables such as the temperature on the day, with body heat and dehydration being major limiting factors; fitness levels, training and psychological factors also have some impact. If the replacement of the units or individuals fighting on the front lines was a major factor, how was that done? In essence, how were medieval battles fought?

CHAPTER 3

The Black Hole of Knowledge Regarding Medieval Combat

The actual seconds and minutes of battlefield combat are never described in medieval manuscripts, but in general the hours are. Nevertheless, the actual detail of what went on cannot be found. However, a typical Wars of the Roses battle might run along the lines outlined in the following paragraphs: Firstly, both sides maneuvered to gain the best ground, preferring to be on higher ground than their enemy. A line of retreat was necessary, and it was preferable that both flanks were protected by a land feature. Cliffs, rivers or boggy ground were looked for, but care had to be taken not to have features such as a forest on their flank, which might provide cover for surreptitiously advancing enemy. Then again, they might decide to accept battle with such a feature there, and guard against a flanking attack by investing the forest with their own troops beforehand.

Both sides would survey the ground and the timings. For example, they would not want to arrive at the end of a forced march and have to fight when they got there. If both the possible site for the battle and the amount of time for a fight were suitable, the two sides would hold their ground, overnight if necessary.

Often, however, one side would realize it was being maneuvered into the worst site – there might be ambush concealments for the enemy on the wings, for example – and a commander would make the decision he was being manipulated, and so either not turn up at the potential battleground or march away if already there.

A commander might also realize that his force was being deceived into *not* fighting, even though the ground or timing was suitable. For example, the enemy might gently retreat, and so hold out the temptation of fighting later. But a careful commander might understand, especially if his intelligence sources told him another force was on the way, that this enemy deception was to keep him there until more troops came up, and then he would be heavily outnumbered. In such a situation, a commander would march his troops away, or might choose to force the engagement by a rapid advance.

Sometimes a force had to fight despite realizing its disadvantage. Before the battle of Edgecote, for example, in 1469, the two sides were settling down for the night for a fight likely to be on the morrow, when Humphrey Stafford, the Earl of Devon, withdrew his troops several miles after quarrelling about accommodation. This left his own side gravely weakened with a fight looming.

If, despite all of these caveats, the two sides turned up for battle, they would generally be in three groups. This would be in column of march on the road – the centre and left and right wings, under commanders A, B and C, and sometimes with a Reserve D under a separate commander. The forward section was the place of honour – and also the less dusty – and sometimes this would present a difficulty when turning off the road, as the overall leader, often the monarch, usually commanded the centre in battle.

Hopefully the other side, if both wanted to fight, also appeared, usually in the same formation, and would turn off the road to form up across the potential battlefield. But it was not always the case of a leisurely forming up. If a commander thought he had an advantage by being ready before the other side, or a weakness was sensed, then a cavalry charge might result, in the hope of a quick victory or serious exploitation of the situation. For instance, at the battle of Bosworth in 1485, the cavalry of Yorkist leader King Richard III tried to seize an opportunity as the battle lines were forming. It failed; Richard died and Henry Tudor won the day.

However, carefully handled, the immediate deployment of bowmen prevented such a commencement. Both sides dismounted, for fear of their horses being shot down, and formed their columns off the road into lines facing the enemy. Horses used as mere riding mounts were sent to the rear, but cavalry mounts might stay closer in case of the possibility of deployment as a shock force. While forming up, a commander might take the opportunity to ride up and down the front, accompanied by his bodyguard, and give encouragement to his soldiers.

Both sides usually had bowmen, and soon arrow fire was exchanged. Usually one side or the other – or both – decided not to endure the arrow fire, and that the only way to stop being so 'galled' by the enemy was to close with him. As the foot soldiers advanced, arrow fire would be in danger of hitting one's own side, so it was stopped. Both sides now engaged as infantry, either in a wing or the centre, and eventually the whole line might be engaged.

If cavalry was present, their commander – usually subordinate to the infantry commander, although operating with a great deal of freedom – might seize an opportunity for a short charge, deployment and quick withdrawal. One side might try a flanking extension if superior numbers allowed, although this was easily seen and countered in most battles, and therefore not so common. But if it was successful, this often led to the disintegration of the receiving side. If not, fighting continued. (The actual means of fighting on the front line in detail has not previously been hypothesized, and is one of the main subjects of this book.)

An army could be reinforced, with more troops arriving along the road – this happened at Towton and Bosworth. Eventually a side broke, or much more usually, one force was weakened and their line began slowly disintegrating, in the fashion of a loose thread being pulled, leading to more and more damage. Often the entire battle line could begin to collapse, with men simply walking off; refusing to stand up if they had been resting, or panicking outright and running.

Pursuit of the losing side was then begun, usually with mounted troops, in what was known as the rout. However, this book asserts, this was likely not as clear-cut as might be thought. Rather than a mere riding down of fleeing troops and dispatching them, a hypothesis of this work is that reality was somewhat different.

The battle was thus described in fairly general terms, except the major leaders on each side were often described as doing valiant things, or less usually, as behaving badly.

The battle of Bannockburn in 1314, for example, was described by medieval chronicler Sir Thomas Gray as three Scottish groups attacking by surprise an English army, who tried to flee by horse. They weren't quick enough, and the English were forced into a crush and their horses disembowelled.[1]

Another example is from Polydore Vergil, a Tudor historian, who wrote an account of the battle of Towton, although he didn't arrive in England until 40 years or so later.[2] Vergil's account runs to a mere 639 words – for an action where reportedly over 20,000 men died. Around a third of Vergil's story is more concerned with the political repercussions of the conflict.

All Vergil gives us of the action itself is 99 words summarily describing hand-to-hand fighting for 10 hours. There is no description of tactical arrangements, just that the fight went back and forth until suddenly the losers 'fled the field'.[3]

Sharon Turner, writing in 1823, has the Towton action well enough described in its preliminaries and its aftermath. A six-page description, however, has the battle being fought at night, while the actual fighting itself occupies only two pages.

Even within such accounts, the actual minutes and techniques of action are glossed over. Turner writes that both sides were 'to advance immediately into close combat'. After some phraseology describing how evil warfare was, then 'Henry's side gave way'.[4]

Why is it the case we never see matters beyond such general terms? The story was usually influenced by who was doing the telling, and which side they were on. This type of scenario was not surprising. But many other factors prevented more accurate recordings. So why do we not know what really happened?

First, there were not usually professional writers present at the battle. Literacy was not the norm in the medieval period, with only around 5 per cent of the population able to read and write.[5] Indeed, many rich landowners and people of distinction had clerks to do their reading and writing for them.

This is not as surprising as it may sound: there were few books available for reading, most of them being contained in monastery libraries. There was no printing press at all in England at the time of many medieval battles, this mechanical wonder – as invented by Gutenberg in mainland Europe – only appearing in 1439, with books before then being hand-lettered. Many people of wealth and power did not regard reading and writing as something with which they should be concerned, and in fact felt it was beneath them: that was the function of clerks and monks.

Pictures were a more common form of communication of an important message for the illiterate. Church windows were a powerful example of this, sometimes showing mythical allegorical scenes such the dragon being slain by Saint George, or more realistic portrayals of the martyrdom of saints or the actions of Christ. There seem to be very few examples of combat in medieval windows, however: the fragility of the medium, the effects of weather and war, and occasional revulsion against the concept – that they were decoration rather than devotion – have militated against their conservation.[6]

Some windows depicting medieval fighting are actually not medieval themselves, and therefore cannot be regarded as an accurate depiction by artists of the time. For example, Dante Gabriel Rossetti's 'The Fight Amongst Sir Tristram and Sir Marhaus' is the creation by an 19th-century artist. While he shows some medieval armour in the picture – the helmet, for example, of one of the fighters – Rossetti was in fact showing one of the knights of King Arthur's court, the warrior-king of England who was said to have reigned around AD 580.

Stained-glass window from Soissons Cathedral, Picardy, France, thought to date from the 13th century, giving some detail of the weapons then in use. (Public domain)

Another medium of communication was the tapestry, a cloth embellished with needlework which also showed pictures. There might be a series of such works telling a story, for example the famous Lady and the Unicorn Tapestries, now housed in the Cluny Museum in Paris, also known as the National Museum of Medieval Arts.[7] One advantage of the tapestry was it could be rolled up and carried from location to location for display. Its length could also be used to display pictures progressively, in which manner it was rather like a modern comic book.

Perhaps the most famous work of this type in the world is the late 11th-century Bayeux Tapestry's literally lengthy message – 70m (230ft) in length and 50cm (20in) in height – depicting William the Conqueror's victory and successful invasion of England in 1066. This is a typical illustration of a story being told, but its message is more political than religious. The Bayeux Tapestry's original purpose was to be displayed in public for locals to inspect, thus illustrating the legitimacy of the Norman Conquest. In the case of the Wars of the Roses, the invasion of 1066 was only 400 years in the past, and the Norman Conquest had been far from quick and easy. So in this manner, famous historical events utilising illustrated wall hangings were often displayed in churches for illiterate members of the public to view a story which related to them, and how their world was organised.[8] Some of this could be propaganda: for example, Halley's Comet appears in the Bayeux Tapestry, signifying the sky signalling the end of Harold's reign and the legitimacy of William's, for the heavens themselves had shown their approval. Therefore, a powerful argument for the suppression, or illegitimacy, of any revolt was created.

There was nevertheless a lack of interest in recording the actuality of battle. For example, much of the Bayeux Tapestry records the events leading up to the Battle of Hastings, where King Harold was slain and King William conquered. What mattered in the use of images of battles – as is the case now to a degree – was what had caused the conflict, who won it and who were the good and bad people involved, even if they weren't proclaimed as such beforehand.

For example, Henry Tudor's Bosworth victory was quickly retold to depict Richard III as the evildoer, this even being magnified to argue he slew the 'Princes in the Tower' and had a body misshapen by evil. Richard actually had scoliosis, a sideways curvature of the spine, which was magnified in later pictures to show him as hunchbacked. Physical

The battle of Crecy in the 14th-century *Chronicles* of Jean Froissart. Note the bows are much longer than those shown in the Bayeux Tapestry. (gallica.bnf.fr, Bibliothèque Nationale de France, Bibliothèque de l'Arsenal, Ms-5187)

and mental abnormalities were often seen by many people then as being god or devil-given, and thus confirmed appearances: a twisted man, so the thinking ran, had a twisted mind, and so on. The arguments about the disappearance of the two boy princes, who had a claim to Richard's throne, continue to this day.

Kingdoms rose or fell on the result of a battle, and messengers were often hired, by those who needed to know to know quickly, to take the news of which side had won to important cities such as London. This preoccupation with the causes and effects of battles, rather than the fighting itself, is still the norm today: history courses in secondary schools and universities around the world focus on few events within the wars themselves. Encyclopaedias, for example, usually devote around 90 per cent of an entry to describing the causes and effects of a war, but only some 10 per cent to the events within the conflict.[9]

Even when articles expand into summaries of the war itself, most of this is concerned with the strategies and grand tactics of how a war was carried out: the army of a country invaded *here*; various plans were put together to bring about a decisive battle *there*; and only some general remarks are made about the numbers involved and new technologies being employed. Almost nothing is said about how the battalion units of basic soldiery – the infantry – were deployed; how they were supported by artillery, logistics, airpower, armour and so on – the technical descriptions of how a war is fought.

There is indeed little recorded about such aspects of battle. For example, down at the company level in World War I – the actions of 150–200 men – there is a degree of written evidence if venturing into archival records, often within individual regiments. Yet at the platoon level (30–50 men), there is often little record, unless one manages to read an individual soldier's diary, but that will usually be concerned with the diarist's personal situation and his reaction to everyday events. Descriptions of how the battle was fought at squad level are rare, but they do exist. However, modern audiences are given the impression from movies that World War I soldiers were commanded as a vast horde who were told, for no real reason, to 'go over the top' every day by incompetent commanders – a depiction so far from the truth it does criminal injustice to the officers of the Great War.[10] But there is a great deal more evidence of how battle was carried out in the early 20th century, a hundred years and more in our past at the time of writing, than existed in the medieval world, simply because most participants knew how to write, so there was a much greater chance of an individual's perceptions being recorded.

To expand on this, it is probable that popular film and television has managed to cement into the minds of the viewing public a concept of how trench warfare on the Western Front in World War I was carried out. Two examples serve to illustrate how warfare reality can be subverted by warfare dramas – and in popular understanding of the medieval world it has been just as misunderstood and misinterpreted.

The first example is the TV comedy show *Blackadder Goes Forth*, set in World War I in 1917. While funny, well-written and having reasonably accurate sets and uniforms, it also badly misrepresents reality in several ways. All senior officers are portrayed as incompetent, whereas any unsuccessful generals were actually quickly withdrawn by all sides. Junior officers such as Captain Blackadder, meanwhile, seem to have no responsibility for the 200 or so men who would have been under his command. And the stunning stupidity and uselessness of Private Baldrick is a far cry from the actual average Tommy, who was intelligent, capable and well-trained. The whole series, particularly the comi-tragic final episode, reinforces the concept of 'lions led by donkeys' – a very popular depiction of the Great War which arose in the 1920s, partly as dislike of supreme commander General Haig permeated the popular consciousness of Britain in post-war analysis of the enormous fatality count.[11]

The reality of the Great War was that it locked millions of soldiers into fixed defences where they struggled for supremacy. The Allies won the war, but afterwards an understandable revulsion set in at the scale of the casualties. Much of this manifested itself in (often unfair) condemnation of the military and political leaders. In the main, the commanders, junior officers and troops were brave, resourceful and committed soldiers.

In the end of course, *Blackadder* is just a TV comedy. History it isn't, and nor does it claim to be. But the point made here is that the *how* to handle troops in World War I battle is rarely demonstrated accurately in television and film. Most members of the public, it is suggested, think that infantry soldiers spent their lives on the front line, and that their attack technique consisted of jumping over the front of their trench and advancing into certain death.

While nothing could be further from the truth, the myth of troops advancing to certain death is perpetuated time and again. The big budget film *1917*, produced in 2019, while stunningly photographed, persists in advancing these notions once more, in an international production widely acclaimed. In the final scene, the infantry troops which are the narrative's focus advance into battle – without artillery support.

Yet advancing into prepared enemy fields of fire in this scenario is suicidal. There were techniques known and universally practiced for avoiding the loss of your essential strike force, the only troops who could achieve victory for you by taking and holding the ground you wished to conquer. The last thing commanders would do was squander their men's lives. An infantry commander would request artillery to bombard the enemy positions, thus keeping them down in their dugouts and not firing at his men, with a creeping barrage of fire to burst in front of his infantry as they advanced.

The trouble with the Western Front is that both sides knew this was how to win, so both sides prepared against it. Systems of trenches, barbed wire which the artillery could not cut, deep dugouts and so on were deployed. Tanks were eventually devised to cut through in the place of the horsed cavalry which previously exploited a breakthrough. Airpower spotted for the artillery more accurately or delivered munitions themselves.

The point being made here is that historically correct technical accounting of such situations is rare. It was difficult to understand, and even more difficult to describe to outsiders. The ability to actually write home in the Great War was variable, but it was enormously higher than in medieval times. Literacy levels had been climbing: magazines were popular, and had grown in circulation strongly since 1890.[12] However, it was common for men to only be able to write their own name and recognize up to 100 words. Writing was so difficult for many that it was common in the armed forces for those who could write legibly and with some degree of literacy to be asked to do so for others, who paid a fee for the service. There was a wide range of hobbies and sports available at the time, and some effort to continue these would have continued in service life. 'Swimming, diving, yachting, surfing, tennis, shooting, polo, sculling, rugby, rollerskating, jujitsu and, most particularly, boxing' were all popular, according to a research paper into 1913 activities, and magazines supporting them – requiring an advanced reading ability – were growing enormously.[13] So we might well expect there to be a higher number of soldiers who kept a diary which described what the actual combat was like, or how it was carried out – the use of the platoon in attack, for example, was a complicated affair, as will be explained later, with many varying roles, duties and weapons. If there had been diary writers around in medieval armies, then this analysis of how combat took place then may not have been necessary.

Medieval times, a survey of the sources shows, were different. Writers were rare men of skill who were likely deliberately employed to set down the account of one participating side's leader. Any writing done about the battle was therefore usually concerned with two aspects: what political factors had caused it, and who was the victor. These two points might become embellished with further detail, but that revolved around numbers of people, the weather, unusual events, timings and aspects of bravery or cowardice. It is worth emphasising that the writer was employed to write, and therefore he would write what was wanted, which might not necessarily be the truth.

The Wars of the Roses, which raged across England for decades, changing the leadership of the country, also received less attention than 'normal' wars. Battles between countries – especially decisive battles, upon which the direction of a country changed – were of more national significance. We have better accounts of the battle of Agincourt, which in 1415 led to France's defeat, than of the massive changes which occasionally occurred in the Wars of the Roses, with Lancaster's fortunes reversed by York, or vice versa. To a large extent, which royal house ruled England mattered little to the bulk of the people, except of course where they were swept up by the conscript system of the time to fight for a few weeks, after which they were released.

Recording the battle also had little point. Few people had the literary skills to appreciate a written account, and the concept of selling books for profit did not exist. The telling and retelling of history was often done by travelling minstrels rather than a schooling system, which hardly existed anyway. It was common for the children of field labourers to be in the fields themselves from the age of seven, with some instruction in very basic lettering and numbering – how to write your name and count to 10, for example – in parish schools instructed by the local priest on

Sundays. Learning how currency worked was important, and in particular girls needed to know whether they had received the correct change in a market transaction. Tradesmen learnt more, but it was still basic stuff.[14]

There was also great difficulty in recording the actual battle. Even hundreds of years later, the Duke of Wellington said of such matters:

> The history of a battle, is not unlike the history of a ball. Some individuals may recollect all the little events of which the great result is the battle won or lost, but no individual can recollect the order in which, or the exact moment at which, they occurred, which makes all the difference as to their value or importance.[15]

This is hardly surprising. Even small battles utilised thousands of soldiers, and observers could hardly see all that happened at once. Sometimes a better viewing platform might be possible: the English at the battle of Crecy had a windmill at the top of their hill to see from, and it is said King Edward III viewed the action from it and even commanded from there. But most battlefields were too large to see all of the events unfolding easily, with the front of an army extending for many hundreds of yards. And whether a battle was good for an individual or bad could depend on whether they were on the winning or losing side, as well as whether they had been wounded, took a prisoner for ransom, found some useful bits of armour for themself or were distinguished by their bravery, and were perhaps therefore rewarded.

Further difficulty for anyone recording the action occurred with the necessity of staying well out of the way of the combat areas. Arrows have little discrimination between observer and combatant, and neither might a soldier discriminate in the target of his spear, lance, mace, poleaxe or bill. He might be battle-maddened, angry, vengeful, and a potential observer merely equipped with quill and paper would doubtless appreciate that quickly, deciding discretion was the better part of valour.

Finally, the actuality of a battle, with its massive scale of death and injuries, was hardly enjoyable to watch. Andrew Boardman rightly observes: 'Mentally, medieval conflict must have been an extremely harrowing experience. Therefore, it is perhaps hardly surprising that both laymen and monastic chroniclers shed very little light on what actually transpired in such battles.'[16]

The propaganda effect

It was also the case that there was little point in recording what went on in a battle if your account did not favour the prevailing power in place afterwards. A case in point is the battle of Bosworth in 1485. The prevailing power before the clash was the Yorkist side under Richard III. The rebel claimant to the throne, Henry Tudor, had landed with mercenary troops, and comparatively few English people flocked to his cause. In the battle that ensued at Bosworth, Richard made a flawed tactical decision, and, hampered by some of his supporters changing sides, lost the encounter and his life as well.

Afterwards, with Tudor taking the throne as Henry VII, there was little advantage to anyone writing a history of the battle that showed the new king in anything other than a positive light. Indeed, there was every disadvantage, as the victorious monarch was able to use the process of an Act of Attainder to legally confiscate the property – or take the life – of someone deemed to have acted against the state. There was therefore no reason to be, but every reason *not* to be, a truth-telling author who was praising Richard and condemning Henry in their conduct of the battle.[17]

There was indeed every reason to show that the victorious side had acted with courage, wisdom and daring – even if they had not. It would be wise to minimise the presence of Henry Tudor's mercenaries, for example, and enlarge the numbers of Englishmen coming forward to fight for him. But given these constraints, and not knowing what really happened, there was encouragement to describe the battle only in general terms, with a few sentences here and there to say that 'Lord X', or whoever the writer's chief sponsor was, engaged in heroic, brave and even superhuman conduct. Thus we might find words such as 'Lord X slew 14 of the enemy personally' being the norm.

Difficulty in storing records

There has also been a general difficulty in the survival of records of medieval battles over the years. Cataclysm has been a fact of life – and death – in British history, and great conflict and conflagration has destroyed an enormous quantity of records.

There were many destructive events in the times after the Wars of the Roses which damaged records. The Great Fire of London was a three-day conflagration in 1666 that destroyed hundreds of buildings, while the Great Plague of 1665–66, the last massive occurrence of bubonic plague in England killed around 100,000 people in the London area alone, with resultant disorganisation affecting public and private buildings. A great storm in 1703 caused thousands of deaths and widespread structural damage. Massive aerial bombing raids on the major population centres between 1939 and 1945 during World War II inflicted a death toll in the hundreds of thousands and destroyed countless buildings.

The destruction of buildings and massive loss of life in such events has understandably endangered the safe preservation of records, while in fact destroying many. Less violent events such as floods, rodent infestations and poor preservation techniques have also caused much loss.

The myth of the medieval battlefield

Another aspect of the problem is the mythology surrounding medieval combat. Much of this has been derived by romantic notions surrounding knighthood; concentration by storytellers and balladeers of the time on the royal and noble cohorts, and a lack of recorded accounts of what life was like for everyday people. Many of the reasons given above also come into play here.

So a reader has their understanding coloured by books and movies which depict the horsed rider inevitably as a knight, while this was not the case. Most of the armoured soldiers of these times, horsed or not, are more accurately described as 'men-at-arms'. These were the professional soldiers who constituted garrisons, bodyguards, road escorts and the like, usually in the employ of someone rich. Cavalry components were not composed entirely of distinguished men, which is what knights were, although they may have had humble beginnings. The English knight was someone who had been given a measure of national honour. But it brought no measure of a family being distinguished by a title of any sort beyond the knight's life, and no automatic wealth, although the granting of land which sometimes accompanied it could indeed bring an income, and some monarchs granted a stipend. But many knights were soldiers who had merely been recognised for their bravery, a feat of arms or some other act. Conversely, the professional soldiers of the time, even though they were plated and horsed, were in the main not knights.

The notion of chivalry also surrounds the concept of the knight. We have been brought to believe he would always behave honourably. In actuality, the concept of ransom and looting held deep attractions for anyone who might have been made poorer by the costs of his horse's upkeep and the need to provide his own armour and weapons. The Wars of the Roses also saw a great deal of resentment towards the other House – York or Lancaster – which saw little quarter given on the battlefield, or indeed afterwards, with executions of the losing side's leaders usually taking place.

The modern understanding of the medieval combat world was changed forever in our understanding by the Victorians in the 19th century, who adopted with enthusiasm a concept of all of the plated and horsed individuals on a battlefield being knights. This was embellished by the works of novelists such as Sir Walter Scott, who wrote the most popular romantic novel of the time, *Ivanhoe*. Widely read writers were joined by a host of illustrators who took on everything from the Arthurian era to the Wars of the Roses and beyond, portraying those times and deeds with gusto. Clothing, armour, horses and equipment – all became romanticised. As one commentator put it:

> The golden days of pageantry, chivalry, honour, valour. Sounds wonderful, does it not? The ideas of that age were so legendary that during the long reign of Queen Victoria of Britain, chivalry came back. Everything 'Mediæval' was fashionable again during her reign in literature, art, and society.[18]

Battle concepts were also romanticised. Knights were said to have fought to strict codes, which would preclude not 'fighting fair'; for example, inflicting blows from behind, striking an enemy who was down or using numbers unfairly to overwhelm an enemy. The concept of the rout, where a winning side would pursue the losers and cut them down, is absent from such works, at least by those portrayed as 'good'. The notion of cavalry riding down fleeing infantry and slaying them would have struck at the heart of the concept of chivalry. That is not to say that chivalry did not exist; rather, as Stephen Turnbull has put it rather neatly, it had to exist alongside the evils of war, and it did, to a degree.[19]

Some rectification of this picture has been made since then, however, by various historians. John Keegan's account of Agincourt in *The Face of Battle* is a noble effort, Ian Mortimer's *The Time Traveller's Guide to Medieval England: A Handbook for Visitors to the Fourteenth Century* is not to be missed, and Sean McGlynn has also made some excellent points.[20]

So what did medieval battle look like? We can gain a fairly accurate picture by studying medieval images of combat, so long as they are ones made at the time. For example, a picture captioned 'Mounted knights are unhorsed and killed during hand-to-hand fighting in this 15th-century depiction of a battle during the First Crusade, c.1096–99' actually shows a poleaxe and sword encounter. But the former weapon was then unknown – the artist had put a weapon from his time into a picture depicting a military action of hundreds of years before his time.

The brasses of medieval churches show armour and equipment, but not the tactics of battle. A brass was an engraved metal plate, which was cut to show a likeness of the commissioner of the piece, and usually secured onto the top of the tomb of those shown. Brasses can be 'rubbed' with a heelball and paper, rather in the manner of how a coin face can be shown on paper by rubbing a pencil point onto the paper on top of the coin. (Brass-rubbing has been a hobby for some for hundreds of years, with a small fee often asked for the privilege by the church in which the brass lies.)

Some brasses are life-sized in dimensions, others smaller. This often depended on cost, for they were a one-off, especially commissioned work of art, and were expensive both in the transference of the image of the subject and the making of the brass itself. As much attention was given to detail, they are a very reliable source of knowledge for what armour, weapons and clothing – for females too, as wives were often the subject for a well-off knight or lord – was being used around the time they were commissioned.[21]

There is actually little we can draw upon to show off tactics of the time. But an examination of the Bayeux Tapestry, brasses and other medieval pictures highlights the following:

- Horsed cavalry were a feature of battle
- Bowmen were used in battle. This is the short bow, rather than the longbow which was developed after 1066's battle of Hastings shown in the Bayeux Tapestry

- Mail armour gave way to plate gradually over hundreds of years, but the change was not uniform, and mail was retained where plate was not available
- Edged weapons were always a feature of the battlefield, with percussive items such as axes and hammers also utilised.

These items of equipment, and how they were used, can still be studied as they are used by re-enactors. However, there is considerable danger in not analysing such depictions carefully, as will be explained.

There is one other area that can be draw upon in this study: to use military logic. The following questions can be asked: how would a soldier use events; how would he exploit a situation; and what action taken gives him the best chance of victory? This type of examination is arrived at by the author's own experience in warfare, and in formalised training as an intelligence analyst. There is a name for this type of reasoning: 'Inherent Military Probability'. This is a process devised by British Army officer and, later, military historian Alfred Burne.[22] In his theory, he argued that in any military situation across the ages demanding a decision, the one chosen would be that which a modern military officer's mind would take.

The author's modern military officer's mind and its equipping to suggest 'Inherent Military Probability'

The author originally trained as a high-school teacher, along with some sidelines as a divemaster, parachutist and journalist. In academic pursuit, he combined a Master's degree thesis into American science-fiction with a study of Cold War Politics. Recruited into the Royal Australian Navy as an Intelligence Officer, he worked in counter-terrorism, and strategic studies, while studying enemy combat preparedness in a tri-service (air, sea, land) environment. Essential to this type of study is predicting the future: what the enemy will do tomorrow, next week, next month and – if he lasts that long – next year. It also studies the art of attack; not only strategic, but operational and logistical, with some tactical understanding.

> The author took these trainings to war in the Middle East, where he commanded a US forces team in Baghdad at the height of the war in Iraq. Although the war there involved extremely 'high-tech' methodologies including satellite, aviation, armour and ground troops of all types, it developed into guerrilla-war thinking, such as the use of Improvised Explosive Devices (IEDs) – how to cope with them and defeat them – and how to block and if necessary kill combatants masquerading as civilians.
>
> The author used the available technology for movement and protection – armoured vehicles and aircraft, radar, artillery and so on – but he also wore body armour and a helmet constantly, and was armed with an assault rifle, pistol and combat knife for every hour of every day. The war was at its height; gunfire was heard constantly, and the explosions of mortars, rockets, IEDs and bombs were a constant.
>
> In essence, much of the author's life has been spent with military equipment, and his job involved predicting how military matters would take place in reality, a major contributing factor in being able to formulate a new hypothesis in how medieval battlefield combat was carried out.

The concept of *how* battle was fought in the ultimate age of armour; that of the heavily plated foot soldier, is not so much shrouded in mystery as frozen in time. We can see in this fog the plated man standing there with his visor closed, impervious to much injury, but around him swirls the mists of a problem – he could not, as will be shown, have simply marched forward and stayed there, swinging his weapons with ferocity, for very long, for rapid exhaustion prevented that. So what did medieval battles really look like?

The following can be used to form a hypothesis of what plate-armour combat looked like:

- Examination of real artefacts: weapons and armour
- Use of these with real people – re-enactors
- Historical warfare experience
- Military logic applied to the problem – Inherent Military Probability.

By combining all of these measures of analysis, it is possible to end up with some conclusions. But first, it is necessary to sketch out an overview of the weapons used.

Weaponry

One of the most interesting aspects of this study is the necessity to make a judgment call on how the poleaxe was deployed. It seems certain that bills, poleaxes, swords, spears and bows were all constant weapons of the Wars of the Roses. The weapons are mentioned in many accounts of the time: '…the Summons given by the Heralds of Arms that Spear, Poleaxe, black Bill, Bow and Arrows should be set a work the day following.'[23] But in what proportions were they used? Contamine suggests that polearms may have been used 'when fighting at a distance' and readily swapped with war hammers and axes, presumably surmising this because of the length of the weapon.

However, maces can be seen as useful secondary armament – more useful than a sword – as it can be used one-handed and has good percussive power against armour. A sword by comparison is defeated by good armour and negated by even medium protection. But in general it is likely that medieval soldiers fought using *one* long weapon overall in company groups, gathered around their leader. There are few rare records, such as the Bridport Roll, showing war hammers and axes in quantity. Both are short-shafted weapons, which would be outclassed if used by a group when facing an enemy using longer-shaft implements such as the bill or poleaxe.[24] Just making a weapon longer had its limitations, however, as the development of the pike showed. Yet this formidable spear is not good in close-quarter combat, being too lengthy – sometimes reaching 18ft/4.5m – and in reality being developed for defending against horse soldiers.[25]

Swords were useful, and had been a good weapon for both cavalry and infantry soldiers in the past. But the improvements in armour meant that swords were becoming less useful against armour, although they still had their place against mail, or brigandine or jack (the latter terms will be explained later). Even the big hand-and-a-half swords were not as effective against plate.

The sword was an effective enough weapon when used by the plated soldier if – and only if – he was fighting another man armed with the same weapon. Each could thrust and, by skill or luck, slide his blade between plates, although good armour was designed against this. A slash might smash through at the join between plates. Delivered with force, a heavy cut with a strong sword on top of the helmet might drive an opponent to his knees, and a sideways cut against his helmet could finish matters off.

Sword versus mace would be a one-sided affair if both soldiers were equal in skill and stature. The mace is not designed for the strong finger and wrist work whereby a man could deliver a sword slash, have it miss, and then within milliseconds turn the blade and bring it back again for another try. (A look at modern sabre or epee fencers in slow motion is instructive.) The mace-wielder could not deliver a series of quick cuts, slashes and thrusts that a capable swordsman could. The mace fighter was committed to follow through and try to bring his weapon, without a usefully manoeuvrable hilt and guard, back for another try, although he might be more effective with a strong strap to secure the shaft to his hand. The mace man was also lacking a point and a blade to his weapon – it was designed to be used with a downward smash, although a blow from one side could be useful. Then again, dexterity, speed and skill were important variables: a skilled soldier with a mace could offset a novice swordsman's weapon.

But if the swordsman was facing a poleaxe-equipped soldier, he was likely doomed. Again, two opponents of equal skill, strength and build are assumed for the purposes of analysis. If he was well trained and used his skills, the swordsman would use his sword point as well as the edge, giving him some ability to hold off an opponent. But taking on a poleaxe would not have been a matter of fencing. A poleaxe soldier would aim to bring his shaft back half over his shoulder and run a pace or two forward, bringing it down with a good overhand blow. The swordsman would of course try to evade the strike, but the poleaxe soldier could still guide his axe in its course, and he would probably make contact. Even if he missed, he could bring the axe up underhand and use the blade in an uppercut. He had the additional advantage of using the point where he chose. It is impossible to know exactly how many minutes the fully armoured medieval soldier could remain effective in battle, but re-enactors give us some idea: they were limited to around 13 minutes of combat – a finding which will be expanded upon.

The armour of the fully plated man-at-arms made him largely invulnerable to the swordsman. The swordsman's technique of aiming for the joints of the plate was not very effective. His cutting edge had to be accurate to with a few millimetres, or it would glance off the armour. His point also had to be just as accurate. Some armour with overlapping sections was not even that vulnerable. Then again, it is important not to generalise in this field. It was always the case that armour and weapons changed and developed, for there was more at stake than just protection in the case of the former. As Hanson observed of the Greeks: 'There is evidence too of a gradual trend over some 250 years toward lighter and less cumbersome armament, showing the hoplite's increasing desire for greater mobility and manoeuvre.'[26] Armour was heavy; it slowed the wearer down, and in effect the soldier was trading off speed and dexterity for protection. Hanson notes a reluctance to put on body armour and pick up the shield until the last moment, with an 'aversion towards wearing arms and armor until their life-saving potential was more significant than the inherent discomfort'.[27]

No-one seeing a poleaxe-wielding man fighting a swordsman in medieval combat – as opposed to a tournament melee – would have backed the swordsman to win. Of course, civilised matches such as those fought in tournaments depended not just on weapons. Knowledgeable audience members, having seen the middle-aged but fit Sir Roger fight with the sword before, might well back him against the younger and stronger poleaxe-armed Sir Geoffrey, knowing that Sir R would evade the first panicked slash and himself slash sideways at Sir G's helmet; his favourite strike, knocking the latter knight down, where he was primed for surrender. But the poleaxe had indispensable advantages, which if all other factors between two soldiers were equal, meant it was the best weapon for foot combat. Later in this chapter, the techniques of the poleaxe are analysed in detail, especially as used in company-sized formations, and this point is proved.

Captioned as 'Mounted knights are unhorsed and killed during hand-to-hand fighting in this 15th-century depiction of a battle during the First Crusade, c1096–99', this picture shows poleaxe versus sword – the former weapon then unknown. (Public domain)

From studying the weapons themselves, both in their static examination and in the hands of re-enactors, it is suggested that the poleaxe was the weapon of choice for the fully armoured man-at-arms. His companions, all less formidable than he was, were lesser fighters, such as the bill-wielding lightly armoured soldier and bowmen used as light infantry with clubs, swords and daggers. But billmen, or spearmen as they were often called, made up the biggest other cohort on the battlefield after bowmen. The rationale that the billmen made up the majority of the infantry is that the bill was an extension of the farming weapons that part-time soldiers would have been familiar with. Derived from the billhook, a simple pointed blade on a pole, the bill could be used to trip soldiers on foot with its hook or slash at their legs or perhaps their torso – although its length militated against that – while the point was a weapon sufficient to do damage to either a horseman or man on foot.

Bills were in plentiful supply – Boardman notes that they were kept handy as a household weapon for use against lawless intruders.[28] Strickland and Hardy cite a list from Oxfordshire in 1480 of 31 men of a village, listing them as '18 were bowmen, 7 were billmen, 5 had staffs and 1 an axe'.[29] In 1452, Westmoreland squire Walter Strickland contracted with the Earl of Salisbury to supply 290 men from amongst his tenants: 69 horsed bowmen, 74 horsed billmen, 71 bowmen on foot and 76 billmen on foot.[30] The authors of this citation go on to note that the makeup of these men in battle is unknown: were they mixed into a unit together, or did billmen and bowmen fight in separate units? We will have much more to say in a later chapter about the deployment of the soldiers and their unit formations.

By comparison to the bill, the poleaxe required much more skill and specialised strength to use. The choice of weapon presented by the warhead needed instant expert assessment as to which to bring into play. Its use required constant training for a soldier to remain skilled and supple enough to bring into use the muscles of both arms, the wrists and the shoulders. The fingers needed to grip the poleaxe for long use must have also been very strong. The poleaxe was the weapon of the professional soldier, while the bill was a clumsy weapon sufficient to allow the less-skilled farmworkers to play a part in a battle. In lists of armouries, poleaxes are noted as being a substantial part of the armoury of professional soldiers. Ten poleaxes are listed in the Bridport Muster Roll: 'the second most numerous staff weapon after the glaive', a blade on the end of a pole.[31]

So who fought as billmen? Ian Mortimer suggested medieval people thought of themselves in three categories: those who fight, those who pray and those who work. The first group secured society's safety, the second its souls and the third its food. Mortimer was referring more to the order of those warriors who made up the monarch's organisation for running the country. Briefly, these are first of all the lords of England: dukes, earls and barons. Under them came about 1,100 knights, who usually retained some fee from the monarch – the 'knightly fee' – and then the esquires and gentlemen. The sheriff was the king's chief officer in a county, more of a civil servant than anything, although he often lived in a fortified house or castle and kept a garrison.

Apart from these, there were the clergy – sometimes containing a warlike abbot or two – and then a class of merchantmen. Although technically all able-bodied men owed a duty of service to the monarch, they often seem to have been exempted. The vast majority of the soldiers were drawn from 'those who work'. However, their service seems haphazard. In times of peace, there were not many professional men-at-arms: Goodman suggests that 'in peaceful times the English government had a total garrison establishment of less than 2,000 soldiers'.[32]

Goodman makes some excellent points on the composition of forces, and the picture he draws is one of haphazard organisation, with every lord's composition differing from the next, and the skills and equipment also varying. Boardman draws a similar picture, citing the individual abilities of some village men in 1460. They ranged from a high of 'Richard Slythurst – harness and able to do the king's service with a bow' to a low of 'John Pallying – harness and not being able to wear it'.[33]

Given the paucity of professional soldiers, and the limitations on the ability of the levied men for training, it is likely that only a small contingent made up those with full armour – 'harness' – and the heaviest weapons. This work contends therefore that the poleaxe was one of the major weapons used by the most formidable fighters, the men-at-arms of the Wars of the Roses, but was not used in quantity. The poleaxe soldiers were the professional men, employed as garrison troops, knightly bodyguards, enforcers and a means of providing the force owed to a monarch. This weapon was their means of maximising their own effectiveness on the battlefield. The billman was his poor cousin, a part-time soldier gathered up in quantity in the levies. He likely fought with the bills in a line, as did the poleaxe men, but the billmen must have been more defensive in nature: the weapon is much more suited to poking forward, or trying to pull a man down by tripping him, and too long for a slash. Its point, however, would have delivered a nasty wound, possibly lethal, to a man who was down.

Out of all of the weapons employed in the Wars of the Roses, the poleaxe was likely the most lethal. It is the one which would most likely have done the most damage during pitched battles such as Towton. One analysis concerning the dead excavated from Towton graves concluded: 'Most were square wounds to the head, which are from poleaxes.'[34]

CHAPTER 4

Misunderstanding Medieval Tactics, Armour and Weapons Through Modern Books and Movies

The impact of modern movies on the popular understanding of how medieval battles were conducted has much to answer for. The depiction of combat in film relies much on impossible thinking. From the stirring speech given on horseback in *Braveheart* – how many people would hear it? – to the same film's finale of the battle of Stirling Bridge, such movies give a totally unrealistic portrayal of reality.

Then again, popular fictional films do not have a duty to be accurate. They are stories put out there by writers and directors for mass entertainment. Quite excusably, they do not and cannot reflect reality to any great degree. For example, a soldier's life, even on a battlefront, is often uneventful and boring, and if a movie reflected that accurately – by showing nothing much happening – then people would leave the cinema in droves. Sadly though, many if not most people nowadays get their historical knowledge from movies, so it is important to point out their fallacies.

The finale of the movie *Braveheart*, for instance, has two lines of soldiers running towards each other to join combat with edged weapons. Yet the English are armed with pole weapons – bladed and pointed metal fittings on the end of staffs – upon which any English commander would simply allow the enemy to impale themselves, aided by the force of the running Scots.[1] The running towards each other is implausible too. After 100 yards, laden with protective armour and their weapons, these soldiers would arrive too exhausted to fight well. Running also disperses the close shoulder-to-shoulder formation most armies want to maintain. In short, it is doubtful anyone ran as depicted here.

Braveheart himself – actually the nickname of Robert the Bruce, not William Wallace, whom Mel Gibson depicts in the film – performs feats of cut, slash and parry with his heavy claymore sword – impossible with a real such weapon, and anyway not actually in use until centuries later. Actors perform with much lighter movie props instead of the real thing, and are thus able to swing them with much more dexterity. Additionally, the English soldiers depicted wear uniform, something not done in England until hundreds of years later in Cromwell's time with the New Model Army during the Civil War.

This 'Hollywood' depiction of how medieval battles were fought, however, has now become widely accepted by many. Movie-watchers know no better, for they have likely never picked up a genuine edged weapon hundreds of years old, tried fencing with it or fought against another similarly armed person who wants to harm them.

Books, which of course preceded movies, started the misinterpretation of medieval times quite deliberately. As mentioned, one of the most famous novels depicting the period was *Ivanhoe*, a romance written by Sir Walter Scott and published in 1819. Set in England, it is a colourful romance interwoven with tournaments, individual combats and a castle siege, with Richard the Lionheart, King John and Robin Hood all making appearances. The battle scenes are brief and vague on overall details. For example:

> 'Who is down?' cried Ivanhoe; 'for our dear Lady's sake, tell me which has fallen?' 'The Black Knight,' answered Rebecca, faintly; then instantly again shouted with joyful eagerness – 'But no – but no! – the name of the Lord of Hosts be blessed! – he is on foot again, and fights as if there were twenty men's strength in his single arm – His sword is broken – he snatches an axe from a yeoman – he presses Front-de-Boeuf with blow on blow – The giant stoops and totters like an oak under the steel of the woodman – he falls – he falls!'[2]

There are no descriptions of how the men are organised or deployed in battle – is it a vast mob, with the valiant struggling to the front; is it two long lines of individuals facing each other; is it small groups of soldiers?

George R. R. Martin's books of the exceptionally popular *A Song of Ice and Fire* series – televised as *Game of Thrones* – are much the same. They might be best described as 'sword and sorcery'. There is a lot of armour, and violence using medieval weapons, but most of the stories concern individuals and small groups, with battle scenes referred to rather than described at length, although there is some battle planning depicted. For instance:

> The captains and commanders argued over the maps like fishwives over a bucket of crabs. Weak points and strong points, how to best employ their small company of archers, whether the elephants should be used to break the Yunkish lines or held in reserve, who should have the honour of leading the first advance, whether the horse cavalry was best deployed on the flanks or the vanguard.[3]

The average viewer's understanding of depictions of 'reality' becomes further blurred by similar portrayals in the world of fantasy. Such books and movies are vastly popular today. While many readers might think on reading or seeing such materials that this blurring doesn't matter, as the works are centred on a fantastic world, the depictions still show humans battling out disputes, even if a commander might summon up mystical or magical forces for aid. And it is from these two great genres that a modern average person's understanding of the world of medieval combat is formed.

As an example, the 2014 fantasy movie *Maleficent* portrays a simple engagement of two lines of combatants running at each other. There are no flanking attempts – troops on the end of the line making an effort to get around the end of the enemy unit and attack from the side. There is no analysis of the opposition's weapons and strengths by the commanders, or decisions as to which of their own missile or edged weapons to use, just a simple engagement until one side runs.[4]

This is also the case in the well-received *Chronicles of Narnia* series of older children's books by C. S. Lewis. The four movie versions of the stories feature somewhat bloody battles between forces of humans and fantasy beings such as centaurs, and various talking animals. Once again, in the *Prince Caspian* film of the series, despite having supposedly militarily wise leaders, there are two vast lines keenly engaging each other. A small cavalry charge from flanking positions would seize the day, but none occurs. In the style of Kenneth Branagh's 1989 production of *Henry V*, sensible helmets are rarely worn, so we can see the full range of emotions on hero and villain. Armour is generally glamorous,

Brass of Henry Parys, 1427, in Cambridgeshire, showing details of the shoulder and knee armour of the period, as well as his helmet, more of an experimental type, and of which he must have been very proud. (Public domain)

whilst also being useless in that it strangely leaves vast areas of the body exposed to a cut or point thrust, with not even the protection of lesser mail instead of regular clothing. This is the same in the graphic (picture) novels of *Game of Thrones* and its TV series: armour is often as much decorative as protective, with omissions which would have left the wearer vulnerable. There's a similar problem with the Tolkien movies, such as *Lord of the Rings*: vast groups of warriors rushing towards each other, with fight scenes that show nothing of how combat would be sustained.[5]

Speaking of *Henry V*, and moving back from fantasy to reality, Kenneth Branagh happily ignores not only tactics, but sensibility and armour as well. English cavalry engage French cavalry, in defiance of all accounts of the 1415 battle of Agincourt, which almost entirely record infantry with some cavalry versus bowmen. King Henry is, again against the contemporary accounts, in the thick of things on a horse. Depicted without a helmet, he nevertheless survives the melee, whereas even a slight blow to the head – a favourite and obvious target – from an edged or percussive weapon would have wounded him to the extent he could not have fought on. Strangely, Henry seems to have no bodyguard of soldiers, yet he is wearing a distinctive jacket, which would have made him even more of a target.[6] Henry's lack of a helmet is even more surprising given that in reality he was shot in the face with an arrow at the battle of Shrewsbury when he was 16 years old. According to historical record, though, in this earlier incident Henry was indeed wearing a helmet; one which incorporated the design of a crown.[7] At Agincourt, especially given his previous experiences, he would certainly have been wearing a helmet.

The armour of the soldiers of Branagh's *Henry V* is of great variety, which actually was the case, as there were no factories turning out identical sets, but the film's armourers place leather straps connecting two pieces on the outside of plates, where they would be vulnerable to a cut, which would make the plate come loose or fall off. Some soldiers have no armour at all, not even the metal flexible covering of mail, which was being superseded by plate at the time. Even the poorest of soldiers would in reality have worn a brigandine or a jack. Around half the cast of the battle scene are not wearing gloves of any sort, let alone the popular metal-clad gauntlets which had been on the military scene for hundreds of years. (The author remembers well from his own fencing days, how even a small jab by an opponent's foil tip against your Kevlar-gloved hand taught you quickly what a sword hilt was for – to protect the hand, but only if used properly.)

Why do these book and movie depictions matter? We live in an age where electronic media is more prevalent than ever, where many households do not own reference books, and where people instead get their ideas of the past from television and the cinema. The television series *Game of Thrones* played to enormous audiences world-wide, and depicted much political infighting and bloodshed, just as the real Wars of the Roses on which it was apparently based were marked by savagery and lack of mercy. Here too the battle scenes are infantile in their depiction. One commander even routinely has his own force's bowmen fire on his own troops, so desperate is he to urge them on to slaughter the enemy – the viewer might well wonder why just one bowman did not alter his aim to take out his commander and save his friends.

A major battle scene in the *Game of Thrones* episode entitled 'The Battle of the Bastards' contains the whole gamut of badly depicted medieval combat.[8] Here are the warrior leaders Jon Snow and Ramsay Bolton fighting without helmets against edged weapons wielded by their enemies, yet largely surviving. Viewers are invited to believe this is by prowess of arms, yet even being a valiant leader is no prevention against a blow on the head from behind.

Here too are warriors fighting in a welter of blood and mud, with no attempt at tactics: no force attacking from an angle, nor even a reserve held back to intervene decisively. It is, as is the case in most films, all or nothing, in defiance of contemporary accounts that at least describe three 'battles' (individual units) and often a reserve. As usual, the combat is fought between two forces who simply engage without ceasing until one side falls in defeat. No thought is given by the scriptwriters as to how long an armour-clad soldier could swing his weapons before being overwhelmed by exhaustion and dehydration. Actors instead are wearing lightweight replica armour – mail is often depicted by woollen clothing – while the weapons are lightweight blunted replicas. Furthermore, the actors can stop between takes, thus avoiding the problem of exhaustion, which – as will be shown later – is a major factor in reinterpreting how medieval combat was actually carried out.

In *Kingdom of Heaven*, an ambitious depiction of a time just before the Third Crusade, reality again is sacrificed for movie drama. No horsed Christian soldier of the time initially charged into battle, as depicted, waving his secondary weapon of the sword – rather he used a lance, and preferably time and again if he could, using his big Western European horse's weight and speed to smash the smaller Turkish cavalry. The Crusaders are shown halting once their charge strikes home, whereas cavalry commanders of forces through the centuries knew that to be effective they should try to charge their force through the enemy troops before rapidly re-forming to charge again. Cavalry are shock troops, and should be used as such. Fighting with sword versus sword on horseback was ineffective; worse still, it made the horse and rider an easy target for anyone on foot with an edged weapon – one slash against the back of the horse's lower legs would hamstring it and bring it down.[9]

All sorts of strange practices are given to the Crusaders in *Kingdom of Heaven*, presumably to make negative points about them. They burn the bodies of their dead, whereas in reality Crusaders buried them. Saladin, the Islamic leader, is depicted as noble and merciful. While a most capable soldier, he rarely showed clemency, routinely having the religious Orders of the Hospitallers and Templars slaughtered wherever he could find them.

The siege engines used in *Kingdom of Heaven* are given far more power to hurl missiles than they had in reality. If they were as powerful as depicted, hurling huge heavy missiles hundreds of metres, then medieval siege engines would hardly have given way to gunpowder artillery. The 2019 production of *The King* – another *Henry V* remake, and a very bad one at that – also has trebuchets hurling fiery missiles at the walls of Harfleur. The difficulties of loading material which could be set fire to before the trebuchet launched, while not burning parts of the machine itself, is ignored, which is just as well, as it would have been extremely difficult for most medieval engineers.

Moviemakers defy historical reality with sweeping generalisations, thinking nothing of making their characters make a thousand-year jump in their costuming. The Arthurian saga of the 5th century has been brought into the age of plate, which was almost a thousand years later, time and again. One of the most notorious offenders is the 1991 film *Excalibur*, which features jousting armour worn in battle, with huge extrusions and pauldrons (shoulder armour) prominently displayed. At least the helmets are sensible, even if they are 15th century rather than 5th century, when Arthur likely lived as a prominent High King of the Britons, giving hope to the islanders before they were engulfed by Saxon hordes.[10]

In reality, the medieval military world was governed by brutal necessity. There was every reason to demand maximum efficiency with one's protection, in the same way that weapons were designed primarily with a premise of what worked best in the field. These imperatives governed not only armour and weapons, but also strategy, tactics and logistics – the arts of war – all of which are examined below.

CHAPTER 5

Armour in the Medieval Period

This chapter draws upon the author's observation and use of armour and weapons over 50 years, ranging from several years of fencing with foil, sabre and épée, to travels through European museums and decades of sword and edged weapon collection; through studies of armour in use at jousts and festivals, as well as in static situations, to wearing modern armour in a combat theatre for many months.[1]

However, the chapter is not a discussion of the many types of armour through the medieval period and precisely how they worked in their many variations. (The reader is referred primarily to the works of Tobias Capwell for that.) It is more an explanation of how armour developed, and when. The analysis is more how armour forced weapons and tactics to develop, but also ensures the reader understands armour's essential place on the medieval battlefield. For armour played a major role in compelling the use of certain weapons on the field and the lessening in use of others. What follows is not complete, but rather biased towards analysing the rise of the ultimate armoured warrior: the plate-clad man-at-arms.

At its most basic, armour needed to protect the soldier's chest and back. Plates sewn onto leather could be utilised for this. Leather could be employed to cover a man's arms and shoulders, with conceivably small plates used there too. The importance of the word 'conceivably' in the previous sentence requires explanation. It is very difficult for those in the 21st century to understand how developments in armour occurred over time. There was no central place to go and buy all of the latest protection. Individuals setting up a small business selling armour either made a profit and survived, or went under. If they were innovative, they might be seeking to continually improve the armour they sold, but being basically an inventor and a metalworker were two different things. Some came up with new ideas, but others did not. Some developed a small venture, which succeeded and became a big, even famous business, while other armour makers remained as individuals. Italy and Germany, in particular, saw family businesses manufacture armour for many decades, selling costly suits of plate to the nobility and royalty of many countries.

As previously outlined, simple protective clothing such as a stout jacket gave way to leather – or even wood for the Japanese – with iron plates later secured onto the body pieces. The technological metalworking of the time limited how extensive that was – it was not possible to make a single metal plate covering that fitted the body exactly, as it would have been impossible to put on. Mail was the answer, in effect allowing the soldier to have a metal skin. Mail, however, was vulnerable to the thrust of a heavy sword or bigger weapon, and a powerful cut could part the links of which it was made.

There was no easy way over the centuries of obtaining new ideas about how the best armour was to be made – there were no newspapers, communication was slow, and there was difficulty in explaining ideas as there was no photography and not everyone could draw. If one imagines how to explain the hinged bascinet helmet this becomes clearer: it was very difficult to communicate this new idea verbally. In addition, armour and its associated weapons were primarily concepts of Europe and Asia, so the complication of many languages added to the difficulties of communicating ideas. (Although this book concentrates on English battles and weapon use in a short period of history, the world of such military matters was richly developed in Western Europe, with master armourers and cutlers developing their products in Germany, Italy, France, Spain and many other countries.)

The invention of mail – links of chain connected to each other in rows horizontally and vertically – was the first big step up from leather armour. Grose distinguishes two version of mail – chain and plate:

> Chain mail is formed by a number of iron rings, each ring having four others inserted into it, the whole exhibiting a kind of net work ... every ring separately rivetted. Plate mail consisted of a number of small laminse of metal, commonly iron, laid one over the other like the scales of fish, and sewed down to strong linen or leathern jacket, by thread passing through a small hole in each plate.[2]

Mail was a great development, for it could be made to run around the curves of the body. Basically, the mail-clad soldier wore a metal coat, called a hauberk in many countries, and a pair of trousers. If they added a helmet, some heavy shoes with strips of metal on them, and the same concept for the hands – gauntlets – then they were quite well protected. This was the type of armour that the Crusaders wore; primarily horse troops, with some infantry spearmen and others using short bows.

The predominant helmet of the Crusades, known by some as the Great Helm, reflected the limited metalworking of the day. It was basically an inverted bucket. There was an eye slit, usually some holes to assist breathing, and the whole thing was held on by a strap. A cloth cap was usually worn on the head to soften the impact of blows, with a mail hood over that. The problems with the Great Helm were considerable: it cut off an enormous percentage of the wearer's sight, hearing and breathing. One fiction writer described an English squire preparing for a duel in the Middle East thus:

> The helm of that date was a clumsy and ponderous affair, flat-topped, and covering a man's head completely. There were narrow slits for the eyes, and smaller breathing holes. As Llewellyn dropped the heavy weight on to his shoulders, Philip blinked. For the sunlit scene, with the shifting and chattering crowd, the bright colours and the blue of the sky, suddenly vanished, and he was in small world of darkness, warm and stifling. Even the sounds around him died away to a muffled hum.[3]

Helmets went through enormous variation, but any open-faced helmet for the heavy infantry seems to have gradually disappeared. Tobias Capwell traces the disappearance of the 'nasal' helmet (the only facial protection being a nose guard), which was the norm for around 700 years, but 'almost immediately upon the introduction of couched spear combat, however, the nasal began to be rapidly enlarged to cover more of the face'.[4] Plate IX from Grose's 1708 book is instructive. Starting with helmets from the time of William the Conqueror, the 16 illustrations show helmets over 200 years, with large openings featured at the start of the pictures and none at the end.[5] It is obvious that the face was more and more in danger from the weapons and tactics which were developing, so the helmet followed this heightened danger with more evolved protection.

Many soldiers wanted better protection in battle not only for their heads but their torso as well. A series of plates on top of mail were utilised. Joining these together so they overlapped, to prevent penetration by edged and pointed weapons, was the armourer's aim, but he was also limited by cost and time. A soldier wanting the best plate might be able to afford to have several fittings, but each fitting took the armourer time, and the cost could rise prohibitively.

We return briefly to the problem of improving armour overall. The whole concept of body protection went through a steady stream of development, lasting hundreds of years. Some enhancements were unobtrusive – improved metal quality, thickness leading to increased protection, or more steel in the mix meaning greater rust protection – and others were immediately visible: shoulder pauldrons meaning weapon strikes often glanced off, or improvements to the helmet such as the bascinet.

The invention of the hinged bascinet was a vast improvement, primarily in that it allowed the wearer to take food and drink and aided his breathing without him having to fully take off his helmet. The degree of development needed in the metalwork was considerable. Developments such as the hinged bascinet reflect the improvements in metalworking techniques over time. The hinged section of the helmet had to operate well: it had to stay open when desired, and also had to shut firmly enough to stay closed in combat. The helmet also had to take punishment: it would be more than embarrassing if the helmet was so damaged in combat the wearer could not take it off. The bascinet came into operation despite these difficulties, and its use spread. An armourer somewhere made one, it sold, it was proven, and the knowledge of it widened. Tournaments and fairs advertised such items, then other armourers would see if they could develop the same idea. Patenting such a development was not possible, and it would not have been too hard to hear of an item or see it, and then start experimentation – the concept known today as 'reverse engineering'.

To a certain level, armour dictated the weapons employed on the battlefield. Leather armour was vulnerable to a pointed sword and, to a degree, to a slash, but mail was less so. Swords got heavier, to deliver that cut, until around the Crusades, when it was a cruciform shape wielded one-handed, but with a hilt long enough that both hands could be used to swing with more power.[6] This heavy sword was also a percussive weapon. If brought down strongly on a shoulder covered with mail, it could break a collarbone, and if a blow was delivered to the top of a helmet or to the side of it – even to a Great Helm – the receiver would be concussed, even knocked off his feet. Duelling was not uncommon at the time, so a Crusader might find himself trying to break through the armour of a similarly protected opponent. Turkish armour, worn by those who constituted much of the opposing forces, was lighter and the helmets were more open-faced. Shields were carried by both sides; they were generally made of wood covered with metal strips, so the sword had to be heavy enough to try to break through this protection. The Crusader cavalryman's primary weapon was a heavy lance, which was chiefly used to knock opponents off their horses.

Battlefield behaviour had few rules, so in addition to back and breastplates, more armour to protect a man's groin area was essential. However, the ability to create plates that fitted here was more difficult, so mail trousers continued to be worn, with plate added as the individual armour manufacturer found inspiration. The plate work was not all done by hand: limited machinery was beginning to be developed, such as the trip-hammer, which could deliver the hundreds of small blows needed to pound plate into shape. Iron gave way to steel as the process of developing this improved: iron can be improved by adding carbon, which makes it stronger, with improved compression and tension properties, and less likely to rust. If chromium is added it becomes stainless steel.

Ironically, back and breast protection plates was the last armour to survive in quantity on the battlefield, with English cavalry retaining them in the Civil War of 1642–51. Cavalry plates persisted in various forces right up until the 19th century, with several units utilising them into the Napoleonic Wars (which ended in 1815) and beyond. The growing power of the firearm begin to count against armour from then on, although there were some attempts in World War I to furnish soldiers with protective plates. Interestingly, at the beginning of the Great War, British Army officers all sharpened their swords to take into battle; by the end of the war, they had been abandoned for all except ceremonial use. Armoured plate was finally rendered useless by the modern shaped bullet driven from the end of a cased cartridge with tremendous muzzle velocity: 3,000 feet per second being a common velocity, compared to the musket ball's 400 feet per second. Modern armour really only appears from the development of Kevlar in the 1960s – its 5:1 strength to weight ratio making it widely used for battlefield protection from then on.

Following the widespread implementation of mail, it was inevitable that further experimentation with plates would evolve. A determined thrust might break through the links of mail, and those links were only as strong as the riveting which joined them. In addition, the percussive shock of a blow from a weapon such as a heavy sword or mace was considerable, and plate would lessen that injury.

It was recognised early on that the joins between plates were the most vulnerable point. In particular, the way one plate joined to another, or simply was held on to the body, was a weak spot. Having a securing strap on the outside of the plate made for ease of putting on and taking off that armour, but a slash through the strap would mean losing the plate. Grose makes reference to studying 'the lobster's tail',[7] with each plated section sliding securely over or under the adjoining plate. This may be seen to this day in King Henry VIII's armour at Leeds Armouries: a remarkable depiction of the armourer's art at its best, constructed for foot combat at the Field of the Cloth of Gold in 1520. There are no gaps in it; it is a complete metal suit, with all pieces sliding over or under the next piece as the wearer turns and moves.

Henry VIII's armour is likely the best surviving example to show both the armourer's craft at its height and a suit made to withstand real combat. There is little for an enemy to exploit: no vulnerable gaps to cut through, no weak plates, no areas left unarmoured or only covered by mail – a typical vulnerability for the poorer knight or man-at-arms. A man wearing a suit of plate such as King Henry's was all but invulnerable, as modern re-enactors have found. One re-enactor said in a poleaxe combat match: 'You can't really kill a man in armour until you get him on the ground.'[8]

Henry VIII's armour is plate carried to its ultimate. It also shows that fighters needed all of its features for the highest degree of protection in combat. The monarch, at the age of 29, was 'a tall, muscular, fit king who took part in tournaments and was particularly good. He complained when he did not have good enough opponents and score-sheets survive that show he was a very good jouster.'[9] But logically, the armour also shows what a combatant must have in order to be protected: if there was one person in the land who needed that protection, it was the king. So this, *ipso facto*, is what armour should look like in popular depiction. Tobias Capwell sums it up well when he says that by the middle of the 15th century, armour 'had evolved to become a complete articulate exo-skeleton of hardened steel'.[10] The knight or man-at-arms who could afford it took best advantage of such protection.

But if plate armour could make the wearer all but invulnerable, and even mail offered reasonable defence, why do popular images of the plated soldier feature weaknesses which would have been most unlikely in reality, and which would have quickly left them dead or seriously wounded?. At one point in the film *Kingdom of Heaven*, soldiers discard their shields before a battle, for no apparent reason. In another fight scene in the movie, the central character of Balian discards, strangely and illogically, his mail hood, known as a coif. Furthermore, many of the helmets are wrongly depicted for the time: for example, the hinged visor did not appear on the military battlefield for over a hundred years. Rather, the Great Helm was the standard method of protecting the soldier's head from the curved scimitar with which the Infidel – as the Crusaders called their enemies – fought at close range and the small bow that the Turks used effectively from horseback.

It is in the depiction of armour, rather than weapons, that modern films are most often inaccurate. Armour is often worn by cast members so the film-makers can make the viewer instantly understand that the times depicted were dangerous, and that violence was a means to an end. It is also an easy method of giving characters an aggressive look. Characters wear armour not only at events which have a martial tone, such as parades or investitures, but at feasts and even in lovemaking. Poor Guinevere in *Excalibur* is only one character who must have found the whole occasion rather painful, not only in the depiction but in the actual making of the movie itself.

In actuality, as ancient and medieval armies marched, the armour of each soldier was carried, often on a horse or in wagons under the control of others. Hansen, for example, notes a reluctance in the hoplites of Ancient Greece to put on body armour and pick up a shield until the last moment; there was an 'aversion towards wearing arms and armor until their life-saving potential was more significant than the inherent discomfort'.[11] Only when battle was imminent did anyone put on their armour. This is only logical: armour was constrictive, heavy and very hot, aspects which still relate to soldiers of modern days. (The author, for example, sometimes divested himself of whatever armour he could in the Middle East, even when enemy weapons were being fired within earshot.)

Armour is little understood by the modern reader, but one fact must be made clear before proceeding further: more than half of the soldiers fighting in battles such as those of the Wars of the Roses had no defensive armour at all, save for a helmet. This is known because the Bridport Muster Roll, a list from the time of 201 soldiers reporting for duty, shows that they are equipped with very little indeed – this will be shown in detail later. It is also known that only knights and professional men-at-arms could afford armour, and that there were not many knights in any particular kingdom.

Armour was 'mixed and matched' to suit, and came from a great variety of sources. Items of 'harness', as armour was called, could be inherited, purchased, pilfered or pillaged. The variations needed to suit a person's differing physical characteristics would have seen a great deal of swapping or buying and selling.[12] Gauntlets for a big man's hands might have been swapped for an item of plate stripped from a small man killed in battle. The acquisition of an extra helmet from an aged relative retiring from the battlefield might have been usefully bartered for a pair of sollerets, the armoured shoes usually worn.

While foot soldiers were usually equipped with brigandine or jack – the former containing plates and the latter merely quilting – they would not have been averse to strapping on an item of plate here or there. Pieces of armour such as mail hauberks, that were gradually becoming outmoded, offered better protection for these poorer fighters, and they lasted for decades or even centuries.[13] Boardman gives an excellent description of both brigandine and jack,[14] in particular emphasising that brigandines gave reasonable protection against arrow fire.

Italian writer Dominic Mancini noted in 1483 of English soldiers he saw in London that they always wore swords, and divided them into two groups; those who had plated brigandines and those who wore 'tunics stuffed with tow' – the jack. He noted that almost all soldiers were wearing helmets.[15] He does not divide the lesser protected men further, but it is more likely it was the bowmen who wore jacks, for the flexibility their task of firing arrows demanded of them would prevent them being armoured with anything too heavy or cumbersome. Bowmen also wore open-faced sallets, as the helmet of the time was generally known – a bascinet would have obscured their vision too much to shoot accurately.

Plate armour's quality changed over time. Developments in the manufacturing process of metal led to improvements in resisting penetration.[16] Breastplates or helmets did not just remain the same over centuries. For example, the Great Helm of the Crusaders, a ponderous piece of metal, had to be unstrapped and removed whenever necessary. The hinged bascinet, meanwhile, was a great improvement, allowing a man to be reasonably protected even when the visor was raised for better visibility or simply to escape the choking confines of a full helmet for a while. Armour was in a continuous process of change. The man-at-arms who fought at Crecy in 1346 was on average much less protected than his equivalent at Towton over a century later.

Although this work is not a study of armour, but of how battles were fought, armour gave some direction to what battles looked like. This was because of the effectiveness of weapons. The armour plated man, the main target of analysis here, was the ultimate warrior of foot combat; the heavy tank of World War II and today, the equivalent of the cavalry dragoon over hundreds of years. And the better his armour became, the more dangerous he was, so long as he did not overreach himself and become too heavy and cumbersome.

It is instructive to use weapon systems from other centuries to illustrate this. In the use of cavalry, there are not just armed horsemen. For example, cavalry are divided by aspects such as the size and weight of their horses, men and weapons, and into types such as cuirassiers, dragoons, hussars and lancers.[17,18] They can be generically categorised as indicated below:

Horse cavalry	Horse	Man	Weapons	Role
Cuirassiers	Heaviest	Heaviest	• Heavy sabre • Eventually large-calibre single-shot 'horse-pistols'	• Offensive • Equipped with armour – hence the cuirass
Dragoons	Heavy	Heavy	• Heavy sabre • Often long firearms	• Defensive • Often used the horse to transport the man, who would then fight on foot
Hussars	Medium	Medium	• Sabre • If firearms used, pistol	• Aggressive reconnaissance • Probing • Attack
Lancers	Smallest and fastest	Light	• Lance • Light sabre	• Reconnaissance • Pursuit

In the modern day, the army equivalents of the old horse cavalry are armoured vehicles. Although there are other sorts of modern armour, the main battlefield weapon is the tank. As with the horse soldiers of old, they are divided into three types: the main battle tank, medium tank and light tank:

Modern armour	Weight	Armour	Weapons	Role
Main Battle Tank	Heaviest/Slowest	Heavy	• Offensive	• Win the battle by punching their high weight and weapons capability forward
Medium Tank	Medium	Medium	• Offensive and defensive	• Carry out roles of both Main and Light tanks depending on their battlefield survivability assessment
Light Tank	Lightest/Fastest	Little or none – use speed to offset	• Defensive	• Use speed and concealment to probe enemy positions and report back

The time of the arrow, and of edged and percussive weapons, gave rise to a need – or a desire not to have – a degree of armour. The bowman, for example, could not have existed if he was cased in plate; he could not have drawn his bow, as the heavy arm and shoulder plates, apart from their weight, would have restricted his movements to such an extent he would be impossibly constrained.

This analysis is only general – cavalry in the days of the horse had different roles on the battlefield than modern armour. But it serves to emphasise the point that the medieval battlefield showed the same differentiation in its infantry roles: cavalry were not some amorphous mass simply advancing towards the enemy, and neither were infantry.

It is worthwhile studying very briefly the breakdown of a Great War infantry unit in combat, as the same differentiation can be seen in the use of a platoon in attack on the Western Front. Following a creeping artillery barrage which moved steadily ahead in front of them, a platoon

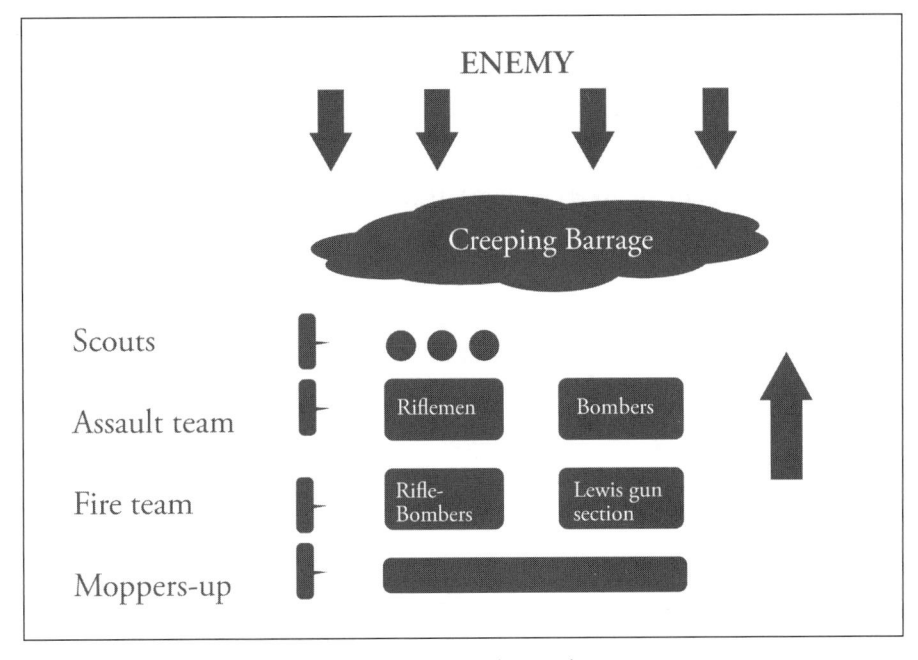

The evolved Allied Platoon by 1916

would move forward, but its 30–50 men had differing roles – they were not, as many movies like to show, simply a mass of men going 'over the top'. As the diagram shows, there were several roles and groupings. While the artillery barrage made the enemy keep their head down, scouts preceded the platoon to direct the best way through shell-holes and obstacles such as barbed wire. The riflemen and grenade throwers were the main fire party, while the machine-gunners moved out to the flanks – it being an enfilade[19] weapon – and the moppers-up did what their title described.

Such a situation was mirrored in medieval England, where the battlefield contained a variety of soldiers: bowmen, sword and spearmen, and plated men-at-arms. The first two categories wore armour of a sort to a wildly varying degree, depending on circumstance, background and fortune. At its lowest level, the spearmen could be mobs of poorly armed peasants. The plated man, however, was a professional soldier, usually employed by a man of substance and property, a knight or a lord. Many were themselves squires, family men of their lord, and of course the lord or knight himself. The plated man was the heavy tank: protected from any threat to a much greater degree than anyone else on the battlefield. Boardman notes that the plated fighter was largely invulnerable to longbow fire, unless he was unlucky enough to receive an arrow in a joint in the armour.[20] But how did these men all fight on the battlefield itself? In general terms, the table below outlines their roles:

Medieval infantry	Weapon	Armour	Role
Men-at-arms	• Poleaxe or • Mace • Secondary sword • Dagger	• Plate • Mail where he could not be plated, or as reinforcement • Bascinet helmet	• Attack where possible • Move forward and break the enemy's line or turn his flank • Defend if necessary
Billmen	• Bill or glaive • Either Sword or • Dagger or • Both	• Helmet, usually of sallet type • Brigandine • Occasional plate pieces	• Pull down the enemy by hooking and tripping • Back up the poleaxe men by dispatching downed enemy/take prisoners • Provide a wall defence against cavalry if necessary

Medieval infantry	Weapon	Armour	Role
Archers	• Longbow • Light sword • Dagger	• Helmet • Jack or Brigandine	• Circulate and dispatch downed enemy/take prisoners

It was always the case that armour and weapons changed and developed; in the case of the former, there was more at stake than just protection. As Hanson notes of the Greeks: 'There is evidence too of a gradual trend over some 250 years toward lighter and less cumbersome armament, showing the hoplite's increasing desire for greater mobility and manoeuvre.'[21]

So in the Wars of the Roses there was a battlefield full of soldiers with quite well-defined roles – although not equivalent to the rigorously organised militaries of today, or even of the Napoleonic battlefield. Nevertheless, these soldiers had particular jobs to do, dictated by their weapons, and to a lesser degree their armour. In the battle they almost universally fought on foot, although there were horse, and horsed, soldiers present, also with clear roles, as will be made clear.

This, then, was the superficial reality of the battlefield. It is now necessary to move towards a study of the longbow and poleaxe, and how they were employed.

CHAPTER 6

The Longbow's Place in Medieval Battle

The longbow was the precursor to battle in most English combat actions, although occasionally it was a winner in its own right, such as at Crecy. Its role will be outlined briefly, as will that of the billmen, as a frequent part of battle, although the main purpose of this work is to show how the heavy infantry fought – a misunderstood aspect of modern knowledge of medieval military tactics.

The longbow's place in English feudal structure is quite well known, but worth restating. The bow was a weapon of national defence, but also a hunting weapon, and had long had a place in almost every peasant's hut. Strickland and Hardy, the quintessential historians of the bow, note: 'Medieval England was a densely wooded country, and a passion for hunting – whether lawfully or otherwise – was shared by all classes of society.'[1] But more than that, each man aged between 15 and 60 was liable for armed service, and had to have 'in his house arms for keeping the peace in accordance with the ancient assize'.[2] While what arms had to be kept varied over time, the longbow and the bill – a blade and hook on a staff – were common to many men, although not all used the bow. When Edward IV 'asked for 20,000 archers to be raised in 1453 [for his European campaigns], he was forced to drop his request to 13,000 archers, and even this number proved too high for the stock of skilled English longbowmen'.[3]

The use of the longbow in medieval battle was in keeping with the tactics of armies using missile weapons as practised for thousands of years. However, this full-size bow – the length of its user – was a more effective weapon than previous missile systems such as the thrown spear, javelin, slingshot or short-bow arrow, the latter continuing its European and Asian usage even while the longbow evolved out of the post-Norman invasion period of England. Jeffrey Singman makes the point that the crossbow, given its excellent penetrating power, even against plate, was still retained for defensive use inside castles, despite its expense and its slowness in reloading: only two or three bolts a minute compared with up to 10 from the longbow.[4]

English armies in the Wars of the Roses were renowned for their efficiency with the longbow. It was a deadly weapon in the right hands. Although it needed physical strength, a high degree of physical fitness and extensive training, in the right hands the longbow could deliver a steady stream of successive shafts. (John Mortimer analyses the different rates of fire claimed for the longbow from many sources, and finally settles on between six and eight per minute.)[5] However, as will be shown, it was primarily a weapon of only the opening stage of the three rounds of a medieval battle: the initial contact, the engagement of the main troops – usually infantry on foot, but sometimes cavalry – and the collapse of one side, usually followed by a rout.

The use of the archers – the initial arrow storm

The primary use of archers in the Wars of the Roses was in the opening stages of the engagement, to gall the enemy into abandoning a strong defensive position, and thereafter they did not play a decisive role.[6] The actor Robert Hardy was a leading authority on the longbow. His opinion was that 'You opened the combat action with your archers.'[7] They were often extended along the entire front line, including the wings, thereby covering all three traditional sections, known as 'battles'. Charles Oman, the celebrated chronicler of war in the Middle Ages, summed it up simply: 'Normally, the men-at-arms dismounted, and threw out the archers on their flanks, settled down to an old-fashioned battle, starting with a bitter archery-contest, and ending with a hand to hand melee.'[8] Hardy adds: 'We know at Agincourt they were on the wings but also along the front in perhaps blocks.'[9]

Robert Hardy, actor and longbow expert, was of the opinion the bowmen were used to 'gall' enemy forces into infantry action. (Courtesy Robert Hardy)

Alfred Higgins Burne, a pioneer of medieval study, has argued that the bowmen were interspersed with the infantry, a concept which John Mortimer contested: 'Burne created the perception that English archers were interspersed throughout English "battalions" in battlefield formation; this idea, however, was one completely of Burne's creation and lacked any real evidence to support the theory.'[10] Mortimer called upon Bradbury's book *The Medieval Archer* as proof that archers were never in the main battle line, simply because they had little protection there against heavy infantry.[11]

Some argue this is wrong. Kelly DeVries, in *Infantry Warfare*, calls it 'the tenacious myth of the longbow'. DeVries' position is that the longbow was not the battle winner it is made out to be.[12] Nevertheless, it is incontestable that it was a major factor, always present in medieval battles: pictures of the time show medieval armies loosing hails of arrows at each other while the men-at-arms wait behind them for the outcome.[13]

At Towton, Boardman suggests the initial arrow storm may have caused 10,000 soldiers to become 'incapacitated', with most of the casualties being incurred on the Lancastrian side.[14] According to the Tudor chronicler Edward Hall, the Lancaster side shot towards the Yorkists, but because of the wind and snow, 'all their shot was lost and their labor vayn', missing their target by 40 yards. After this:

> [T]he Lord Fawconbridge marched forward with his archers, which not only shot their awne whole sheves, but also gathered the arrows of their enemies, and let a great parte of them fly against their awne masters.[15]

Such tactics were a normal occurrence. The usage of archers in combat in the Wars of the Roses was therefore, as has been shown, primarily confined to the beginning of battles, to push the opponent's forces into either fighting or dissolving. Taking on the enemy with bowmen overall was too much to expect. It seems to have happened on odd occasions, but was not the norm.

At the battle of Halidon Hill in 1333, Scots infantry chose to assault a strong English position on a hill. Bravely advancing to fight, the infantry were mown down repeatedly by the English bowmen, until finally the Scots dissolved into a rout. Then at Crecy in 1346, the French carried out the same futile charge against bowmen, but this time with cavalry only. The English bowmen stood firm, and although there was some engagement by persistent and brave Frenchmen against the English infantry lines, in general they dashed themselves to pieces against the rock of the bowmen.

These, however, were isolated incidents in the general use of the bow at the beginning of battles. Another main objective of archery was to weaken the enemy before the battle was decided by the clash of men-at-arms. The archers could only deliver their arrows from a suitable distance. If too far away from the enemy, they could not effectively shoot and reach their targets; if too close, they ran the risk of their adversaries closing quickly and killing them.

Arrow supply was limited, so it was important for discipline and training to play a role. The distance from which bowmen began shooting was again important regarding this aspect, as arrows fired from too far away were wasted. While Boardman suggests bowmen would shoot a continual shower of arrows, this does not tally with them being initially supplied with 24 or even 48 arrows – continual fire would exhaust their stocks in just a few minutes.[16] Even though resupply was possible from spent enemy arrows, these would have to be recovered in the face of the enemy. Wagonloads of arrows being brought forward would be too vulnerable to having their horses shot down wholesale.

Bowmen were also vulnerable to a sudden attack from cavalry, who if skilfully used from an unexpected direction would be on top of them before they could turn and begin defending themselves. In general, however, the extended line arrangement guarded against this, at least in theory and on suitable ground. If there were woods near the battlefield, or dips and folds in the ground, then detachments of cavalry could be carefully deployed and hidden until a suitable moment.

The bowman, once his trusty bow had done its work, became an agile footman of opportunity, seeking to inflict damage where he could, while keeping well out of the way of the sweep of bill or poleaxe. There was, however, a further differentiation between bowmen: some were mounted, and these were more the professional soldier, employed as garrison troops but expert in their deadly weapon of the longbow. Strickland and Hardy make an interesting note on this: the Ordinances of War of Richard II in 1385 stated than if a 'foot-archer or valet' disturbed the cohesion of the army by outcry, then he was to lose 'his right ear'. But if a man-at-arms or mounted archer was to do so, then he would lose 'his best horse'.[17]

The number of arrows and their resupply

Archers were usually equipped with 48 arrows, and it would be generally expected that a bowman would turn up for his service with such a store. Before the battle of Crecy, Edward III had sent home for more archers: '1,200 men, mostly archers, together with 2,450 bows and 6,300 sheaves of arrows (totalling some 151,200 arrows, which suggests over 60 arrows per bow and 2 bows per man).'[18]

Hardy, author of the book *Longbow* and co-author of *The Great War Bow*, suggests that further stocks were supplied, with more bows and arrows, by the quartermasters of the army.[19-21] He suggests two sheaves of arrows were carried at Crecy, and does not demur from that as the usual maximum carried by longbow archers in the rest of his writings. If not expecting immediate battle, the men would often carry just one sheaf.[22]

This is an important part of understanding the capabilities of the archers, and also essential to realising what casualties were being inflicted. The percentage of arrows that were immediately usable again would be affected by some having their points damaged by impact with hard surfaces: armour; icy ground and so on. Others might be snapped in two, or have their flight feathers torn off, but many would not be badly misshapen. Hardy estimates 40–50 per cent would be usable again, and points out that at Poitiers, the archers rushed forward in a lull to get what arrows there were on the ground.[23]

The arrows of either side were usable: this was not a weapon whose ammunition was of differing calibre, available only to the side who had been shooting with it. The bolts of the crossbow archers were a different matter. Shorter, thicker and heavier, they were only reusable for other crossbow archers, and these were a rarity in English forces.

Hardy describes the usual practice of archers being supplied in battles with new arrows:

> [T]he archers braced and shot. Those in the reserve must have run behind the lines handing out new sheaves of arrows, and runners must all the time have been going to and from the wagons and the stacks of arrows to the men in the front who worked ceaselessly to drive their steel arrow points, cold chisel bodkins, through mail and through plate.[24]

Goodman writes of boys from the camp followers retrieving spent arrows, rather like ballboys in a tennis match.[25]

So how effective was the arrow storm? Strickland and Hardy analyse why the bowmen were not more decisive in the battle, arguing that for reasons not entirely clear, 'the archers' role in the principal engagement – as bowmen at least – was far from decisive'.[26] For not many of the fatalities in a battle of the Wars of the Roses were the result of fire by bowmen. Shannon A. Novak, too, examining the Towton mass grave bodies, writes: 'Projectile injuries are the least represented wound type in the Towton series, as only two cranial head wounds [are] caused by projectiles in two separate individuals.'[27] Arrowheads have been found in quantity on the battlefield, but their dispersal does not show a wide field of engagement – perhaps only scores of yards, rather than hundreds.[28]

The arrows were tipped with steel arrowheads. To cleave through armour, the type of arrowhead used was the long, thin 'bodkin' type, as opposed to a broad hunting head, although there are variations on this.[29] Mortimer cites Featherstone and Bartlett's research suggesting 'that archers may have carried a variety of arrows, which were to be used for either volleys or skirmishes'. While English archers carried into the field a sheaf of 24 arrows, buckled within their girdles, a portion of them, between six and eight, were longer, lighter and winged with narrower feathers than the rest. With these 'flight arrows', as they were called, archers could hit a mark at a greater distance than with the remaining heavy sheaf arrows. Sir John Smythe, writing in 1590, stated that in every sheaf of 24 arrows, eight should be lighter 'flight' arrows to 'gall' the enemy at longer distances.[30]

The effect of an arrow hitting a plate-clad soldier is not as destructive as might be thought. If the arrow hit at the right angle, it certainly could be devastating:

> At the Siege of Abergavenny (1182) where Welsh arrows penetrated an oak door four inches thick. A knight of William de Braose was hit by one which went through the skirt of his hauberk, his mail hose, his thigh, and then through the leather and wood of his saddle into his horse; when he swerved round, another arrow pinned him in the same way as the other leg.[31]

However, the arrow had to strike at the right angle. An extensive analysis at the end of Robert Hardy's *Longbow* is instructive. Written by Peter Jones, it analyses armour strength and arrow strikes in considerable detail, and concludes:

> It is important to realise that very few arrow strikes were likely to be 'normal', at 90 degrees to the armour. Arrows were likely to reach the target at an inclination determined by the trajectory which could be anything between 90 degrees and

0 degrees to the ground. Further, allowing for the curves in armour plate which delineate the shape of the body, and for deliberate angling of the armour, the number of normal strikes would represent a proportion only of the number of arrows discharged ... Thus it can be seen that as the attack angle increases the amount of penetration decreases until the arrowhead actually fractures.[32]

Jones does not venture into the unknown: that is, how many soldiers were indeed hit at not the best angle for arrow penetration. That cannot be known, for he was not present at the battle, and nor are there lists of such injuries. But in summary, a soldier wearing plate armour was protected from arrow fire by a number of factors, including distance from the bowman – which affected the speed of the arrow – the quality of his armour and the angle at which the arrow struck. If he merely had a brigandine or jack and a sallet helmet for protection, he was not so invulnerable. But in conclusion, it cannot be said that the arrow storm was the end of the battle; nor was it of massive overwhelming consequence. What can be said is that it was dangerous; an annoyance that had to be endured. The warriors of the time understood the arrow storm must be dealt with, and that was done by moving forward to engage at close quarters.

The role of the bowmen once arrow engagements were over

Before leaving the bowmen, it is important to emphasise that their role as the infantry walked forward – their weapons ready to strike – was not now to leave the battlefield or merely to view proceedings.

The bowmen's usefulness was at this stage largely militated by fear of hitting their own. Where both sides employed bowmen, it cannot realistically be stated that either side would close to inflict fire on the enemy's rear ranks: the accuracy of the weapon, and the possibility of opposing fire, counted against this.

The bowmen now moved into a new role, as useful skirmishers. This was nothing new in the Wars of the Roses or other conflicts of the time. For example, at Agincourt, it is said the English bowmen took up their swords, daggers and the mallets they used to hammer in their defensive stakes, and joined in the fight.[33]

This concept of how the archers were used will be explored more in later chapters, placing them within the extended battle between the infantry, for that is what they now become – infantry, albeit of the lightest type. In essence they acted as light infantry, equipped with swords, daggers and club weapons. Their lack of armour and therefore superior mobility – and visibility, with simple, open-faced helmets – here stood them in good stead.

So essentially, the bowmen earned their living with medieval armies in two roles: as archers and then as light skirmishers, the lightest infantry of all.

Longbows against cavalry

The most important impact of arrow fire from longbows was the reduction in the use of horses on the battlefield. Inspection of the horse armour collection at Leeds Armouries, and for that matter in European collections such as that in Vienna, shows pieces routinely secured on the horses' chests, heads and sides. Francis Grose's *Treatise on Ancient Armour and Weapons* shows illustrations derived from horse armour collections showing the entire body and head encased in armour.

Despite this attempt at protecting the horse on the battlefield, equine armour was not sufficient to protect them against all injuries. This is due to three factors. The first was the sheer quantity of arrows which could be directed towards the animals and their riders, and therefore the high chance of some hitting the horses where the armour could not possibly cover: at joints or on their legs. With an archer capable of shooting up to 10 arrows a minute, and the large number of longbow-firing men in the armies of the Wars of the Roses, this meant several thousand arrows converging on the enemy lines over a span of a few minutes.

The second factor militating against cavalry was the much higher impact and effect of the longbow compared against the short bows European soldiers had faced from their enemies in the Crusades. The arrow fired from the short bow arrived with less shock impact from a lower kinetic energy yield, and horses could often continue after suffering the relatively minor injury from such bows. This was not the case with injuries inflicted by longbow arrows, which drove in deeper and caused more painful and debilitating wounds, often fatal, to the horses.

Thirdly, even steady improvements in the quality of plate armour – in thickness, and in changes from iron to more impenetrable steel – was not enough. The whole horse could not be armoured sufficiently, as an example from the battle of Poitiers showed, where when the bowmen's arrows failed to penetrate the horses' armour, the men moved around to a flanking position to attack the animals' hindquarters.[34]

However, this did not mean the disappearance of the horsed rider from the battlefield, or to be more precise, from the overall battle picture. For while the horse and rider were not used as a primary weapon in a battle, that does not mean they did not have a role.

The main cavalry role would have been as shock troops, able to make a sudden appearance with so little warning that bowmen and/or edged weapon men-at-arms would not have been able to defend themselves in time. A group of armoured lance-men could then be of enormous impact: they could be amongst their enemies in extremely quick time, with the horse urged to full speed within 10–20 seconds of starting off.

The effect of the impact of such heavy, fast and accurate cavalry was devastating. The blow delivered from a couched lance at speed would smash plate through or push it aside, and could literally spit a man. The horse itself, weighing around 1,100lb/500kg, would often hit someone with a shoulder, with an impact similar to being hit by a modern motorcar. The horsed man-at-arms would always carry a secondary weapon, and once the lance was splintered or lost, this would be deployed to devastating effect. A blow from a mace or sword carried the additional impact of being delivered from above, and with any retained forward speed. The obvious target was the helmet of the man on foot, and if delivered with accuracy it would be enough to split the helmet and drive the unfortunate foot soldier to his knees or completely off his feet.

So while the longbow had changed the dominance of cavalry on the English battlefield, the effectiveness of horsemen was still enough to keep them as a factor. But just the sight of bowmen in the ranks of an enemy was enough to have the men-at-arms dismount, with the whole subsequent battle fought on foot. This was a standard routine for horsed men-at-arms for hundreds of years in English armies. Strickland and Hardy note that in almost all of the major battles of Edward III's reign, 'The men-at-arms initially fought on foot; their horses were placed in the rear, but were near enough at hand for the knights to remount quickly either to launch a counter-attack or give pursuit to a defeated enemy.'[35]

Well-trained infantry were also not as vulnerable to cavalry as might be thought. If the infantry were armed with spears, and used them in a disciplined fashion to form a lengthy line of pointed or spiked weapons, then horses would not readily charge at the steel hedge. The lances of the cavalrymen were not particularly effective as some sort of poking weapon. Medieval cavalry were still useful, but proved not nearly so successful as they were in the next several hundred years, when they developed into a role as shock troops, proving decisive if used at the right time and place. In this role, they became highly successful for both the French and their enemies in the Napoleonic Wars. Earlier, under the Duke of Marlborough, British dragoons – the heaviest cavalry of all – had become almost mounted infantry: riding into battle, but dismounting to fire their muskets as volley troops.

Horses enabled medieval armed riders, used carefully, to attack a battle line and very occasionally, if used at the right time and place, achieve the aim of all commanders – a decisive breakthrough. But more often, once a line was broken by infantry, then cavalry could be used with skill to exploit the opening, in conjunction with the victorious footmen. In this situation, the battle line was in pieces, and those on the losing side broke into isolated groups of leaders with their localised or household groups. The situation was exceedingly grim for them in such situations. On foot, and probably pressed in from three sides as the winning force enveloped them left and right and from the front, they could not rely on others to help them, unless another such group managed to link up with them.

Meanwhile, the cavalry of the winning side could, it is thought, pursue the defeated survivors with impunity. (This practice is examined with suspicion below.) The bowmen's defence was probably limited to a few shafts being loosed by isolated groups, but the archers were in no situation for a lengthy battle when deprived of their former covering of plated men-at-arms and billmen. They too would turn to flee. Masses of fighters, their morale dashed, would turn and begin to depart. Hampered by the weight of their weapons and armour, in most situations this was discarded as fast as possible. But even a running unladen man was no match for a horse at speed. Armed with lances, swords, maces and flails, the victors would often massacre the fleeing soldiers.

If this exploiting of an opening was the second role of the horsemen, there was another that had brought the battle about in the first place. The horse enabled scouts to range far ahead of an army, and not only locate the enemy, but bring back vital information such as their strength, what their disposition was – the proportion of bowmen, spearmen and men-at-arms – how many were horsed, and their direction and to which ground they were heading. So while the horsed rider could apply the *coup de grâce* to a successful battle, he could also have helped to bring it about.

CHAPTER 7

The Fight of the Poleaxe Soldier

The poleaxe occupies a unique position in the history of edged and percussive weapons in Western Europe. It uniquely combined an axe edge with a spike, plus a hammerhead on the side opposite the edge. But how was it used, and who used it? It is of primary importance in this study because it was the premiere weapon of the heavy infantry: the plate-armoured man-at-arms.

The poleaxe is a shorter and more rugged type of halberd, an axe on the end of a pole. Its usual form has a shorter axe blade with a straight edge and a four-pronged hammer replacing the beak. Other variations can have a convex edge, a beak and even a flat spear instead of the usual triangular one.[1]

The poleaxe can trace its ancestry through the long-handled axe in use several centuries before the Wars of the Roses. Depictions of warriors wielding these axes can be seen in the Bayeux Tapestry, which may still be seen today in all its glory in the Normandy town of Bayeux.[2] There are different spellings of poleaxe and indeed arguments as to the origins of the word – pollaxe is common, for example. Originally designed for combat, it was also used in fighting in tournaments. Neither is there universal agreement as to the exact design of the weapon; like the sword, it may be found in a variety of types, weights, lengths and designs. Francis Grose, for example, writing in 1708, discusses 'Morris pikes' and 'halberts' in detail, before moving onto 'pole axes', but in essence they are all the same in concept. Its poorer relative, the bill, is longer and more designed for thrusting at the enemy and pulling soldiers off horses, rather than slashing or delivering a percussive strike, for which it was not designed.[3]

A point made before, but worth making again, is that weapons and armour of the medieval period were a matter of individual preference for the wearer or the innovation of the armourer trying to sell a new concept to satisfy a demand from a customer. A man-at-arms might attend a tournaments see a new variation of poleaxe or armour piece, and then return home to visit his local armourer to explain his choice, and the armourer would then set about trying to make one. Every weapon was slightly different from its predecessor. The poleaxe was a continued variation on earlier battleaxes, and its changes in design came from the best proving ground of all – actual combat.

The poleaxe is said by many historians to have been the weapon of choice for dismounted combat in the Wars of the Roses period. Many surviving examples are of high quality and decoration, which supports the idea that they were used mostly by well-to-do soldiers. This is not exclusive: item A925 of the Wallace Collection in London is an example of an unadorned poleaxe. It is commonly acknowledged that poleaxes were also favourite duelling weapons. There is even a slightly modified type, called a *hache* in French, which was used primarily for duels. This weapon had a 6–7-foot long haft and a rondel guard on each side of the grip.

A useful analysis of these edged and percussive weapons lineage can be found in *Fighting Techniques of the Medieval World*, which contains a perceptive discussion of the relationship between bearded axes, glaives, bills and so on, culminating in halberds, which seem to have eventually become a ceremonial

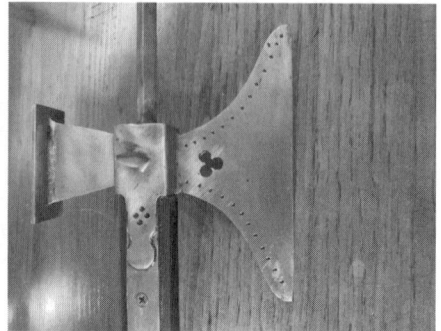

Warhead of a modern reproduction poleaxe. (Author collection)

weapon. Indeed, the latter can still be seen today in use at the Tower of London and at other ceremonial centres.[4] Britain derived the generic battleaxe for use in combat from the development of a variety of weapons fused together by their Anglo-Saxon and Viking users, together with techniques and materials brought over by the Normans in 1066 and beyond.

Bennett *et al* gives a perceptive illustration of the battle of Falkirk in 1298, where a Scottish force was defeated by an English army. The Scots army consisted of 'massed pikes with sword and targe [shields] men, and others carrying axes and bills'. Edward I of England used his cavalry to drive off the Scottish horse, and then had his bowmen shoot down the opposition infantry. The cavalry finished off the massacre.[5]

A careful examination of 14th–16th-century art reveals that warriors were often depicted using poleaxes in mass battle. This suggests that the poleaxe was used more widely than popularly thought. Indeed, the German name for poleaxes, *fussstreihammer*, is roughly translated by John Waldman to mean 'infantry warhammer', indicating that poleaxes were used by infantry or dismounted forces. Foratio *et al* and Blackburn *et al* concluded that skull trauma evident on bones from the mass graves of Visby in Scandinavia and Towton are consistent with wounds caused by poleaxes.[6]

How was the poleaxe used?

The poleaxe is three weapons, or even four, in one combination. As such, the poleaxe man-at-arms had to make a choice each time he swung. He had to choose whether to strike with the axe-edge, the hammer, the spike or even to use the shaft in a manner rather like the quarterstaff.

The quarterstaff, much ignored in history, was a length of wood used as a weapon used by the lower classes. Being only a length of wood, it has not survived to find a place in museums. The quarterstaff's best-known appearance is the fictional fight on a bridge or in a river ford between the legendary outlaw Robin Hood and Little John, the latter being bested by Robin and becoming one of his most faithful followers.

The quarterstaff was about 8 feet long and 4 inches around. It was likely capped at the ends with metal, and could be used for both attacking and defensive strikes.[7]

In fights, the user sought to crack ribs, heads or preferably knock his opponent off their feet. In Robin Hood's legendary struggle, both antagonists are evenly matched, fight but remain uninjured. In reality, receiving a full sweeping head blow from a quarterstaff would be quite injurious, even fatal.

The staff's length doubtless varied depending on the height of its user: the taller he was, the longer was the staff. The same would be the case in its diameter, and the choice of wood is a consideration, for some woods are heavier and stronger than others. It may be that quarterstaffs were much shorter than outlined above, or thinner. Some consideration was given to these factors for this study. Author and underwater spear-gun maker Ric Fallu, who has worked with wood weights, measurements and strengths for many decades, suggests an oak quarterstaff of the dimensions Docherty gives above would be far too heavy to use. This would especially be so if the quarterstaff was made of oak, and smaller measurements or a different choice of wood would be essential for shorter users: their own height would be a deciding factor.[8]

The quarterstaff was either swung, or the point was pushed sharply forward, in a manner rather like a spear. If swung, the user's best technique was to grasp it in both hands, perhaps 2 feet from either end. The section of impact against the adversary was the last 2 feet of either end, which travelled at speed for a full blow. It follows that the longer the staff, the faster the further end was travelling.

There was an emphasis on speed as well as striking the most significant part of the opponent's body. Cracking the skull of the enemy with a full-blooded swing was desirable, but the quarterstaff could also be used to sweep the opponent's legs out from under him or smash a rib or two. It was also effective to use either end of the staff sharply against any portion of the body.

The poleaxe derives from a combination of the quarterstaff and the axe. The original length of the poleaxe is not accurately known, taking into account variations to the shaft's size as required by the user, and to the warhead itself to the end of the spike. There was also the necessity for a regular replacement of the wooden shaft: a crack or split was a dangerous liability for further effective use.

No poleaxes have been found with metal shafts. It was probably beyond the capability of the metalsmiths of the day to make a metal shaft that was strong, of the required length and yet light enough to be vigorously used as an integral part of the weapon. Lances used by cavalry were also wooden, probably for the same reason.

What is certain is that the poleaxe was a two-handed weapon; experimental use by either original or replica weapons has shown it is impossible for the average man to use it one-handed. This is a problem in itself: two-handed use means more force required from the user, thus making him tired, and impacted upon the poleaxe shaft, the most likely part of the weapon to fail.

Given the tremendous pressure exerted on the poleaxe shaft in a full swing – this will be developed in later pages – one of the biggest liabilities in terms of weapon failure must have been the shaft breaking. A slight crack could easily develop into a split. Further, the shaft would have suffered cuts and abrasions in the course of normal usage. For that reason, a careful and sensible user would have inspected the shaft of the weapon regularly for any signs of a split or a cut developing.

Thus, it is highly improbable that an original shaft – that is, one fitted to a Wars of the Roses weapon – would have survived. Henry Yallop of the Leeds Armouries notes that 'almost all of our medieval staff weapons have later replacement shafts'.[9] After a major engagement, an expert soldier would have replaced the shaft if there was the slightest possibility of it failing him, for a broken poleaxe meant he was disarmed apart from his sword and dagger, neither of which were sufficient in a melee. That is why staff weapons were developed, because they were superior – i.e. much more lethal – than an edged single-hand weapon.

Enough warheads, for want of a better word, have survived to give an indication of what the 'average' – for these were all individually made – poleaxe weapon looked like. Warheads on average are 225mm (8 inches) in length, excluding the langets securing the head to the shaft. This is a little longer than the head that is fitted to the average felling axe. The average length of seven poleaxes contained within the Leeds Armouries is 1.7m, or 5ft 7in. The one depicted in the Armouries' picture of Henry VIII seems too long – perhaps 6ft 4in, given Henry's height is described as 6ft 2in.[10]

This poleaxe was to fight at the Field of Cloth of Gold tournament in an arena. Given that shafts seem not to have survived, it cannot be accurately said what the actual length of one would have been, but two combatants who may be seen in an online video by the Academy of European Medieval Martial Arts are indeed using poleaxes longer than they are tall.[11]

The poleaxe was the best and most effective weapon to use on a medieval infantry battlefield. The user of the poleaxe had the advantage of a metal warhead, with its weight and durability, to cause more damage to the enemy. The sharp edges of the head's blade or hammer could shear through mail, while the hammerhead could dent or perhaps split plate. Good armour, however, was made to resist such blows, and it would only be possible to open a cut if the poleaxe blade was delivered at high speed at the end of a full-blooded swing. To deliver such a blow called for a combination of balance, precision, practiced ability and essential timing on the part of the user. The spike was also probably used on occasion to push an enemy back, and if the user was lucky, to penetrate at an armour joint.

Choice of weapon face

A capable poleaxe fighter would choose carefully which part of his weapon was the best choice for each moment of the fight. While a cut might be desirable, an instant estimation of his opponent's armour might suggest otherwise. He might judge his blade had no hope of penetrating the thickness of the plate of his enemy, but the use of the hammerhead could be skilfully employed to smash an opponent to his knees with a full blow on top of the helmet or a shoulder. The spike could be employed if an armour plate was broken or had become dislodged.

This choice was made in a matter of a second or two. A soldier would deliver a cut, a hammerhead blow or a lunge with the spike, then he would recover to make another strike or to parry a blow, unless his action had been decisive and no further attack was needed. However, in melees he would have had little time to stop fighting, for his enemies were many and lined up left and right in front of him. In almost every case, he had to decide within a second what his next blow would be, and with what part of the poleaxe he would strike.

A capable fighter would be able to parry a blow made against him by a poleaxe-equipped enemy by meeting a strike with his own warhead. He would need to be careful to avoid meeting a strike from a blade with his poleaxe shaft, for a serious cut could be the result. However, if the shafts were metal-covered – as they were at the langets – then that made them more effective in defence.[12]

Poleaxe blades, the hammerhead and the end spike

The edge of the blade was best used not so much against armour plate, but against the joints between two plates. The best armour was even proof against this, as the makers knew the joins were a weakness, and therefore sought to make ribs and flukes to divert strikes, and to overlap plates to prevent against a cut through on a joint.

Whether the blade could cut through a plate was a mass of variables. It was a complex question composed of how well-tempered the armour was, how thick the plate was and whether the plates were in good condition. If they were brittle through exposure to the wrong elements, if they were weakened by being rusty and not cleaned for a long period or if the plate was old and not well made originally, could all be factors making the armour not as strong as might be expected.

Conversely, the blow being delivered by the poleaxe was also full of variables. The weight of the warhead, the length of the shaft, the place where the shaft had been gripped by the user and therefore the speed of the attacking edge, were all variable factors which could heighten or lessen the effectiveness of the blade's cut. One other massive variable was the physique of the person using it. A 190cm (6 feet 2 inches) tall man in the prime of life, skilled in arms, was going to add much more lethality to the weapon than a shorter novice.

So, given favourable factors and in the right hands, the poleaxe blade could shear through armour plates. But, it must be stressed, there was no such thing as 'Blade A' being always able to penetrate 'Plate B'. This was warfare before the age of the production line.

The hammerhead of the poleaxe was a percussive weapon. It would be unable to split armour plates, unless they were already weakened by previous blows or cuts, but it could certainly cause damage to the body beneath any plate it hit. A full single blow could be enough to shatter a collarbone, or bones of the upper or lower arm. A roundhouse strike to the side of a helmet could knock a man over, while a hit to the top of the helmet would drive him to his knees and probably result in a fractured skull or concussion. Boardman suggests that repeated pounding by a poleaxe hammerhead may well have been a technique,[13] but the author's practice with the weapon suggests it was too long and unwieldy to be used in short, sharp blows. Nevertheless, it was doubtless the case that, if time and the melee permitted, several strikes against the head could have been inflicted until a combatant was *hors de combat*. These could even have been inflicted by several of his enemies attacking at once.

Some of the inhabitants of a mass grave at Towton have injuries that attest to such injuries, showing several blows to the head which may have been inflicted after they were incapacitated.[14] However, it must be borne in mind that we have no way of knowing whether those in the Towton grave were buried after the battle in which they fell, or whether they were the victims of post-battle execution by a vengeful enemy. It is difficult to ascertain too whether they were wearing armour over the point where a penetrating injury occurred. They have also been victim to the blows of many enemies rapidly in succession, either in combat or in hot-tempered execution.

Sometimes the hammerhead has the addition of a fluke, or spike, in the middle of the hammer face – for example, see Item VII.1542 in the Leeds Armouries, which also has a handgrip in the rondel fashion, a circular piece around the shaft to stop a gauntleted hand from slipping. Experimentation with the use of a spike in the middle of a hammerhead would have been a special innovative idea by an armourer or someone commissioning a poleaxe warhead. It could also be used to hook into an opponent's armour to pull him over.

Like so much of medieval combat, the best use of the poleaxe would have been the subject of a constant forwarding, discussing and trialling of ideas. Men-at-arms may have keenly discussed the latest concepts, bringing forward something they had had made: a new helmet hinge, a sword guard or a pair of knuckledusters built into gauntlets.

It was not the case that one effective blow would always end matters between two evenly matched men-at-arms; indeed they were not usually evenly matched. Many factors could give an advantage to one combatant over the other. While a sweeping blow with either hammer or blade could bring a man down, the spike, although the most easily parried, could have been decisive if it penetrated at the right place, preferably between armour plates.

It is worth repeating that this analysis is dealing with theoretical situations, whereas the chaos of war was not simply a matter of two men-at-arms battling it out. Real warfare was much more likely to have seen a well-armed and armoured soldier pick a weaker target than himself. Around him was likely a mob of billmen, maybe a plate-armoured friend and some foolhardy or brave bowmen trying their hand. In reality, battle would have seen screaming, shouting and savagery in a confused, mad slugging match, with the full gamut of bravery, cowardice, ability, idiocy and first-timers versus veterans, all mixing it up without regard to any rule save the best, nastiest, luckiest and most savage warrior winning.

The spike would also have been an effective psychological weapon when jabbed at the face of an enemy soldier. Its point was closer to the enemy than the blade or hammer, and would have caused an instinctive recoiling, which would have meant a momentary hesitation, a mistake in defence, allowing a split-second blow inside their guard.

Some accounts[15] refer to a spike on the foot of the poleaxe, but this has not been found in any weapons examined. But a spike on the foot would have been useful in a number of ways: as a weapon itself, and in allowing the shaft to be more securely grounded if the poleaxe was used as a support for a tired or exhausted soldier. Given that shafts were replaced on a regular basis, refitting a foot spike would have been another necessary task each time the shaft was renewed.

Secondary weapons

No poleaxe soldier would have gone into combat unless armed with a secondary weapon, as the shaft of his poleaxe could break or he could be disarmed – separated from it in the melee of an attack, where two groups clashed and neither gave way. He needed something which was effective and as lethal as possible, but which could be carried without too much thought and taken up easily when needed.

It cannot have been something as lengthy as another poleaxe, for the shaft prevented it from being easily carried at the waist, and straps holding another along his back would have been easily cut and tangled in combat. The most logical suggestion is a mace or sword, the latter without a scabbard, for once the sword was withdrawn a scabbard would be an encumbrance. Maces have survived in quantity from the period, as have swords, chosen for strength and thrusting ability rather than length, which would have made it difficult to swing in a crush. Oakeshott has noted that most of the swords from this period are built along these lines.[16] The Roman gladius was more an inspiration – 1,000 years after the Empire collapsed – than the sabres and smallswords which were beginning to appear at the time.

Maces often have heads that contain protruding sharpened metal lines, which would add to their ability to split armour at the joins. This is where the sword would have been deployed, between plates rather than trying to pierce them. However, it must be emphasised that any soldier who was using either of these weapons was at a disadvantage against a poleaxe-equipped man, who could use the length of his weapon to hold off swings, and with timing could deploy one of the formidable blows which was the primary purpose of the poleaxe.

Combatant height, strength, endurance and fighting ability

The height of a soldier gave him an advantage if he was taller than his opponent. The helmeted head of his enemy was then a constant target, for a good sidestroke could well knock his opponent over, while a blow swinging upwards might penetrate the gap between helmet and shoulder plate, and a blow full on top of the head could bring an opponent to his knees. There was always the hope too that a swing with the axe side of the poleaxe would penetrate a plate. The taller opponent always had an advantage in the swing downwards to the top of the helmet, for he could see what he was aiming at, and gravity helped his efforts.

The shorter fighter was disadvantaged in a converse fashion. If too short, he might not even be able to see the top of his opponent's helmet. If he was distinctly shorter, his poleaxe might not even be able to reach that elusive target, as the angle of the shaft would never reach the horizontal in its downward stroke, the shaft being blocked by his enemy's body.

The enemy's head was the ideal target for edged or percussive weapons, and was indeed a popular aiming point. An examination of the Towton mass grave bodies produced the following conclusion from Shannon Novak: 'In general, the head exhibits a dramatically higher frequency of perimortem trauma than the body.'[17] It presented a weaker target in terms of armour, for the heavier the helmet, the less quickly a soldier was able to move his head. In general, helmet armour was thinner and less laden with ridges designed to deter blades than breastplates or shoulder pauldrons. A strike to the head could be successful even if it was not fatal or even seriously wounded the opponent. The recipient could be left dazed and confused by a good blow, meaning he might withdraw from the fight or present an easy target for another attack.

The poleaxe warhead, arriving at its target, had an impact governed by a number of factors. The first was the speed of the blow; a faster blow carries more kinetic energy. Also, the heavier the warhead, the more impact it would have. A strong soldier was able to bring these two factors to the fore: the stronger he was, the faster he could swing and the heavier the warhead of the poleaxe could be.

Strength is not the same as endurance, in the same way that a sprinter's abilities are not the same as those of a marathon runner. In some ways, the two are the converse of each other. A fighter who could deliver great crushing blows was obviously extremely dangerous, but if he could only fight for 12 minutes or so before becoming exhausted, then he reached his limits very quickly. Meanwhile, a soldier who might lack strength, but instead could keep swinging comparatively less dangerous blows for longer, was dangerous in his own way.

Techniques acquired over a long experience of war were invaluable. Thus, a soldier who was older than the average might still be a dangerous opponent. Instead of wasting his time on furious blows, he might just avoid his opponent until the edge was taken off his enemy's enthusiasm, much in the same way a boxer will defend initially until his opponent becomes exhausted. One decisive stroke in the right place and at the right time could then end the matter.

The poleaxe in summary

While the poleaxe plate-armoured soldier was the ultimate fighter on the battlefield, for all his power he was, ironically, still limited. His armour, the best on the battlefield, protected him to a high degree, even against other poleaxes. The richer he was, the better the armour; and a lord or knight of means would have worn the latest pattern he could obtain.

It is not possible to test the poleaxe's ultimate capabilities. To do so would mean two plated men fighting it out without curbing their blows in any way. The swings of their blade and hammer would be at full power. Their use of the spike on the poleaxe would be given a full thrust. They would be aiming at the weakest points of their opponent, the joints between plates in particular, and they would show no restraint or mercy.

Such a test would mean injuries which could be life-threatening. Who would take part in such tests? Re-enactor engagements are in fact rehearsed and choreographed 'fights' that are designed to see both participants walk away and fight again. Rebated, blunted and pointless poleaxes are used. Finishing up one engagement for the camera, one of the Academy of European Medieval Martial Arts coaches in *FACT Open House 2012 – Poleaxe in Armour* says: 'This is simulated for this' – showing a sharpened and pointed poleaxe compared with the blunted and pointless one he has just taken from a re-enactor. 'Because if we did with *this* what they did with *this* – we'd be calling an ambulance.'[18] The engagement coach goes on to note, however, that in their opinion armour guarded even against full blows – unless the opponent was downed, which would leave him open to being hit hard with percussive hammer or edge, or the spike being used, and the inability of the prone body to recoil from the impact would lead to much greater injury.

Having seen what combatants were armed with, this analysis will proceed to examine how they used their weapons on the battlefield itself and reveal two previously undiscussed aspects of medieval combat.

CHAPTER 8

How Were Medieval Battles Actually Fought?

What is advanced here is a hypothesis only. As is shown repeatedly throughout this book, definitive proof of how medieval battles were fought is substantially lacking. It is safe to say that more is known of how the Greek and Roman armies of antiquity deployed on the field and advanced their cause than how English battles of the medieval period played out. The reasons for this have been outlined within this work, but it is useful to repeat them:

- A lack of need for the battles to be described by the winners or the losers
- A scarcity of readers, due to low literacy levels
- A lack of a means of spreading any word through books, as the printing press was in its infancy
- A difficulty in storing records, with libraries confined largely to monasteries

Without any accurate recording of how battles took place, the historian has to turn to using logical analysis, Inherent Military Probability and examination of re-enactor practice to virtually reconstruct the battlefield. But these three analysis techniques have limitations.

First, soldiers do not always behave logically on battlefields. Factors such as emotion, reliance on traditional practice and kinship come into play. For example:

- King Harold's army at the battle of Hastings was in a good position in their fight against William's Norman invaders. However, according

to some they abandoned their position in the face of what was falsely perceived to be a withdrawal by William's troops to pursue them. It may well have been that, scenting victory, their exultation and a wish for revenge on their attackers overcame any suspicion of a trap. As a result of excitement – emotion – overcoming logic, they lost the fight.
- The French cavalry at the battle of Crecy persisted in charges despite the obvious superiority of English bowmen in fixed positions. Some say they charged repeatedly out of pride and a refusal to believe their highly armoured and skilled horsemen could be defeated by mere arrow fire. As a result of pride and a reliance on their old established practice, they too were defeated.
- The Old Guard of Napoleon's army at Waterloo refused to surrender in the final stages of the battle. They were musket infantry who had accompanied Napoleon around Europe and beyond in his numerous victories, and occasional losses, for over 20 years. As a consequence of their virtual kinship to their emperor, they refused to give in to an overwhelming enemy even when they were surrounded and helpless.

However, with some exceptions such as these, soldiers usually behave logically, especially in the planning and initial stages of battles. As explained before, the medieval commanders knew their Vegetius, and would have studied older tactics closely. Most medieval battles were lost not because of lack of logic or emotional factors, but because of one side's greater numbers, superior ground, better skills or a surprise reinforcement.

While advancing the suggestion that some idea of how a battle was fought can be derived from logic, and army practices taken from guides such as *Epitome of Military Science*, an understanding can also be gained from how re-enactors go about recreating the look and feel of battles. However, there are some limitations and constraints that need to be understood about the latter source.

The limits of analysis using re-enactors

For this analysis, time was spent interviewing re-enactors at the 2016 Tewkesbury Medieval Festival in south-west England. Seeing over a

Re-enactors begin a melee at the Tewkesbury Medieval Festival. (Author photo)

thousand re-enactors take to their field in their armour, with weapons, and engage in some limited 'combat' was a stirring sight. But interviews and careful observation reveal the full extent of what can be learnt from examination of re-enactments.

There are limitations if using re-enactors to analyse battle techniques of previous centuries.[1] Re-enactors do offer valuable insights into how weapons and tactics might have been used, but they remain just part of this overall study – part of a hypotheses rather than proof.

The first limitation is that re-enactors are not trying to kill each other. Usually the purpose of their re-enactment is to create a spectacle, which looks reasonably dangerous but is not. However, for those seeing re-enactors – especially in mass formations – for the first time, it is easy to get the impression that they are indeed behaving in a fashion which will bring injury or even death to those on the receiving end of their weapons. Poleaxes and maces swing at opponents, men-at-arms are hit with fairly full blows on their armour, and sometimes a re-enactor falls to the ground, or at least appears to do so. Occasionally there are actual injuries, ranging from being winded to bruises and cuts. However, re-enactors sometimes arrange such a fall as part of the entertainment.

Perhaps the most important deliberate limitation that re-enactors make is to use blunted weapons. Poleaxes in the Wars of the Roses had sharpened blades, designed to cut through mail or plate if possible, and honed spikes. Maces had sharpened sections on their warheads, swords and daggers had sharpened blades and points, while spears had sharp tips. All of these weapons, when used by re-enactors in combat against others, now have blunted edges instead.

Re-enacted engagements – where two replica armies advance towards each other and 'fight' – include a general agreement not to aim blows at each other's heads. Even if wearing a padded cap and a good helmet with thick plate, receiving a strike from a replica poleaxe can cause serious injury. Helmets have eye slits, and given the clash of metal against metal, there is a small chance a splinter, either from the weapon itself or from the helmet, might become detached and injure an eye. Modern jousters – as may be seen for example at the *Medieval Times* attraction in Los Angeles – usually wear modified motorcycle helmets with eye mesh and ballistic eye protection, the latter the same as soldiers of modern Western forces wear on the battlefield.[2]

Also important is the extent to which blows are delivered. Even with a blunted blade, a poleaxe using a 1.5 metre-long shaft delivers a lot of kinetic energy when its warhead strikes something. These weapons are percussive in their impact, as well as cutting. Re-enactors generally 'pull' the blow at the last second, and do not deliver a swing with the same savagery that would be found in battle, especially by members of two forces who hated each other in a manner beyond that of normal warfare. Some of this can be seen in filmed re-enactment at websites such as that of the Academy of European Medieval Martial Arts.

In medieval warfare, there was often a good reason not to use full force. Normal military campaigning, for example in Continental Europe, saw lesser savagery applied or the good reason that ransoming – demanding money for the safe return of a prisoner – was a normal and much-appreciated part of war. A defeated and captured but still alive knight, squire or even well-off man-at-arms might be held until his family and friends handed over a suitable sum of money in return for his freedom.

The Wars of the Roses, by contrast, saw much revenge, anger and spitefulness that would have leant more ferocity than usual to a combat action. For instance, almost every recorded battle has post-battle executions as the norm, carried out by the winning side against the losers. Some of these were arranged formally, such as when, with the Yorkists on top after the initial stages of the battle of Edgecote, Sir Henry Neville was beheaded by order of the Earl of Pembroke. The next day, when the battle swung the other way and the Lancastrians emerged victorious, both Pembroke and Sir Richard Herbert were executed by the House of Lancaster.

Many other executions took place informally and with great savagery: the Towton graves, for example, reveal edged and percussive blows against unarmoured heads – this suggests beheading of stripped prisoners, although it is by no means certain these were executions rather than men who fell in battle. The executed men were buried haphazardly within the grave pits, with no formal Christian burial.

Re-enactors, therefore, are using neither the lesser blows which might knock an enemy soldier over, nor the deadly blows more common in heated combat by two sides who hated each other. Wars of the Roses battles would have witnessed vigorous use of the body and its armed plates to punch, knee, strike and generally bash the opposition. All of the blows common to boxing, and those common to wrestling, would have been used, ignoring the 'below the belt' rules of such sports. Striking an opponent vigorously with a mace, and then seeing him off balance and open to a kick to the groin, would have given the fighter with the upper hand the opportunity to deliver such a strike. Furthermore, a sharp blow from an armoured elbow would have been nearly as devastating as a short poke with a mace head. A full kick against the helmeted head of someone who was momentarily on the ground would also have been used, to devastating effect, especially as the aggressor would have been wearing armoured shoes known as sabatons or sollerets.

Men-at-arms would have used their daggers when they could to exploit the joins in armour, in a way not carried out by re-enactors.

Re-enactors await an engagement at the Tewkesbury Medieval Festival. (Author photo)

Plated armour was, as has been explained, of considerable variance, but in most cases it would have not been of the beautifully fitted and interlocking type seen in Henry VIII's armour displayed at the Leeds Armouries. There would be parts of the body on most people's harness where the plates did not interlock, with protection only from mail underneath. Where possible, a sharp stab with a dagger would have been made at such a weak point. It would not take an 8-inch penetration to prove debilitating; depending on where it was made, a stab only a few inches deep could have been effective, at least in slowing the recipient and maybe making him vulnerable to a blow from another weapon or a second stab. Adrenaline would have somewhat lessened the effects of such blows, but even shallow stabs would have eventually counted against the recipient's ability to keep fighting.

Finally, re-enactors observe the niceties of groups of people who are united by a common enthusiasm, rather than brought together to sort out differences by the ultimate means. If an opponent falls, re-enactors step back; if an opponent seems hurt, they stop their combat re-enactment and lend assistance. They know that the people who are watching are not there to see real violence.

But for all that, re-enactment is the closest that can be got today to really understanding how arms and armour of the 15th century were actually used. For that reason, an examination of tactics using re-enactors is invaluable, and its findings will be referred to in the following analysis of the formations in which medieval soldiers fought.

Ground

The ground underfoot for two battling combatants was a constant factor. If it was slippery from rain or snow – as it was at Towton – then the effectiveness of each man's parries and strokes was less as his balance was constantly undermined. In such situations, the person who was the most experienced in these circumstances had the advantage, while the weight of armour and weapons began to be negated. The advantages of the plated man became less the worse the ground became. As Oman put it, referring to Agincourt: 'The archer was effective not only with his box but with his axe or mallet, when once his adversary was tired out and hampered in the mire.'[3]

The fighter who was on higher ground held an advantage: it requires more strength to swing uphill, and is more tiring, with the constant drag of gravity a factor for the poleaxe warhead to reach its target. If combatants were fighting on a slope, then the soldier who had the higher ground held that advantage, whether he was being forced up it by enemies advancing, or he was coming down it as his line moved forward.

Commanders knew full well the gain or loss that height and condition of the ground gave them, and would often seek the height advantage if they could. But this advantage only applied if they could hold the higher ground for the entire battle. Consequently, commanders of evenly matched forces generally sought out level ground where either side had a chance of victory. However, a general who wanted to employ defensive tactics – perhaps to weaken his enemy by attrition – might have sought a gentle slope at his men's backs in order to gain an advantage.

Weather

Often overlooked by analysts, weather was a primary factor in determining battles – and for that reason is even today still the first consideration in battlespace assessments. The author was part of a Battlespace Upgrade Assessment (BUA) team in the war in Iraq at its height. The BUA was a daily appreciation of the war, given to an assembled audience of several hundred, but more importantly, to around 1,500 military personnel via videolink. The author, as an intelligence analyst, was sometimes there to give the 'Intelligence Appreciation', but always took second place behind the meteorologist – the weather could always 'stop play'.

Coping with the weather in medieval times was just as important as it is today. For the bowman of the times, the wind worked against him if he was shooting into it, lessening the flight duration of arrows (just as it does today for bullets, artillery rounds and missiles.) Wind can also move the projectile off course, either left or right. Bowmen were taught to allow for the wind when shooting, so shot their arrows slightly off target to allow the elements to correct the aim. In gusty conditions, however, this was a very difficult task to perform.

Rain reduced visibility for all concerned. It was also a primary factor in lessening the power of the longbow when the bowstring became wet. Bowmen were taught to unstring their bows if rain was approaching, and anecdotally, as happened with the rainstorm which preceded the battle of Crecy, they often coiled them and put them under their hat or helmet. This of course meant the bowman was disarmed, and he could neither shoot offensively nor defend himself with anything but his wall of stakes hammered into the ground in front of his position and his personal weapons.

For cavalry, rain was also a limiting factor, with slippery conditions hazardous to the horses and lessening their ability to accelerate and manoeuvre. The first squadrons to cross a wet battlefield would have turned it to mud, with horses following on behind inheriting the disadvantage. It was the same for foot soldiers. The use of pole weapons meant a considerable turning momentum, that could cause a loss of footing on wet ground if one missed the target or even hit home. Thrusting weapons were a better choice in wet conditions, but were, as outlined above, generally less effective.

Cold was a significant factor for some soldiers, but curiously not for the plate-clad soldier. Ninety per cent of re-enactors interviewed by this author said that cold weather was something they liked, or even desired.[4] Re-enactor Ewen Cameron said: 'The colder it is, the easier it is to keep going.' Several made the point that it was heat exhaustion that was the most limiting factor when wearing plate.

Heat meant that a soldier would have constantly had to replenish his hydration levels, or else he would fall due to heat stroke. Although hydration was poorly understood at the time, soldiers would know that they had to drink. Wine or ale (a type of weak beer made without hops) would have been one choice for this necessity: the general practice of the day was not to drink water as it did not store well.[5]

Liquid carried in flasks around the waist, however, could have had the retaining straps easily cut or torn asunder in combat. Helmets were another factor in rehydration, with the sallet-wearing man holding an advantage. A fully plated soldier wearing a bascinet would have had to withdraw from the line in order to drink, which would have necessitated him raising his helmet visor, making him a target even at a distance for any enemy bowman. Taking off one's helmet or raising the visor could be the cause of a serious wound or a fatality – this is what is said to have caused the death of Lord Dacre at Towton and Lord Clifford the previous day at Dintingdale.[6]

Communications

There is little evidence to record the use of trumpets on the battlefield in the Wars of the Roses. However, battlefield commands were in use from ancient days. Hanson notes of the Greeks that: 'Orders to advance or retreat were given by blasts of the horn.'[7] Dando-Collins cites the Roman legions, who had players of the lituus, a horn made of wood covered with leather. On the battlefield they used audible commands for movement directions as well as more complicated commands relating to weapons.[8]

Vegetius wrote: 'Trumpeters, hornblowers and buglers normally launch the battle.'[9] Such general command signals were probably confined to individual companies, however, rather than the overall army. Commands could have been easily formulated by medieval forces for essentials such as 'move forward' 'halt', 'make one half turn left' and so on, as per the Roman days. It would be unlikely there would have been a command for 'about turn' or 'retreat' – these could lead to misinterpretation or panic – but there may well have been one for all ranks to take five steps to the rear while still facing forward, for example.

Trumpet commands would necessarily not follow a widely understood series of calls, for one side would have been able to understand what the other was about to do, and of course use their own trumpeters to confuse them. In later years, under commanders such as the Duke of Marlborough, the use of trumpet 'cavalry calls' evolved to a much more advanced system than outlined here.[10] Drummers were also used, as were martial bands with fifes and side-drums, in particular to arouse martial emotions.

At a lower level, the medieval rank arrangements would have been commanded through the sergeants with whistles and shouts, sometimes unheard in the overall din, and necessarily repeated. Words of command could also have been passed along the line from soldier to soldier: 'Halt – pass it on', for example. Such commands, however, would have been kept extremely simple, as they were open to misinterpretation through indistinctness caused by the enveloping helmets, especially of the plate men. Vegetius notes that hand signals and gestures with whips and weapons would have been well understood in armies, and practiced constantly before battles.[11]

The handling of individual medieval companies would have been managed through the movement of their standard and other commands. Trumpet blasts could have been used by a force's main three commanders: the centre leader and the two flank captains. This was noted at the battle of Bosworth as being the main signal the army was waiting for at the beginning of combat.[12] However, it may have also been the practice to use what in later years were called 'gallopers' – mounted messengers with a note – as the din of the battlefield would have prevented effective communication at the highest levels.

Why medieval soldiers were loyal in battle

Although more has been learnt about soldier psychology in the last 100 years than ever before, it has always been an important factor in battle.

Loyalty, as Lawrence LeShan pointed out in a collection of thoughts from 20th-century combat veterans, is a most powerful driving force.[13] 'We were closer to each other that we were to our wives', was one significant comment he mentioned. Historian Stephen Ambrose noted that virtually without exception, those he interviewed said that their closest friends – 'The men from whom they have no secrets, the men with whom they would gladly share their last piece of bread' – were their combat comrades.[14] The medieval soldier was no different: he may have fought for his lord, but his primary loyalty in a fight was to his friends.

World War II Australian Warrant Officer Philip Jones was eloquent on the subject. 'Your mate was your tender companion, the rough-house drunken bum you went on a spree with, the bloke you could depend on in life or approaching death, who would never let you down.'[15] US paratrooper Don Malarkey wrote of his experiences: 'There is not a day that has passed since that I do not thank Adolf Hitler for allowing me to be associated with the most talented and inspiring group of men that I have ever known.'[16] Private David Webster of the US 101st Airborne Division could have been withdrawn from his unit through several methods – experience, parental influence at home, promotion or his two combat wounds – but he wanted to stay with his friends. On one journey by truck, surrounded by his comrades, he described his return to his unit as to a 'bright home full of love'.[17]

Despite the stresses and horrors of close-quarter combat, soldiers will often return to it rather than let their comrades down. Poet and British infantry officer Siegfried Sassoon went back to the horrors of World War I trench warfare because he could not live with the thought of his comrades being there without him: '…he couldn't bear to think of poor Old Joe lying out at night in shell-holes and getting shelled'. His poem 'When I'm asleep, dreaming and lulled and warm', is about the ghosts of soldiers he had had known reproaching him in his dream for his absence.[18]

World War II US Marine E. B. Sledge, at first puzzled by why former members of his unit would want to return to the horrors and dangers of fighting, concluded that it was because no-one else would 'understand what we had experienced, what in our minds seemed to set us apart forever from anyone who hadn't been in combat'.[19] In Vietnam, wounded in the arm by a white phosphorous grenade, Sergeant John Setelin had received first aid and was due to be helicoptered out of the battle of Ia Drang. He changed his mind, took the sling off and went back into battle, explaining: 'I couldn't in good faith get on a chopper and fly out of there and leave those guys behind.'[20] The author experienced such emotions when going on leave from the Iraq war, leaving his own unit behind and then, back in his own country, finding he wanted to return to the war early.

The closer to combat one is with one's comrades, the more one bonds. Wehrmacht soldier Guy Sajer transferred from a transport section to the infantry during World War II, and while he noted that the decision almost cost him and a like-minded comrade their lives, he did not regret belonging to a combat unit: 'We discovered a sense of comradeship which I have never found again, inexplicable and steady, through thick and thin.'[21] US paratrooper Leo Boyle, who was wounded in combat in World War II and never returned to his unit, commented: 'I never became fully resigned to the separation from the life as a "trooper" – separated from my buddies, and never jumping again.'[22] Marine officer Philip Caputo thought that the US Marines in Vietnam fought as hard as they did because they would rather do so than be a deserter, who 'ran out on his friends'.[23]

Shared fears make for self-stabilisation. World War I British soldier George Coppard thought that 'the daily comradeship of my pals, whether in or out of the line, gave me strength'.[24] In World War II New Guinea, Corporal Lofty Cox told his mate that after seven straight days of fighting and being shelled, the only thing that stopped him jumping out of his position and running was that he had 'a bloke like you alongside me', only to be told in reply that his friend felt exactly the same.[25] Thus, the last thing a soldier will do is inform authority about his battle-partner's behaviour, leading one to surmise that such behaviours as discussed in this work may very well be widespread but unreported.

The worst thing anyone can do as an infantry soldier – or as anyone engaged in close-quarter combat – is to let down their friends. World War II US battle surgeon Brendan Phibbs took part in an assault by his infantry company in the Battle of the Bulge which was not supported very well by the two companies on either side, and noted the pained giving and taking of the comments that followed its bloody aftermath: "'Where were you guys, for chrissakes? We needed you on our right' ... exquisitely painful when a wounded man points a bloody hand at a friend from another company, [and] mutters, "Where the fuck was you, Tom?"'[26]

Aggressive leadership – a necessity in medieval battle

Medieval warfare necessitated a commander within each unit who led by example. He would have been necessarily aggressive. He showed his men, fighting on foot with them, what he wanted them to do, and demonstrated that he shared in their fears, difficulties and successes whenever possible.

Little has survived showing such a commander, although in William Shakespeare's *Henry V*, the king inspires his troops at Agincourt:

> And gentlemen in England now-a-bed
> Shall think themselves accursed they were not here,
> And hold their manhoods cheap whiles any speaks
> That fought with us upon Saint Crispin's day.

The real Henry V probably did make an inspiring speech, but he doubtless had to make it several times, riding along his broad front of men before they had advanced to their battle-line, rather than once, as depicted in the 1989 film starring Kenneth Branagh.[27] (Incidentally, the lead actors on the English side fight without helmets in the final melee, which in real life would have likely led to their demise.)

Stirring words did make a difference, as Philippe de Commines noted of a 15th-century engagement on the Continent that he witnessed, judging that the enemy only stood and fought because of the inspiring words of their king.[28]

Elizabeth I is said to have made a speech to her land troops, waiting at Tilbury to repel any landings from the Spanish Armada in 1588. Some of her reported words declare her willingness to die alongside them in battle: 'to live and die amongst you all; to lay down for my God, and for my kingdom, and my people, my honour and my blood, even in the dust.'[29]

It was not just in speechmaking beforehand, however, that a commander had to excel. He had to be a committed and aggressive leader. There are many examples from later wars, where meticulous records have been kept, which illustrate the sort of leader necessary in close-quarter combat.

Men in battle behaved the same in medieval times as they do today. The role of the aggressive leader was as important in the 1400s as it was in World War II and as it is today

A World War II engagement, related to infantry surgeon Brendan Phibbs, was proof enough that one aggressive leader could get unwilling men moving, and then operating as an effective group. Pinned down, awaiting mortar fire with dread, a platoon was urged into combat by its lieutenant. He first called down artillery on the enemy position, and then berated the men into following him while the enemy was thus occupied, shouting: '"If they can't see you, they can't hit you; those guns are to shoot with you know. You shouldn't be lying' on them; you can't fuck them", and he walks along the platoon kickin' asses and pretty soon we're all standing' up bangin' away.' The officer got rifle grenadiers and bazooka teams firing, rans ahead of the men, who followed, and then he

> gives a scream like a wild fuckin' Indian and we all start yellin' like maniacs and runnin' after him ... we were all different inside. Them Krauts must have thought they were up against some kind of murderin' lunatics, 'cause I never saw so many white faces under them big helmets and handkerchiefs wavin'.[30]

It was necessary not to show fear if you were a leader. An officer in the South Nottingham Hussars, who were waiting to go forward into an attack in North Africa during World War II, was asked by one of his men if he was scared. '"I'm as scared as you are," he said, "but, being an officer, I have to hide my feelings."'[31] Another officer, a lieutenant leading his British platoon during Operation *Market Garden*, commanded his men to charge, and leapt forward, but none followed. He turned back and exhorted them to follow, and still none moved. Finally, 'he said furiously: "If you don't charge, you bastards, I'll shoot you!" and at that they moved.'[32]

US paratrooper Richard Winters was a well-known officer by the time World War II was over. He exhibited excellent leadership throughout his training and in combat. After the D-Day landings, his men were attacking at night, but the advance was not going well. Exhausted, without preparatory fire on their target, the troops were lying on the ground but were then ordered to assault. Winters, running, led the way, but a machine gun opened up on the men and the company was split, with most taking cover on either side of the road. Winters yelled at them to move, but they did not, so he resorted to running across the road from side to side, under fire, kicking their backsides, yelling and screaming, something that was very out of character for him, for he was a well-liked and respected officer who led by example. Eventually they followed him – and the action saved the flank of that section of the army.[33] Stephen Ambrose, who interviewed many men of Winters' association, came to the conclusion that Winters provided 'not only brains but personal leadership. "Follow me", was his code. He personally killed more Germans and took more risks than anyone else.'[34]

World War II British Commando officer George Knowland was leading 24 men who were besieged by 'platoon after platoon' of Japanese in the Far East during the final stages of the war. He led his men in a vicious fight for high ground the Commandoes had taken:

> He himself was everywhere, hurling grenades, manning a Bren, encouraging his hard-pressed soldiers. He was last seen engaging a horde of Japs with a 2-inch mortar, firing it right in their teeth against a tree. His first bomb slew six men. Then the Japs surged forward.[35]

Knowland was killed in the assault and received a posthumous Victoria Cross, but the stand he took and his leadership meant that the position was held. Some of the American generals fighting in the Pacific certainly believed in setting a direct example. General Simon Buckner, who commanded the Tenth Army, was known to appear at the front, and on at least one occasion spent some 'ten to fifteen minutes' sniping at the enemy. General Claude Easley, of the US 96th Division, was also known to visit the front lines for the same reason.[36]

Commando officer Lieutenant Colonel A. C. Newman, of the Essex Regiment and 2 Commando, was leading a detachment during the

St Nazaire raid in March 1942. Newman's men suffered several setbacks, and then 'His blood was up. He was damned well going for it bald-headed now. Observing one man struggling, he shouted at him angrily: "Do you want to live for ever?" The effect of this startling challenge ... was magical, and (soon) ... they had all become charged with the same burning ardour.' Newman was awarded a Victoria Cross for his valour in the raid.[37]

A VC was also awarded posthumously to Colonel H. Jones of the 2nd Parachute Regiment in the Falklands for similar reasons. His unit was delayed by the enemy in front of them, and finally the colonel, urging on his men, went forward with a sub-machine gun but was shot down by an outflanked Argentine position. There has been some comment on the wisdom of being so far forward,[38] but as one of his men said: 'Hero or lunatic, he was a leader of men.'[39] The same might be said of Lieutenant Colonel J. H. C. Pearson, who led Canadian forces in the storming of a bridge in 1944. His men, demoralised by the experiences of the previous day, were refusing to advance. Pearson got out of his armoured carrier and walked forward, with a walking stick and a red rose in his hat. He was shot down, but his men went forward, encouraged by his example.[40]

Philip Caputo was taking his US Marines platoon further into jungle in Vietnam, chasing some Viet Cong forces they had fought. Eventually, with the trail growing cold, he had to make the decision to move on or not, with one of his men looking at him with the expression that Caputo thought every infantry officer has seen: 'What are you going to do now, mister officer?'[41] Caputo went on, admitting to himself that although he was afraid, he also wanted to get into the fight to prove himself, and that the Marines had pushed such aggression into him. Later, in an action he was leading, the Marines took on some Viet Cong and beat them thoroughly, with his men going into a 'frenzy' and wanting to get over a river across which they had exchanged fire to finish off the enemy. Caputo could 'feel the whole line wanting to charge across the river ... and smash the life out of anything that stood in its way ... [I] wanted to level the village and kill the rest of the Viet Cong in close combat. I wanted us to tear their guts out with bayonets.'[42] Caputo was on such a 'high' that he later walked up and down in a clearing, shouting insults at the enemy and trying to draw their fire so their positions would be exposed.

In medieval times, just as in all combat, it was the aggressive leader who was most necessary in close-quarter battlefield command. He had to be almost someone who enjoyed being there. Richard I of England – Coeur de Lion, the Lionheart – was said to be such a soldier.

His descendent, Richard III, the infamous 'hunchback king' of the Wars of the Roses, was reputed to be the same sort of fighter. At Bosworth, effectively the last battle of the wars, he made a distinctive aggressive command decision, to cavalry charge the centre of Henry Tudor's troops. It was to be the last decision Richard made, and he was the last English king to die in battle, leading his troops from the front. But it was a fair gamble, and typical too – to be aggressive, charge forward and lead the way was a necessary part of what constituted war in the Middle Ages.

What the supreme leader showed by example, his lesser leaders would have to emulate. Whether commanding a wing or a detachment of 150 or even just 30 soldiers would not matter: the leader had to lead by example. If he was not resolute, then his men would melt away. It was necessary to show this in every way, by being at the front, striking hard and first, and encouraging his men verbally, with his actions and by his very stance. A piece of advice the author received in his own military leadership training comes to mind: 'Don't look back. If they're right behind you it doesn't matter. And if they're not you'll show them you're afraid and doubtful.'

A capable commander of a household group in the Wars of the Roses might have organised his men as follows:

The poleaxe men would go to the front in two to three lines. The forward line would fight, and be relieved after a decided period – 10–15 minutes – by the second line. If a third line was present, it then went forward in its turn.

The lines rotated in this fashion for the duration of the battle, but a mobile reserve could have been used to give 10-minute breaks. If the battle was protracted, men would have been withdrawn fully from the fighting for perhaps 30–45 minutes for extended repair and refreshment.

The reserves were 'plugged in' to the battle by relieving the third line. The reserve thus formed a fourth line, and at the word or whistle of command, the third line would step back, with the reserve taking their place. The withdrawn third line then became the reserve.

The billmen might be the second section of the line. Then again, a different commander might have used them on the wings – this was no army of the Romans, with a definitive overall style, being rather household groups, with localised loyalty and individual techniques. As the battle moved forward, the billmen could be tasked to take care of any fallen poleaxe men whom the army literally walked over as they progressed. Men still fighting would be dispatched, and prisoners taken – if prisoner-taking was indeed the commanded practice of the day. The Wars of the Roses, as has been observed in this work, was characterised by a viciousness that often manifested itself with an unwillingness to take prisoners and the summary execution of those who were captured.

If there was a break in the poleaxe line, the billmen could have used their bills as best they could to hold off the poleaxe enemy fighters with their points, while their own poleaxe men regrouped and re-formed. The billmen would have also utilised a reserve concept.

The bowmen would have circulated independently to the rear of the lines. They would dart forward in packs to attack any enemy poleaxe fighters or billmen who were isolated. They also might take prisoners, if prisoners were being taken, and escort them to the rear under guard. However, on rare occasions the bowmen could become a decisive factor: they were an immediately available force, and constituted the bulk of the army. At Agincourt, for example, they acted when the extremely muddy ground took its toll on the exhausted French attackers: 'The chroniclers speak of the embogged knights as standing helplessly to be hewn down, while the archers beat upon the armour with mallets ... and rolled them over one on another till the dead and wounded lay three deep.'[43]

The aim of the battle

The overall aim of medieval battle commanders, which all but the newest soldiers knew, was to break the enemy line. When that happened, it was the wish of every battle captain to exploit the breakthrough by rushing into place new troops – preferably fresh, keen and strong.

Attacking the enemy not only from the front but from the side was a major problem for medieval commanders. The average man-at-arms could not deal with such a move. He could cope with an enemy in front of him, but being attacked at the same time from the side gave him more problems than he could handle; he could not fight in two directions at once or see multiple threats which might be approaching at the same time.

The enemy realised a breakthrough was a major problem, and would do all they could to stop any such rupture. It was therefore by no means certain that what appeared to be a breaking of the main line would continue to be so. A commander, rushing forward his reserve, could patch it and repair the problem.

If it was not possible to break through, then it might be possible to outflank the enemy. This meant getting around the end of the opposing line with his troops. In the event this happened, the soldiers at the end of the line had the same problem as any coping with a breakthrough – they were fighting an enemy in front of them and others swinging weapons at them from the side.

Panic was the companion to a breakthrough. If soldiers were in such a position, they might well hesitate in their fighting, and hesitation could be fatal; it showed, and it spread. Hesitation might well turn into retreat. That could manifest itself in turning away from the enemy and simply walking off the battlefield, or in just taking a few steps back, causing confusion in the ranks behind. There could also be a full-blown panic, with weapons thrown down and groups of men running away.

The flank commanders knew very well that the enemy would try to extend their line beyond the end of the soldiers they had facing them. But that might itself weaken the line and allow a breakthrough, so it was a matter of careful calculation and control. It was possible to cope with a flank extension by a means of 'refusing the line', which meant to form a sharp angle against the oncoming enemy, but often this caused confusion and chaos resulted. For example, during the battle of Barnet, fought in dense fog in 1471, a flanking manoeuvre by the Lancastrians resulted in some of their soldiers mistaking their own men for the enemy, with disastrous results.

One problem facing the side weakest in numbers was that they could have their line broken simply because they did not have enough men to meet the enemy in equal strength along the entire front. A commander using, for example, two ranks of poleaxe soldiers backed by two ranks of billmen and roving bowmen could be outmatched by an enemy front which had three ranks of each. The weaker side would be steadily worn down in battle by the ability of the other side to fight for longer. The toll of wounded and dead on the weaker side steadily ate away at their ability to resist.

Related to this was the overall commander's willingness to fight in the first place. He would rely very heavily on his forward scouts before consenting to fight, to establish that he was at least the enemy's equal in numbers in types of infantry and quantity of bowmen, and to assess the quality of the opposing troops. If he was markedly inferior, he would avoid combat if he could, while waiting for reinforcements or finding ground markedly in his favour. As historians Smail and Verbruggen have pointed out, commanders usually went to a great deal of effort to avoid a battle if they could win by other means.[44] This might include simply ensuring rumours of his superior numbers, fighting ability or equipment reached the enemy force, overawing the enemy on the day itself so he would flee or occupying a strong position first. They may not have heard of the sixth-century BC Chinese strategist Sun Tzu, but they certainly understood one of his maxims: 'The supreme art of war is to subdue the enemy without fighting.'

The formation of the battle line

So what did a medieval battle look like? In general, there seems to be a collective adherence to the list given earlier, in that the opposing sides formed up into two lines facing each other, each line often composed of several ranks. The men were, however, still collected in their household groups, following the important person whom they were serving. These are best thought of as 'companies' of infantry:

some 100–200 men clustered around the banner of their leader would be a typical company. This would make a block perhaps four men deep and 50 men wide for a 200-man company, or perhaps 4 deep and 40 wide, with a 40-man reserve: a manoeuvrable formation in the right hands. It must be emphasised that there was no set rule about this. One company might be experienced and formed up tidily, another an enthusiastic noisy mob. This study will advance a hypothesis as to how heavy infantry *might* be used, if their commander had experience, intelligence and foresight. What is stated here is definitely not the rule for all, and nor is there much in the way of historical proof as to how they were used – instead, there is a suggestion of how they *must* have been used to survive.

The household grouping, with its banner, served as a focal point for this familial host of troops throughout the battle, and indeed followed ancient practice. As Vegetius noted: 'The insignia were inscribed with letters indicting the century's cohort ... seeing and reading this, soldiers could not stray from their comrades.'[45] It was seemingly always the case that banners were used, indicating which household group was which, and that the leader's flag formed an important focal point for a household group. Most companies wore some sort of device, often on the sleeve. The surcoats of the Crusaders – a sort of sleeved coverall, designed to ward off the sun – had long been discarded. All armies did this, and it was deemed most important to get the flags into the right place before a battle commenced, even if that meant delay. John Keegan noted of the French at Agincourt: 'There was a great deal of tiresome struggling, during the period of deployment, to get these banners into the leading rank.'[46]

The soldiers were in three broad groupings: bowmen, billmen and plated men, the last two groups the light and heavy infantry respectively. It is a mistake, however, to call the latter group 'knights'. Dr Peter Williams, who personally visited a great number of the medieval battlefields of Europe, is of the opinion that when surveying medieval army orders of battle (as far as can be known what they were), the 'knights' constituted a very small number. In an army of one or two thousand soldiers, the knights might make up about 3 per cent of the total. That would mean in an army of 1,000, there would be just 30 knights. Ian Mortimer believes that there were 'about 1,100' knights in England in medieval times, and some 11,000 gentlemen and esquires, the latter being the sons of knights.[47] The gentlemen and esquires would also have been of 'the group that fights' in society, as Mortimer put it, and it can therefore be expected that the plated men would have included plenty of this cohort. It is worth noting that there was nothing to stop gentlemen and esquires being professional soldiers too.

Consequently, just having the knights in plate armour with staff weapons would not constitute a large number of fighters. It follows, logically, that a commander would want to have as many as possible of his heavy infantry so armed. Plate armour was the aim of all professional soldiers, and it is known that permanent garrisons and professional cohorts of the castles were made up of such soldiers. It can be safely assumed that such people wore plate and carried the best weapons.

The plated warriors wielding poleaxes therefore did not merely comprise knights. The entire number of professional soldiers at any battle constituted the heavy infantry, apart from two other small groups of minor commanders within the ranks.

The first such minor commanders were master bowmen. These were men who had become the best at using the longbow, and whose role was to lead, advise and command the units of bowmen raised by the Commissions of Array. Their number is not known, but in practice today it can ne seen that one master bowman can command three ranks of 50 or even more – such numbers have been seen by the author at medieval festivals, firing the 'arrow storm' under command.

It would have taken a professional NCO-equivalent to command in similar fashion a group of billmen. Although likely a professional soldier capable of wearing full plate, rather than the brigandine coat with plates the more common soldier wore, it would have been more likely that this commander wore the billmen's harness, and carried a bill rather than a poleaxe, simply to identify with and therefore empathise with his charges.

The bowmen and billmen in the main were therefore not the professional soldiers of England: they were those raised by the levies who turned out for a campaign, or sometimes merely a single battle. They followed the banner of their local knight or lord, and they fought as directed.

While their lord's banner flew and went forward, so too did his soldiers. If the flag wavered and fell, this had a highly negative effect on those soldiers' morale, and a great effort would be made to get it flying again. Mud and dirt were not to despoil the banner, but blood was not a significant negative factor, especially if it could later be linked to a person or event. Anyone who visits a British cathedral can see these military banners hung from the roof rafters and walls, some many centuries old, and many reflecting regimental insignia.

Some historians have argued for distinctive markings on the armour of chiefs and minor leaders within the ranks. Andrew Boardman points out the Duke of Gloucester's 8,000 white boar badges which marked out his men.[48] This was only logical.

A block of 100–200 men forming several ranks deep around their banner, with their lord front and centre, was therefore the tactical building block of a medieval army.

The preliminary to the foot battle

An arrow engagement was the initial norm. It might be wondered why this was so, for if the armour held off the danger of the arrows, why bother? The pavise – a heavy shield, the lower section of which was rested on the ground – was in use on medieval battlefields, and there is evidence they were employed by English combat forces, although less perhaps in England than in forays to the Continent. They offered a fair defence against arrows, and it would have been sensible to deploy them.[49] Oman suggests they were more often used defensively by the attackers in sieges, and says they were not used 'in normal battles out in the open'.[50] But medieval battles were not won by defending, and sheltering behind pavises offered only temporary protection.

Armour itself was not generally 100 per cent effective in defence. Plate would give a high amount of protection; mail and brigandines much less. But only the best armour could be guaranteed to hold off the arrow storm, and while good plate would protect a soldier, he could still be wounded by an arrow in the eye at a weak spot with inferior plate or mail. Any billmen wearing just a brigandine or jack, along with the bowmen – similarly clad – were also disadvantaged, and would be steadily picked off by arrow fire unless they closed and fought. The best tactic to avert this was to walk forward and fight.

To begin the infantry assault, there was a need for some method of effective communication, such as a trumpet blast, or rather several, with outlying commanders hearing the sound from the centre, then ordering it repeated along the line. The weapons of the bowmen and how they routinely fought has been established in a previous chapter; but how did the whole mass of foot soldiers move forward to engage? They might not always have acted as a single body. It seems from some accounts that a medieval army might almost fight as three forces – left flank, centre and right flank – all with the same general impetus, but with the individual commanders controlling their component in a symbiotic relationship. This was the case at the battle of Tewkesbury in 1471, when King Edward IV, commanding the left 'battle', took the initiative by stationing a small infantry force of perhaps 200 men in a wood to his left to guard against a surprise attack. These men became of critical importance when an attack was indeed made on Edward's left flank.

The arrangement of the ranked foot soldiers

As previously discussed, but now examining the battle of Towton as an example, Hardy – and he is the expert – and others argue the bowmen were only really a factor in the battle's initial stage. They fired off part of their stock of two quivers of 24 arrows each, and picked up maybe 50 per cent of the fallen arrows fired towards them.[51] Oman, by comparison, says the initial Yorkist arrow attack by Lord Fauconberg used a skirmishing line of archers, which then retired. Anecdotally, it appears the Lancastrian bowmen were largely ineffective as they were firing into the wind, with a snowstorm engulfing at least these initial stages.

The Lancaster return arrow fire was thus ineffective, and 'All the Lancastrian arrows fell into empty ground, till their stock was nearly exhausted.[52] It would be doubtful that the arrow storm would have continued for long, but it was important to have enough archers to make it effective – Boardman suggests they constituted half of an army in the Wars of the Roses, a lesser proportion than an English army serving overseas, where he argues for eight archers to every man-at-arms.[53] The army of the Yorkists at Tewkesbury, for example, constituted 3,436 bowmen out of a force of 6,000.[54] Philippe de Commines, writing about his observations of battle on the Continent, thought the bowmen 'must be strong, and very numerous, for few are of no avail'.[55]

It was common to put the most heavily armed and armoured soldiers in the front line. Again, this followed ancient practice, as advocated by Vegetius: 'Those fighting before the standards, around the standards, and [otherwise] in the front line were … the heavy armament … [with] the second line similarly armed.[56] The men with poleaxes, the heavy tanks of the army, likely fought in the front line. Not only were they the best armed, but they were the best armoured as well. There would have also been some competition to be in the front line to show you were brave.

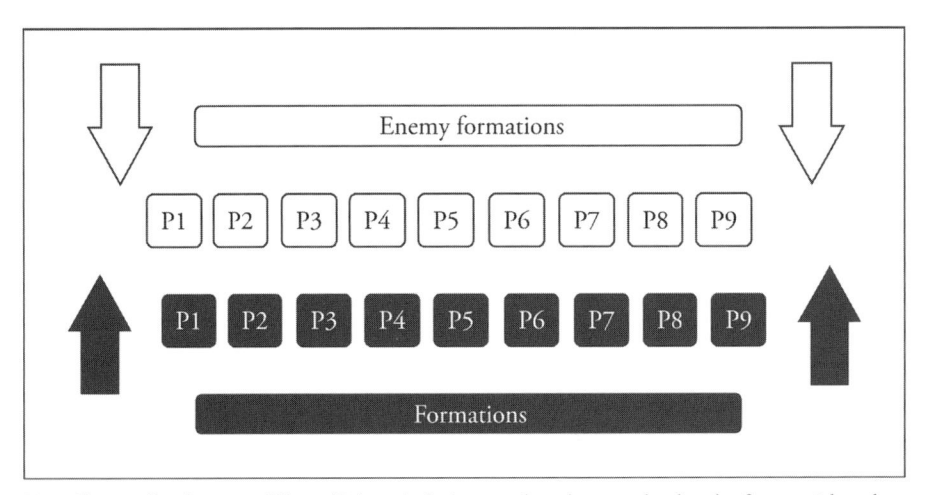

Two lines of poleaxe soldiers (P1 etc) facing each other at the battle face, with other formations of soldiers behind them.

Keegan notes that the French at Agincourt placed 'the grander and the braver in front of the more humble and timid'.[57]

Was this therefore how the battle line looked?

Although this is a start, it cannot have been the whole story. Such lines would have been too thin. The soldiers with bills and glaives were the second line of the army; that is to say they were the second force. Boardman wants them 'mixed in with men-at-arms', but that cannot be countenanced for two reasons.[58] The first is that the poleaxe men fought in a different way, with full swings to take advantage of the blade, or the weapon's hammer faces, against armour. They needed room to swing their blades, and a haphazard arrangement of not knowing whether you had an axeman or a billman to your left or right would have hampered this.

Furthermore, if the other side had used, for example, a line of 10 poleaxe men, then those 10 advancing towards a mixed line of the enemy would have caused much destruction, the lesser armed and armoured billmen being easy targets and going down quickly. For these reasons, this study cannot see the soldiers fighting in mixed groups, but rather in blocks defined by weapons: poleaxe men, soldiers carrying the bill or glaive – for convenience now being called billmen – and the archers, with mobile bands of skirmishers who used their speed, mobility and ease of vision to make up for their lack of protective armour and heavy weapons.

The concept of having differently armed and armoured infantry cohorts is not something new to the Wars of the Roses. Historian Stephen Dando-Collins describes the Roman legions as being supported by 'Auxiliary' forces which were lesser armoured, although similarly armed.[59] It seems in the ancient period this was a common practice across several countries and armies. Sextus Julius Frontinus, who wrote widely in the first century AD on ancient battle tactics, described how a mix of such forces was used, with the light-armed troops hurling javelins and then retreating, circling round to attack the flanks of the enemy as he rushed forward.[60]

The Romans also used a three-line system of fighting, from which it may be possible the medieval armies drew inspiration. The second line pushed through the first and engaged, and after a while they in turn were replaced by their now somewhat rested compatriots.[61] The system was widely used and for many years, and for some time was unique to the Romans – no other army had used such a system before.[62,63]

Returning to the medieval world, Adrian Waite suggests soldiers of all types were organised into groups of 20, one of whom would be appointed vintner, the medieval equivalent of a sergeant. These groups were organised into five blocks of 19 men, with four vintners and a 'centenary', who would be the vintner in command.[64] As with all things in these organisations, this situation would not be fixed, but would depend on the abilities of the commander: one with considerable experience, or indeed a very loud voice, may have commanded more men.

Re-enactors today use such a system. Robert Johnson, aged 35, said of his experience: 'We try and fight in ranks five rows deep. As there is no real record of what commands were used, we used very simple commands from our sergeants.' Andreas Dracocardos, another re-enactor, aged 39, added: 'We can take commands by our sergeant shouting. The visibility when wearing a helmet limits what we can see and anything visually commanded.'[65]

The second argument against Boardman's mix of soldiers is that the billmen were less heavily armoured than the poleaxe soldiers, which

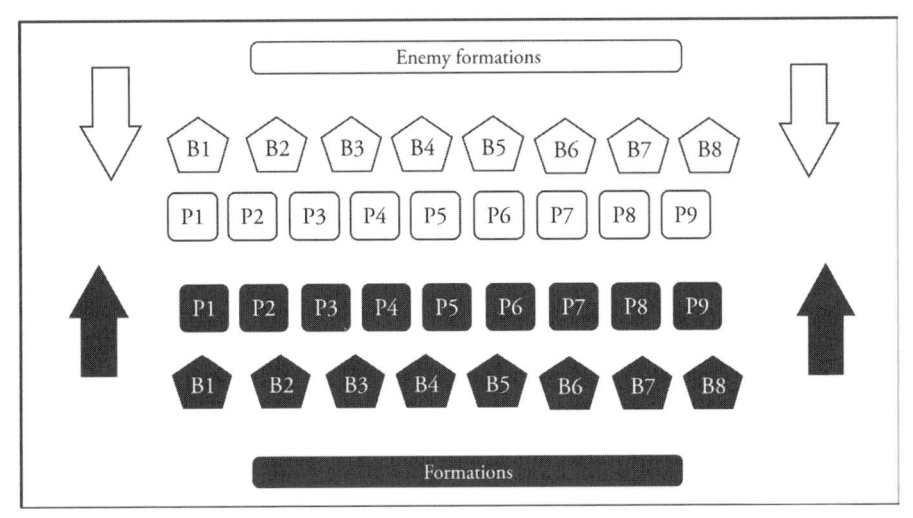

A more accurate depiction of the front line, but this still is not the right picture.

would have made them preferred targets. Instead, the best arrangement would have been for the better-protected poleaxe men to be at the front, with the billmen in a supporting role. This is indeed what the commanders would have taken from Vegetius, who says that behind the front two-line force previously described were 'the light troops and light armament'.[66]

It is not only logical to fight this way, it is the only possibility. The billmen were there to mop up any fallen enemy as the line advanced, or to take advantage of any enemy poleaxe men who were disabled by an effective poleaxe blow. The hook of the bill would have been brought into play to trip up or pull down the enemy soldier, and once down, if the line advanced over him he was much easier to despatch with the swords and long thin daggers of the bowmen, who stayed well clear of the main melee, but acted as light infantry where they could.

As each lord brought his 150-man 'company' to the battlefield, it must be realised that within each such group there was a variety of arms: some bowmen, some professional soldiers armed with poleaxes and some billmen. There must have been a reorganisation before the battle so as to get all the bowmen together with other bowmen, probably in front of their own company, but perhaps sometimes not under their own banner.

It was probably not the case that the billmen and poleaxe plated warriors would have accepted such dispersal away from their lord. To fight with one's friends was the foundation of morale – this is recognised throughout history. To say otherwise is to suggest separating a member of the Black Watch to go and fight with the Life Guards, or a small group of US Marines be placed within the ranks of a US Army battalion. No commander does this, as he knows the loss of morale would be a crippling factor. Consequently, the battlefield must be seen as composed of company groups, which were varied and discrete. One company might have 40 bowmen, 20 poleaxe men and 90 billmen. Another might be stronger with its poleaxe component. But dispersal to fight outside of companies would not have been accepted: the men would have been deprived of their essential morale, which every commander then and now knows is crucial to success. The battlefield must have been highly varied and colourful in its composition: in essence resembling a giant patchwork quilt of soldiers, but each patch was an individualised company grouped under its lord.

This was nothing especially new for the Wars of the Roses: the bowmen had fought in this manner at Agincourt, for example, and Anne Curry vividly describes the variety of their weapons, with all sorts of edged and percussive pieces.[67] Polydore Vergil confirms that the bowmen started the battle of Towton in their traditional manner, and then moved into a role as light infantry.[68] This is what happened at Agincourt, which was a shambles of a battle: the advancing French were deprived of space, pushed forward by their own, and as they spilled out of their advancing columns, came into contact with the English bowmen. Keegan claims: 'The chroniclers are specific that, on the contrary, it was the archers who moved to the attack.' This they did with their edged and percussive weapons, including the mallets they had used to hammer their defensive stakes into the ground.[69]

The billmen may have also had another role: to provide a staff weapon defence against any sudden use of cavalry. Horses will not willingly or effectively charge a wall of spears, and the billmen may have had signals and commands for such a specialised sudden forming of a defensive line. Their bills were probably longer than poleaxes, and more suitable for cavalry defence, which some writers have suggested saw them laying the spear across a knee in a line of men.[70]

But there is a major factor which advances a new hypothesis of the actuality of the combat. Fighting with a single rank of poleaxe men could not have been sufficient. No-one can fight non-stop in full armour while swinging a weapon which requires so much physical strength – as will be shown in detail. It must have been the case that the front row of axemen was relieved periodically. This might have been every 15 minutes, for tests have shown that heavy infantry could not fight for longer than that.

This use of relieving lines is something missed in almost all accounts of medieval battle. For example, Curry and Vergil do not have the front line relieved at all in the battles they are discussing. Similarly, Barker, describing Agincourt, says: 'For three long hours the slaughter continued, as the English hacked and stabbed their way through the vanguard and the main body of the French army.'[71] But soldiers cannot fight in this way – for 'three long hours' or anything like that time. Using percussive and edged weapons for so long is not possible. And only one part of the advancing English, or the advancing French for that matter, was in contact with the enemy: the very front of the two forces. There would have been many French soldiers falling – which saw them replaced, in a fashion – but not so many English, who must have changed their positions in the crush for their companions who stepped forward.

For how long could the front line fight? Interviews of re-enactors give an average of just over 13 minutes, from the initial start of fighting until they need their first rest – that is, being moved to the second line. These re-enactors were all experienced males, fit, with an average age of 36,[72] and were all using edged, point or percussive weapons. Note, though, that they were asked how long they could *initially* fight before they would need that *first* rest – outlined as being a minute or two. The 'rest' was in reality being moved back a row, where they could still face danger if the man in front of them fell, and where they were there to step forward over their comrade to protect him if necessary. Any downed enemy would be stepped over or around by the first rank and dealt with by the second line, and/or the billmen – these measures were especially necessary if the line was advancing, which after all was the main point of a battle. So there was hardly a 'rest' but merely a pause in having to constantly wield their weapon.

Even soldiers used to wearing armour and wielding weapons need rest breaks, for they are using considerably more energy just by being steel-clad than they would otherwise. A test, devised by the University of Leeds, using armour-clad re-enactors on treadmills, 'found that the volunteers expended nearly twice as much energy walking and running while wearing the armor [sic] as when they weren't'. In addition, wearing armour was found to be more taxing than carrying the same weight in a backpack, primarily because of the weight distributed around the lower body.[73] One journalist, writing about re-enactors and taking part in a fight for his article, reported: 'I'm struggling to get used to the weight of the armour. I'm expending a huge amount of energy, gasping for breath and sweating profusely.'[74]

Although there is now a good understanding of how ancient battles were fought, this cannot merely be transferred to medieval battles. Combat actions in the Middle Ages had different weapons – the longbow played a crucial role in English medieval combat – and the bascinet imposed a constraint despite at the same time affording better protection. But some of the limitations the ancients experienced were also encountered in medieval fighting, in particular the lessening of endurance imposed by wearing armour. Victor Davis Hanson, a keen researcher of the phalanx and hoplite of ancient times, taught university students who created replicas of Greek armour and weapons. He noted that: 'After about thirty minutes of dueling in mock battles under the sun of the San Joaquin Valley they are utterly exhausted.' He later concluded: 'Battle quickly exhausted the men in the phalanx, both physically and psychologically – perhaps in little less than an hour's time.'[75] Richard Gabriel also suggests the battles were short – perhaps lasting only 30 minutes – due to the exhausting nature of the fighting, and that only the first two ranks landed blows.[76]

The same considerations for battles fought thousands of years ago with armour and edged and percussive weapons apply for those of medieval times.

There are some minor further considerations. Dr Peter Williams has argued to the author that there is no reason why the two combat lines should not have engaged and then broken off periodically, almost by mutual agreement. Michael Miller, too, likes this concept: 'No man could keep up the furious pace of such vicious hand-to-hand fighting for long, and parties withdrew for a time to recover their breath before charging into the fray once again.'[77] Such a rest period seems initially feasible, and indeed both sides might have indulged in some recovery of the injured, with a bit of shouting at the other side and then – almost by mutual agreement again – a resumption of the fight. It must be said, however, that any such break in combat would be accompanied by much posting of sentries at the front, who probably stood there, visors down and weapons in hand, to guard against any sudden moves by the enemy to their front. The two sides would also have had to remain close enough together to negate any arrow fire coming over the enemy's line into their own. And given there could be no agreement not to engage

122 • MEDIEVAL MILITARY COMBAT

in conduct to gain the upper hand, there could be surreptitious edging forward to gain a flanking advantage.

One fictional depiction from soldier-turned-novelist Ronald Welch is likely correct:

> 'Ware left!' a voice bellowed, and Owen swung round, instinctively pushing out his pole-axe, sending a Lancastrian back on his heels, and then jumping after him, thrusting again, and shouting with triumph as the man toppled over, and another Yorkist hacked down at him.
> 'Rest! Rest!'
> Yorkists were pushing past Owen from behind, the rear ranks coming forward to relieve those who had begun the attack. Not even the strongest could fight for long in plate armour, and as Owen stepped back he realized that his arms were aching and his whole body was afire with heat, his shirt and hose soaked with sweat. Safe for the moment behind two ranks of Yorkists he pushed up his visor.[78]

This passage from Welch is more significant than might be thought. He likely applied the same logical construction of how the battle line must have looked, in his creation of it in his novel, as has this author – using his own war and intelligence analyst experience and Inherent Military Probability.

Obviously if there were three ranks rather than two, the first row of soldiers were getting less exposure to combat by having a further break

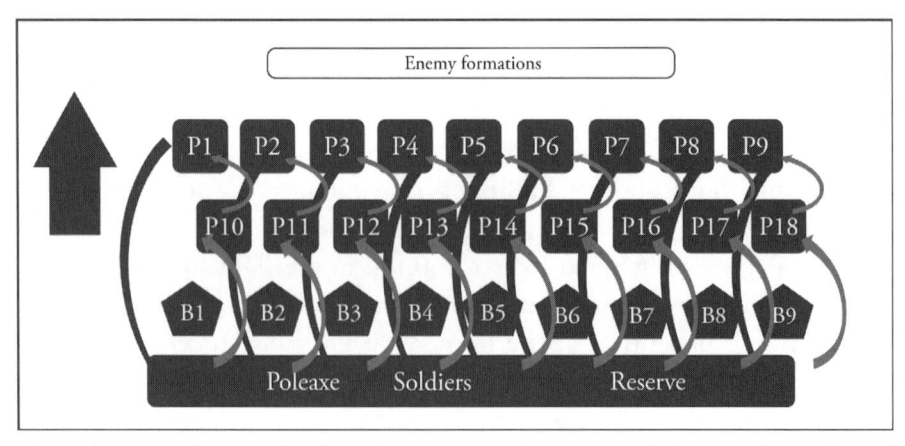

The poleaxe soldiers on the front line, stepping back to the left through the line of medium infantry billmen, and grouping together as the reserve, for the 10-minute break. The reserve becomes the second line, and the second line becomes the new front.

as they moved from the second rank to the third. It might not, however, have always been the case that they fought in three rows: it would depend on their company's strength, their own experience in handling another layer of complexity and the ability of their sergeant and commander in handling them. But they must have had at least two ranks.

If the men-at-arms were asked to fight in this way, they needed a 10-minute *full* rest after an average of 49 minutes in the first hour. That is, they would be able to fight for 13 minutes, move to the second rank for a minute or so, then resume their place in the front line and fight for another 13 minutes, and so on, until they got to around 49 minutes. This precision is not what they would have acted with; it is merely a hypothetical time inserted here from the analysis above. Of course, there were no watches in those days, and a sandglass could hardly be brought to the battlefield, so maybe an estimate of the time intervals was guessed at, or the sergeants counted it out on their heads.

The variations are myriad, not only for time, but of the order of the household group. Maybe it was three ranks: the soldier would fight for a measured time, move back to the second rank for two minutes, then back to the third rank for two minutes, then to the front line for another fighting session. Or maybe he went back into the third from the front line, with six or so steps, with the variation chosen depending on the commander and troop expertise and preference. Then they must be taken out of the ranks completely and put into the reserve, given a full 10-minute break, sitting or lying down, drinking water or wine, or merely breathing properly. The University of Leeds treadmill test showed how necessary this was:

> Wearing plates of heavy steel over the chest and back, while potentially preventing death in a battle, limits how much the lungs can expand and how much air a soldier can breathe in. Not only that, but some of the helmets from the medieval period had only thin slits in the face mask, further restricting oxygen flow.[79]

Boardman disagrees on rest breaks, although he does not examine how medieval armies fought in minute detail. He says instead: 'Close-quarter combat must therefore have been short-lived.' He sees battle time lengths as vastly exaggerated, and argues: 'For the common soldier there could be no respite.'[80] However, the re-enactor examination shows there has to be periods of rest, and battles could hardly have lasted just 20 minutes or so. The reported fatality numbers, ignoring Towton for now, show such short battles were impossible. Note too that the footmen all got less efficient as time went on. Re-enactors will never know how many of the other side they could kill in actual combat, but when asked, their average answer was perhaps one enemy soldier an hour if combat was spread over several hours.[81]

If Boardman was referring just to the billmen, they could have likely fought for longer, not being burdened with the stifling and heavy plate armour, except for a few pieces here and there, but even so they would have needed breaks too. Four re-enactors using spears and bills, asked for how long they could fight initially until a rest was essential, gave an average of 13.5 minutes of combat.[82] If that was the case, there could well have been a fourth reserve line of poleaxe men, who stepped forward when commanded to take the place of the third line, who then became the second rank.

It should not be presumed for a moment, however, that this manoeuvring of the medieval army was a precision affair, with everyone looking alike, moving in strict lines, understanding everything and getting it right. Anyone believing this melee resembled the well-dressed and ordered lines of Waterloo is mistaken. Instead, groups and soldiers must be imagined with varieties of types and styles of armour, weapons and fighting techniques. One household group might well use three ranks of poleaxe men; the next group, united around their lord, may fight with two ranks. One group might have had billmen in another line behind the axemen; the other may have had a loose mass of billmen. Each group would be fighting with what its commander thought the best techniques. Overall, the medieval battle would have been a scene of controlled chaos: metal on metal noise, screams and yells, and the signals of command, be they shouted orders or trumpet blasts.

The positioning of the lesser infantry

Returning to the composition of the lines, behind the poleaxe men as a lighter relief force are positioned the billmen, the medium infantry. In that case the front row must have looked more like this.

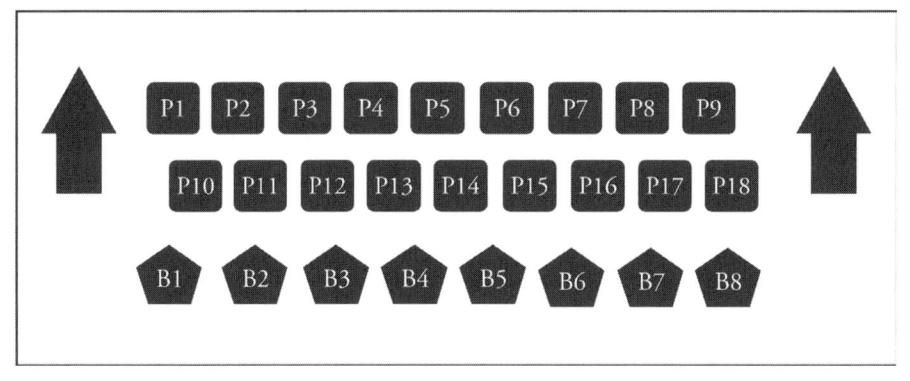

```
 ┌─────────────────────────────────────────────────────┐
 │  ↑   P1  P2  P3  P4  P5  P6  P7  P8  P9    ↑        │
 │      P10 P11 P12 P13 P14 P15 P16 P17 P18            │
 │      B1  B2  B3  B4  B5  B6  B7  B8                 │
 └─────────────────────────────────────────────────────┘
```

Two rows of poleaxe platemen in a household group, with a line of billmen behind to assist or to mop up as they moved forward.

The billmen might have been in two rows, or just in one. As backup medium infantry, they were not as involved in the fight as the very front line, but would have been very much involved in what was happening, They could be part of the action in repelling an attack at any moment or going forward as the axemen advanced, stabbing at downed enemy, taking prisoners and being ready to hold off a determined push by the enemy, with the points of their weapons extended.

The billmen too may have utilised a reserve concept as outlined above. But as their role was more as backup than anything else, this may not have always been the case. Indeed, the billmen might sometimes have constituted the front line, but this would have been done sparingly: they were too vulnerable to arrow fire, and could only have constituted a force to be used against enemy billmen or bowmen fighting as infantry.

The bowmen would have circled behind the whole affair, searching for prey. This again follows on from Vegetius, who says that behind the heavy infantry and then the light infantry were 'archers ... slingers' and what are described as 'catapulters and crossbowmen'.[83] These lightest of infantry would, however, have been very wary of any sudden thinning of the lines in front of them, and a breakthrough of either enemy billmen or poleaxe fighters who would have brought them down if they caught them. The battle line would therefore most realistically have looked like this:

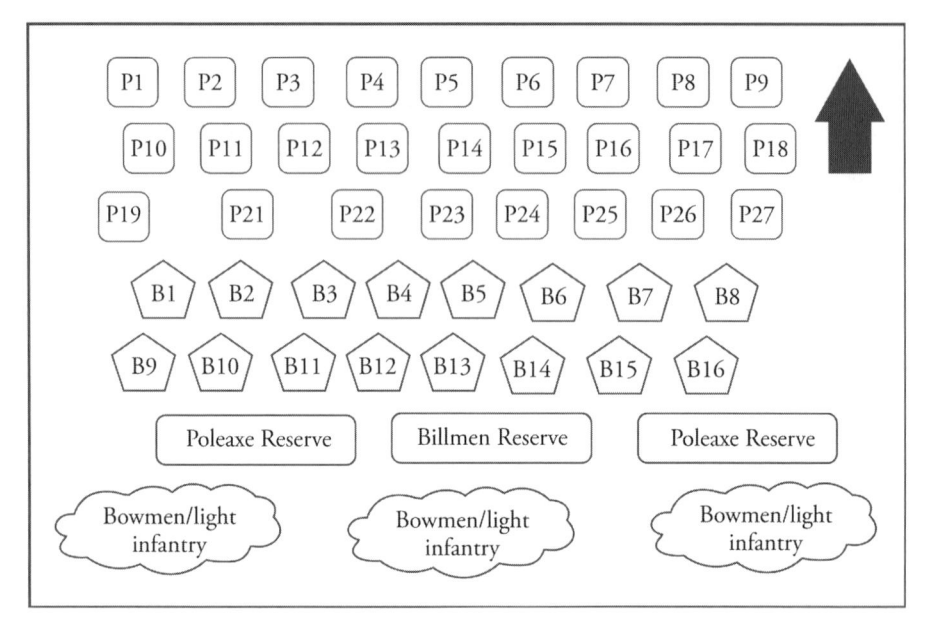

```
P1  P2  P3  P4  P5  P6  P7  P8  P9
P10 P11 P12 P13 P14 P15 P16 P17 P18
P19     P21 P22 P23 P24 P25 P26 P27
 B1  B2  B3  B4  B5  B6  B7  B8
 B9  B10 B11 B12 B13 B14 B15 B16
```

| Poleaxe Reserve | Billmen Reserve | Poleaxe Reserve |

Bowmen/light infantry   Bowmen/light infantry   Bowmen/light infantry

The most realistic composition of the two sides joined in combat. The poleaxe soldiers 'P' bear the brunt of the fighting, with the billmen 'B' as reinforcements. Both move through variations of direct and secondary combat lines and reserve rest units. The archers are deployed as skirmishers.

This is not to say the battleline was a neat, straight affair, and nor did the men keep their lines in a strict dressed formation, as did British redcoats in later wars, such as those of Napoleonic engagements. Boardman suggests accurately enough that 'Pockets, blobs, and patchy groups of fighting men may well have occurred all along the battle line.'[84] But the commanders knew the value of ordered formations, and indeed the practice of rearranging them was well understood. Vegetius gave clear advice, which was doubtless followed:

> Nothing is more advantageous in battle than that by dint of their constant exercises soldiers should keep their appointed ranks in the line. And not mass together or thin out … Then the command should be given that they at once **double the line** [author emphasis].[85]

We must remember that the men were grouped in their localised contingents. Each company of 100–300 men stood in a tight group close to their own standard. If that group weakened, the line was dented inwards. Here is where the main commander – of either the centre or a wing – would have seen what was happening, and with his own staff would have reinforced as necessary by the use of whistles or shouted commands. Trumpets would have been unlikely to be used at the household level: it was an instrument that required specialist skills to play, and if the trumpeter was knocked out of action, a valuable signalling mechanism was lost. Moreover, as discussed above, it was likely the instrument of the three main commanders only.

Beyond what is outlined above, it was likely the case that another mobile reserve was kept in each household group, located well back behind the combat lines. A commander would have rotated the reserve into action and brought the group replaced to be the new reserve. No man would have been capable of fighting continuously for hours on end. When the re-enactor group, analysed here, was asked how long they could keep fighting for in a battle that lasted between six and 10 hours, they gave an average opinion of 30 minutes per hour.[86] Given that occasionally battles went on for many hours, it would have been a

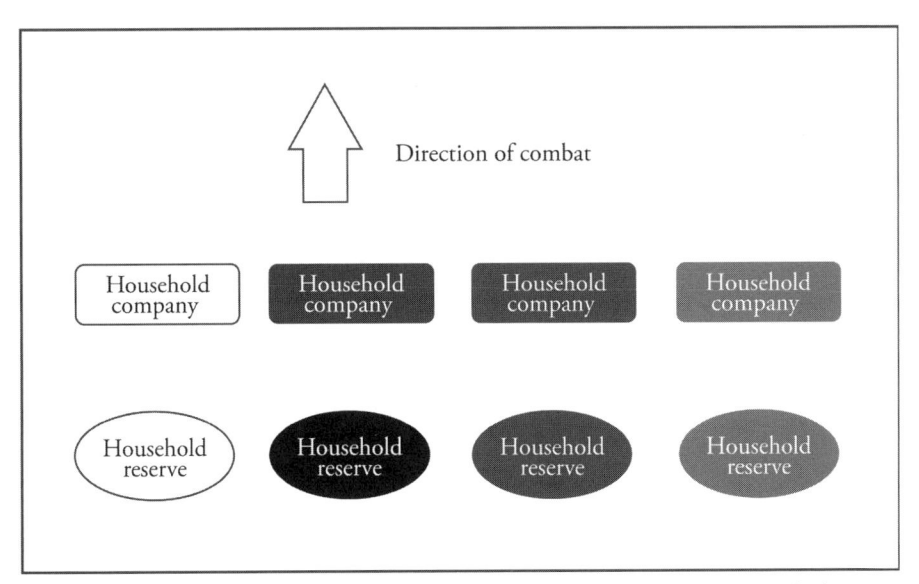

Household companies would have likely relied on their own reserves, simply because the cohesion of the whole company relied on knowing who you were fighting with.

necessity for soldiers to retreat much further into safer conditions. Men would have needed to do this for several reasons: to eat, drink, relieve their bladder or bowels, repair their armour, seek replacement poleaxe or bill shafts, and so on.

The battle rhythm of medieval combat

The modern term 'battle rhythm' is not really synonymous with hand-to-hand combat, but the medieval battle did have a rhythm all of its own, which dictated how events unfolded on the field. Battle rhythm is the military name for the maintenance of an ordered routine, but it generally refers to daily routine. As defined by the US Department of Defense, it is: 'A deliberate daily cycle of command, staff, and unit activities intended to synchronize current and future operations.' Further, it comes into discussion when people speak of, for example, pulling back in World War II in 1945 to allow the Japanese time to surrender. The battle rhythm of, to explain one part of the action, the aircraft carriers' routines of daily offensive operations could not be simply curtailed. If they were then operational, efficiency dropped, and more aircrew accidents were incurred when they wanted to ramp up efficiency again.[87]

Medieval commanders would have had to judge carefully how to compose and order into action their units. Consider a small battle frontage. An astute leader might well have judged his poleaxe-bearing fully armoured men were the equivalent of today's tank on the battlefield, especially massed together. He may have set them up into a murderous phalanx of steel-clad men, some 50 wide and three ranks deep. Together they would march forward to cause chaos and break the enemy lines.

How would the opposition commander deal with this? He may simply have decided to meet this threat with his own team of men. He could bring together two squads with a frontage of 30 soldiers to form a 60-man wide front. Now his men would be superior in numbers. But perhaps that leaves the billmen to form the rest of the front. If he noticed his enemy was doing the same, he could quickly call up a reserve squad of poleaxe men, only six wide, but three ranks deep. They would march forward to break the billmen's line.

But the enemy commander could have been ready for this, willing to pit 200 trained billmen against 18 poleaxe soldiers. They should use their points, he would tell them, and hold off the poleaxes as best they can. If a billman's shaft broke, or he was wounded, he would step back and let the ranks absorb him, to spit him out behind. Billmen would try to trip the axemen, then deal with them when they were down.

Then again, perhaps surprisingly, casualties might not have been as significant as first thought. As re-enactor analysis has shown, the fully plated man-at-arms was quite invulnerable so long as he kept on his feet.[88] Surrounded by his comrades, he had plenty of people to help him keep upright or – protected – stand back up again quickly if he was knocked down.

Such would be the constant calculation necessary to handle the armies in combat.

The fight of the front line

Fighting in the front line must have been a mix of occasional furious bursts of energy and careful management of one's resources of strength and endurance.

One of the matters relating to this would have been the grand tactic of the overall commander. It may have been that a senor commander perceived their opponent's right flank – facing his own left – to be weak. This may have been from a calculation that their commander did not have the experience or courage to sustain his position. So that it where his side decided to push forward.

In this case, the middle section and right flank would fight a holding action – that is, hold their ground – in this particular action. The job of the men-at-arms groups there was to hold their position, that is, not be pressed back in particular, nor to go forward. This might have meant using their points more than usual, to deter the enemy men trying to push forward. A simple command such as 'Use your points' would have been easy to communicate beforehand, and easy to remember. Someone wise years later came up with the maxim: 'No battle plan survives contact with the enemy.'[89] In the press of men, surrounded by noise, pain, confusion, fear and the ultimate in physical exertion, no man could hope to remember instructions for long while he was fighting for his life. But a simple order like 'Use your points', especially when reinforced by the sergeants, could well survive as an instruction.

It may have been that simple deceptive techniques were used as well. At a given signal, a group of perhaps three to five of the front-line men could have fallen back, with the pre-arranged co-operation of the second line behind them, and perhaps the billmen too. This would allow the enemy to confidently come forward, only to be enveloped in a circular trap, with the front men stepping to one side a little and forward.

Such a course of action cannot be proved, but again, using the technique of logical analysis and Inherent Military Probability, it would seem to be something that could and would therefore be done. The example also serves to illustrate that this combat portrait is not one of fixed and stilted behaviour, but something that would have ebbed and flowed. The lines would have gone forward and been pushed back, and all the while capable and clever commanders would have sought – as has always been the case – to gain an edge to bring them victory.

In this scenario, on the left wing, meanwhile, their job was to push forward. This would have meant being more aggressive than usual. What would that mean for a poleaxe-wielding man-at-arms? It could mean to use the blade and hammer faces more. It would mean organising the platemen even more, probably in small groups of 10–15 fighters. The best, probably through a combination of strength and skill, would have been to the front, and beside him two bodyguards, left and right, almost as formidable as fighters. They would form the apex of a triangle which would push forward into the enemy lines.

This might sound complicated, but it was no more than a revisiting of the organisation of numerous armies of ancient times. Richard Gabriel is particularly instructive, describing numerous armies who fought in a 'rest and fight' routine, although he argues the Romans pioneered it. He suggests that the front rank was indeed replaced at regular intervals, with a reserve of spearmen always available in case they were attacked.[90]

The use of all three types of medieval soldier as melee infantry

Sometimes a medieval battle might mean that all three specialist soldiers mixed into a massive melee fight, which was extremely fluid. If poleaxe men were forming the front row of the enemy lines, then it was essential they be matched with a commander's own axe men. There would be a similar situation if billmen formed the enemy front row. Then again, attacking them with axemen, if a commander had enough, would definitely win that section of the line for him.

The bowmen, as stated, had an additional role, which will now be expanded upon. Once combat was joined, and the archers could not shoot at the enemy for fear of hitting their own men, it could be expected that they would fall back through the ranks of men-at-arms and billmen, to be used as light infantry, taking on an aggressive role in which they would harass, injure or hopefully kill the enemy.

Hardy describes the secondary role of the bowmen as a usual practice: 'After the armies shocked together the archers threw down their bows and went in with sword and dagger, maul and anything else they could lay hand to.'[91] Goodman supports the idea: 'When archers entered into close combat, using knives, axes and mallets, as they did after the lines were engaged at Agincourt and at Verneuil in 1424.'[92]

These tactics must have been carefully managed, not so much by the captains and sergeants but by the archers themselves. Lightly protected as they were by their jacks and sallets, they were in no position to take even a non-fatal blow from a poleaxe: a strike by the edge would have cut deep and injured decisively. Given the tremendous kinetic energy contained in such a swing, a cut 6 inches/15cm deep could be expected, of at least the same length.

If a bowman was hit by the hammer side of the poleaxe, the injury would have been just as serious, and such a blow would have smashed bone wherever it struck. Part of the skill of the poleaxe man was choosing which part of his weapon to use, depending on the enemy's type of armour and its condition. He would decide if the axe, point or hammer was best in the circumstances, but all three were deadly.

Given such disadvantages, the bowmen would have fought in groups, using at least two or three against a man-at-arms who was injured, exhausted, on the extreme edge of a group or alone. The best tactic would have been to strike at the enemy soldier's legs with a lengthy edged weapon such as a sword. Even so, their target's legs were usually armoured, but a precise or lucky hit could have cut at the joint between plates or through mail. If the enemy were still in their ranks, disciplined and contained, then the archers could not do this, but if the battle was in its closing stages and the opposition in disarray, this is likely what archers would do.

Working together with spearmen would have also been useful. The long pole of the spear might well trip an armoured man, or the point – driven with at least as much force as a full swing from a sword – had a chance of punching deep into that vulnerable area between the plates.

Casualties amongst the archers, spearmen and billmen who got in the way of the plated men-at-arms must have been steady but not extreme. Any enemy plated soldiers were dangerous targets, and the lesser-armoured billmen and almost completely unprotected bowmen would have kept well out of their way – unless a plated enemy soldier was in trouble. It must have been a matter of 'hover and watch'; keep out of the way, and only move in, with the protection and maximisation of chances in a group, when a target of opportunity was identified. Then there would have been a sudden rush to try to bring down their man.

Bringing the plated man-at-arms to the ground was the best tactic. When he was down, his weapons' power were minimized. He could no longer swing the poleaxe if he was on his back, only push it out in front of him as a momentary protection. His backup weapon of the sword, buckled to his waist, could be drawn only with difficulty. If he fell on his front, he was in a dire position until he could get a knee under himself and regain his feet. If he was in the ranks of friends, he might have been able to get assistance, although the considerably lessened vision and hearing of his comrades would have reduced their awareness of others being down.

If a plated man fell and was out of the ranks, the lighter enemy infantry would have been on him in a flash, frantically trying to keep him down with their weight and numbers. Their daggers would be out, and they would have been trying to push their long thin blades between his steel plates. Daggers may have been a weapon of choice against a downed plated soldier. There was no point in trying for a full-bodied swing from a sword: the plates were protection against that. Lightweight mauls, clubs or even maces snatched up from the fallen would have been less effective in the hands of soldiers not trained in their use. The light infantry would have had little chance before to use a poleaxe, and should one be taken from a fallen man, lacking the skills to use it, would have hesitated to pick it up.

Against downed plated men, a good stab from a rondel dagger could have been the beginning of the end for the man-at-arms. A 3–6-inch penetration would often have brought instant and terrible pain. But not always: adrenaline is a powerful stimulant. There are many accounts across all warfare of terribly injured men who have fought on, only discovering they were wounded, and subsequently collapsing, well after a fight had ended.

The rondel stab would have been decisive if it was made at the right place. The knee joint would have been an excellent target. A piercing there would have meant the man-at-arms' mobility was fatally crippled. He would not have been able to rise, which would have given an opportunity for a second and third strike by the daggers. If his friends were not instantly rushing to drive off the attackers and stand over him, he was finished. This again implies that the poleaxe men's ranks were starting to be a little disarrayed – perhaps at a stage in the battle where the lines were about to be broken.

The downed plated man, however, was not always in a helpless position. If he was on his back, he was better able to defend himself. A strike forward from one of his steel-clad fists into the face of one of his attackers would have caused much consternation, and possibly a pause or withdrawal by a man now with a broken nose or teeth, or damaged eyes. A man-at-arms would have also often carried a sword in addition to his poleaxe, and this could have been dragged, albeit not easily, from the belt where it was carried, perhaps without the sheath. He also had his own dagger.

A downed man needed to do one thing above all – to get back up. The weight of his armour was not a major factor. These men were fit, strong and highly motivated individuals who were used to riding, practicing and fighting in their armour. A roll to one side and a knee brought up were the start of his recovery, with perhaps the shaft of the poleaxe to lean on to help him up, and then he was on his feet again: angry, and more determined than ever to strike down these light infantry who had tried to kill him. Revenge would have been in his heart, and he would have swung viciously and with determination at anyone he could reach. With a compatriot or two, he may have even decided to pursue them a little, if the battle situation allowed it. In general, however, he was constrained by the understood tactics to stay in the battle line.

The billmen were in a somewhat different situation. They likely had better vision as a group, with most of them wearing sallets rather than bascinets. They might therefore have been better able to fight in small packs, with a fluid front line where men fell back on an individualised basis or as lines commanded by sergeants. The bill is more a defensive weapon, or at least one which can hold the line, rather than be used to push forward – the plated axemen were much better for that. For all that, the billmen would have likely been present in greater quantity, and were suited to keeping the line solid.

Turning tail and running from the battle would not be a factor at this time. Soldiers in general only exhibit an unwillingness to fight before a battle, not once it is joined, when adrenaline was combined with a fierce determination to stand alongside his friends. This is common to all wars, and has been written on in more recent times.

The continuation of the battle

This outline of the medieval battle's progress is one of continual struggle, with two great stretched and irregular lines. It is essentially fluid, with the household commanders keeping a very careful eye on their own groups, a difficult affair when they themselves were fighting in the very front line, as they were expected to do. As explained, the rotational system likely saw all soldiers moved in a cyclic fashion to the front lines,

The author at Dacre's Cross at Towton. (Kaylene Anderson)

and any commander was expected to do his bit, to show his heart was high, and he had faith in the men under his command backing him. King Edward IV, for example, fought in the front lines of his army, and he must have been an impressive sight at 6 feet 4 inches (193cm) in his plate armour.

For the overall commanders of the centre and the wings, their job was occasionally to lead by example, but to also keep a very careful eye on the overall situation of the line. Where it wavered, it was strengthened. Where there was the possibility of breaking through the enemy's line, extra pressure was applied. Above all, there was a necessity to keep an eye on morale and to prevent any disheartened lapses in aggression.

There was therefore a need to keep going, to move any reinforcements into use and to maintain pressure. The battle would go to he who could maintain the line aggressively for the longest, and break through as he saw the opportunity. The battle would then move into the closing stages, which often saw the most savagery.

The battle of Towton will now be examined as an example of medieval combat, with, using the outlines above, an analysis of what most likely happened.

CHAPTER 9

Towton as an Example of Medieval Battle

The focus will now turn on the battle of Towton in order to examine how medieval tactics and fighting techniques were utilised. Along the way, it will be seen how confused was the accounting of battles of the time.

By 1461, the Wars of the Roses had been a bitter struggle in the kingdom for many years. The weak King Henry VI, of the House of Lancaster, had transferred succession to the throne to Richard Plantagenet, Duke of York and great grandson of Edward III. However, Henry's wife, Queen Margaret of Anjou, saw the right to the throne of her son, Edward, Prince of Wales being lost, and roused her followers to fight.

Richard was killed at the battle of Wakefield in late 1460, leaving his 19-year-old son Edward as head of the Yorkist faction. The Yorkists declared Edward monarch, making him King Edward IV. The Yorkists were mainly centred in London, while the Lancastrians were more northern-based. Hearing their forces were gathering, Edward marched north to deal with the threat.

There were two skirmishes beforehand. At Ferrybridge on 28 March, Lord Fitzwalter's Yorkists were first attacked by Lord Clifford's Lancastrians. Then a force of Yorkists under Lord Fauconberg fought Clifford's Lancastrians north of Ferrybridge, pursuing them to the village of Dittingdale. After a brief fight, the Yorkists emerged victorious and Clifford was killed. (Archaeologist Tim Sutherland has argued convincingly that all three actions took place on the same day.)[1]

The main battle was fought at Towton the next day, 29 March 1461, in snowy conditions in what are still today open fields. Some say around

28,000 men died in the encounter. The following is one modern account from English Heritage:

> The battle begins with an exchange between the two sides' archers. Because of Lord Fauconbridge's [sic] cunning and the strength of the wind which blew snow into the Lancastrians' faces, the Yorkists get the better of the duel. The Lancastrians attack. Their vanguard, which would have been positioned on the Lancastrian right (i.e. to the west) and which at least both Waurin and Hall agree had Sir Andrew Trollope in the lead, achieved success against the Yorkist cavalry opposing it. According to the *Brief Latin Chronicle* the fleeing Yorkist cavalry ransacked their own baggage train.
>
> The Lancastrian success on the western side of the battlefield accords with a tradition often cited (but for which the evidence is elusive) that they previously concealed men in Castle Hill Wood which, during the course of the battle, emerged in ambush. The assumption therefore has long been that the Yorkist left was under particular pressure. The exhortations of Edward however stabilise the situation. The two sides' main bodies lock in combat.[2]

The ambush interpretation does make sense. The Yorkist ridge is higher and has a better view of proceedings, meaning it would be advantageous

Taken from the extreme right of the Lancastrian position at Towton, this photo shows the slight but still problem-presenting slope up towards the Yorkists. (Author photo)

for a Yorkist commander to take up his position there. The disposition of the battle's opening stages does raise a question about why the Lancastrians deployed where they did. There are two sensible explanations: either they rushed to deploy and so didn't have time to get to the better ridge, or they wanted the Yorkists on the higher ridge, as their opponents would then be flanked by the ambush in the wood. The English Heritage account continues:

> At noon, after about three hours fighting, the Duke of Norfolk's division arrives on the battlefield. Since these reinforcements approached from Ferrybridge it is accepted that they would have marched directly along the road to Tadcaster and emerged on the battlefield upon the Yorkist right. The intervention of Norfolk's men, for want of an alternative explanation, is held to have slowly shifted the advantage to the Yorkists. Steadily, during the course of ten hours of fighting, the Lancastrians were forced back until their line crumbled and the struggle degenerated into a series of combats over the plain stretching towards Towton and beyond.[3]

The usual description has been given here of the battle, outlining only at the most basic level how the main blocks of men and movement were utilised.

Following an arrow storm, a small initial cavalry engagement on the Towton battlefield is described on the Yorkist left and the Lancastrian right. There are two problems with this. The first is that there is a steep bank at that point, extremely difficult for a horse and rider to ascend – and impossible in the wintry conditions experienced on the day, according to all sources, as ice and snow would make the horses' grip on the bank precarious, dangerous and most improbable.

The second problem is that using cavalry in such a preliminary move flies in the face of what is accepted about horses on the battlefield in the Wars of the Roses. With bowmen in quantity on both sides, and the horses not impervious to arrow fire, such a clash is most doubtful. However, no capable commander will ever discard anything out of the routine in a combat action: he will seize the moment, utilise surprise as much as possible and not discard anything merely because of tradition. It is possible there was a small cavalry action at the beginning of Towton, but it may have only been a probing and scouting action to investigate the enemy's numbers, with the manoeuvre stopped and reversed.

Alternatively, could not the possible early cavalry clash be the Lancastrians coming out of the wood on the rear left flank, and the Yorkists responding by moving their cavalry reserve over to meet it? The resulting fighting might not have amounted to much owing to the ground, but this could offer an explanation.

The second passage from the English Heritage account states that the battle lines met each other and engaged in combat for three hours. This would seem reasonable.

The Towton battlefield is potentially quite wide. It extends from the steep banks on the Yorkist left, and Lancastrian right, across the two modern roads and on to the Yorkist right, where it is stopped again by marshy conditions. A possible battle frontage of a kilometre or perhaps even 1,200m is possible. The Lancastrians had their backs to the village of Towton, while the Yorkists were in front of the village of Saxton. The

The rear of the Lancaster position, where a supposed 'Bridge of Bodies' was located. The drop into this depression is steep. That and the stream at the treeline would have been an obstacle, but not one preventing escape. (Author photo)

Lancastrians had a small disadvantage: they had a slight slope to contend with. This slope, mentioned in several accounts, is steeper than it looks, as the author can ascertain, having walked it. The incline would have lessened the Lancastrian infantry's effectiveness by perhaps 10 per cent, making them more tired than normal. The slope also gave the Yorkists the morale advantage of looking down on their enemy toiling up to meet them. Troops like looking down on their opponents: it gives them a feeling of being superior, both position-wise and psychologically.

Why has this situation been presumed, where the battlelines are running east–west? Why can they not swing round, on a more north–south axis? One reason – as can be judged from the map illustration – is that the Lancastrians would have never allowed themselves to be boxed into the corner formed by the River Cock and the Old London Road. There is quite a cliff to ascend to get to that road, and a river at the bottom of the cliff. The Lancastrians would not have committed to battle in this situation. Nor would they have swung around to face east, which would put the steep bank at their backs, allowing for no strategic retreat. Perhaps they relied on the ambush they had placed. However, in the end, that boxed rear right portion of the battlefield was part of their undoing.

An earlier of this study has described how a battle began. It took a degree of co-operation from both sides. If either commander thought the ground he was to fight on was too much to his disadvantage, he would seek to avoid it. Again, if either believed he was severely outnumbered, he might try to march away, but such a move was often impossible at this stage: the deployed lines could not simply form back into columns and leave the field, as they would then be vulnerable to attack.

The medieval battle commander would also at this stage have assessed his own side's morale and that of the enemy's. Morale, Napoleon was to summarise some 350 years later, was to the physical as three is to one. In other words, a numerically smaller force, whose hearts are high, will carry the day in combat against a bigger force with low morale, despite the major numerical discrepancy. Thus, an army of 10,000 could vanquish one of 20,000, and even hold its own against one of 30,000.

Yet the medieval battle commander had to make a careful assessment of the combat force that was against him in more than mere numbers and morale. He needed to know its composition: what was its make-up of bowmen compared to billmen and men-at-arms? As previously stated, the bowmen of these wars constituted about half of a force. If an enemy had too many bowmen percentage-wise, however, that might be a good thing – it meant he was short of medium and heavy infantry.

But what of the nature of the infantry themselves? What were they armed with?

One or both sides may have possessed artillery, that is, gunpowder-fired guns. Primitive guns first made their appearance in English–French battles at Crecy in 1346, and Foard and Curry discuss their presence at Bosworth, more than 20 years after Towton.[4] Although ammunition has been found at the battlefield, and mention has been made of artillery at Towton, it does not figure in any of the accounts of the battle itself, and it would be highly unlikely it was used to any significance.[5] Artillery of the period generally contributed little decisively to either side, such was its inefficiency, although guns contributed to the break-up of enemy lines in the same way as longbows did.

Artillery, like the bow, also impeded morale and the impact of the first clash: no man liked standing there while its fire was directed against him. (Indeed, this was always a problem: battles sometimes disintegrated before they even got started, with men melting away into hedges and woods if they thought it possible to safely desert.) Artillery was to develop significantly over the years, and by the Napoleonic era in the late 1700s and early 1800s it accounted for around 15 per cent of those killed on the battlefield. In the 20th-century world wars, artillery's pre-eminence can be seen through the grim statistic that over half of those killed in battle fell from the effects of explosives delivered by gun or air.

As the two medieval sides met across the battlefield, and neither drew back, the mutual assessment continued. For instance, was there enough light to fight by? Medieval battles were never conducted at night, by almost all accounts, although scouting and even an accidental skirmish were not unknown. (One source suggests that Towton was fought at night, but this is dismissed by all who have analysed the battle in the modern day.)[6] If there was not enough light, then both sides would pitch a camp. If the situation remained the same, there would be a battle the following morning.

Encampments could mean trouble, however. Arguments could develop, and – fuelled by alcohol – they could get serious. Yet it did not take drinking to cause Humphrey Stafford, Earl of Devon, to break off his support for King Edward IV before the battle of Edgecote in 1469.[7] Following a quarrel over accommodation in a village, the Earl led his forces off, and largely as a result, the Yorkists were defeated.

The consumption of alcohol the night before a battle was a means of ensuring sleep and the banishment of fear. Drinking in the company of friends meant receiving mutual psychological support. Philippe de Commines noted bowmen drinking before a European battle in 1465, and commented that 'never men had more desire to fight' due to their 'several pipes of wine'.[8] Keegan suggests that it was 'quite probable' at Agincourt that men went into battle 'less than sober, if not indeed fighting drunk'.[9] This leads to an interesting and arguable possibility: good soldiers would have noted that being drunk took the edge of their ability to use their weapons with precise timing. Then again, alcohol dispels fear to a degree, and drinking in company inspires bonding with comrades with whom one will fight on the morrow.

It cannot be confirmed exactly where the fighting at Towton took place because there has not been sufficient evidence found on the field itself. Once again, the historian has to use logical analysis, but to a fair degree has to assume that the descriptions which have the Yorkists south of the Lancastrians is correct. No sensible Lancastrian commander would have allowed himself to be initially fighting uphill, so it must be assumed that the Lancastrians advanced forward up the slight rise to the top of the ground, near where the present Lord Dacre's Cross stands.

Once the initial arrow engagement was over, the two sides would have closed to fight. Each would have looked for opportunities to turn the other's flank while ensuring their centre was not left too weak. This means the Yorkist left and Lancastrian right would have extended their respective lines until they were terminated by the steep drop to the stream below.

The men-at-arms' engagement would then have commenced, and both sides would have settled down to infantry combat as described in the previous chapters. This could have gone on for some time, depending on the ability of both sides to replenish their front line. It can be expected that with large armies, such close-quarter fighting would have lasted several hours. The difference in the description given here, however, is that it can now be understood, with infantry fighting in companies using lines, how this melee was sustained.

Wintry weather – the few accounts there are say it was snowing – would have made for less telling blows from edged weapons, and for unsure ground underfoot. Nevertheless, the cold would not have meant a lot to armour-wearing soldiers. As pointed out previously, modern re-enactors like cold weather, preferring it to mild or hot conditions. But the lack of secure footing underneath probably meant a reduction in their efficiency by up to 20 per cent.

How long was the battle fought for?

There is no firm agreement between analysts about how long the battle of Towton lasted. Some say three hours, others as long as 10 hours.[10] Boardman argues for 'three to four hours at the most' of fighting occurring in the morning, with the rout following into the afternoon.[11] However, some historians argue Towton lasted for a lot longer. One 19th-century analyst, Ellis, has the battle lasting 10 hours.[12] (It was often thought doubtful, prior to Sutherland's analysis, that a skirmish at Ferrybridge, some miles distant, would be included in such accounts as it occurred on the previous day, and both armies are said to have made camp overnight before the main battle on the following morning.) There would have been over 12 hours of daylight on the day of the battle: sunrise on 29 March is at 6.46am, and sunset at 7.33pm.[13]

Polydore Vergil, chronicler for Henry VII, writing scores of years after the battle, but within living memory of Towton, also claimed that the combat lasted for a total of 10 hours.[14] This was perhaps an exaggeration to suggest the ferocity of the troops that Henry overcame later at the battle of Bosworth, which put a new king on the throne. Vergil's history writing must be tainted by his writing under the Tudor reign, and it would not have been in his interests to make his

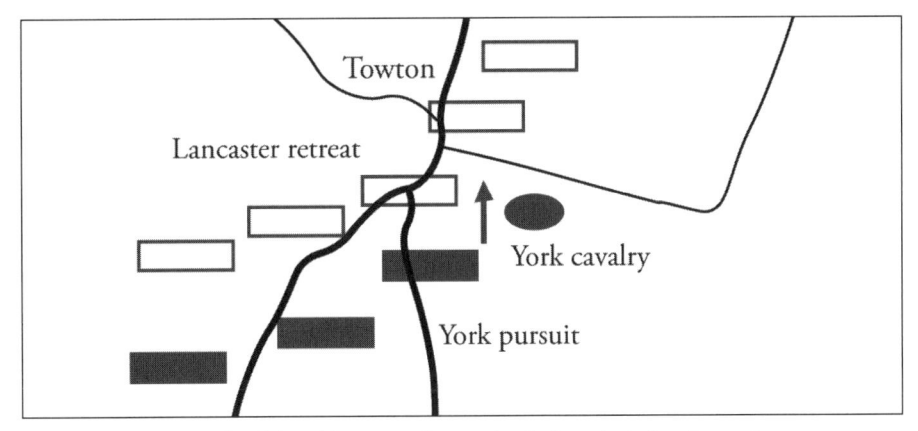

Towton, battle's mid-stages, from a logical analysis by the author.

masters – the victors over the Yorkists, who had won at Towton – in any way look bad.

The Tudor chronicler Edward Hall, who would also have had an agenda, suggested: 'This deadly battle and bloody conflict, continued ten hours in doubtful victory.' He goes on to say: 'The chase continued all night, and the most part of the next day, and every northern man, when they saw or perceived any advantage, returned again and fought with their enemies, to the great loss of both parties. For in this three days were slain (as they knew it wrote) on both parts 36,776 persons.'[15]

These accounts of 10 hours' fighting are not borne out by any other evidence. They must be dubious, given the previous chapter's showing how little time medieval soldiers could actually fight. One major factor not considered by many accounts of the battle is this physical exhaustion factor, which precludes soldiers being able to fight for such a lengthy engagement.

The battle continues

Given high morale on both sides, if the two armies were evenly matched in skill and numbers, there is no reason to suppose anything other than hand-to-hand engagement continuing for some time. The two lines would have moved only a little backwards and forwards. Here and there, bold and brave commanders would have taken forward their part of the line, and then just as resolute a reaction would have pushed it back again. Wounded men would have been dragged backwards and clear by their friends. Dead soldiers would have lain underfoot. The front line would have been replenished in the way outlined in previous chapters, with the second line replacing the first, the third the second, and so on, and completely exhausted soldiers going to the rear. But neither side would make a clear gain.

Two early accounts of the battle – by Vergil and Hall – make no mention of the Duke of Norfolk arriving to change the course of the battle. This appears to be have been introduced by later chroniclers. But it seems certain that the battle began to go the Yorkists' way, and maybe the Duke of Norfolk's men arriving was the catalyst for this. Fresh and eager to prove themselves, they would have arrived along either of the two roads which are in clear sight of the battlefield, and importantly, they would have been arriving in full view of the Lancastrian lines. It is not know whether they were horsed, but if so, the sight would have had the enemy bowmen changing their role back from skirmishing light infantry and running for their bows. However, it can be assumed the Yorkist reinforcements would have anticipated this, dismounting quickly rather than have their horses shot from under them. Then they would have walked forward in a body towards the fray.

It would have taken some time for the Yorkist reinforcements to deploy from the column they would have been in: each man would have had to dismount, hand over his horse and walk forward. They may have preferred to wait until they were all on foot and then move forward in their group. The column would have had to deploy into a line left or right of the road, or straddling it, to strengthen the Yorkist front.

Although the Duke of Norfolk's men may have swung the battle for the Yorkists, perhaps there was just a strengthening of heart amongst them, led by capable leaders. Maybe the arrival of any 'Norfolk force' was piecemeal: a trickle of fresh warriors arriving up the road. But it could also have been the precipitating factor for an uneasy ripple to run the length of the Lancastrians, the precursor to them losing heart and being

Towton battlefield, looking from the Lancaster centre up the hill towards the Yorkist centre. (Author photo)

steadily pushed back. If the Lancastrian right began to break, then this would account for later stories of men eventually being pushed down the banks towards the streams that bound the back of their position and their right. The Lancastrians were being pushed into the box which bordered their backs, and which they had tried to avoid by advancing up the slope.

What happened when the lines broke?

Banners would have occasionally wavered on both sides as a household head or lord listened to his supporters agitating for a quick escape. The first to leave the battlefield would have the advantage of the vast number of Lancastrians still fighting, forming an obstacle to any pursuit. Those who fled early thus had a much better possibility of getting away. However, they also risked the danger of being branded a traitor. Whatever

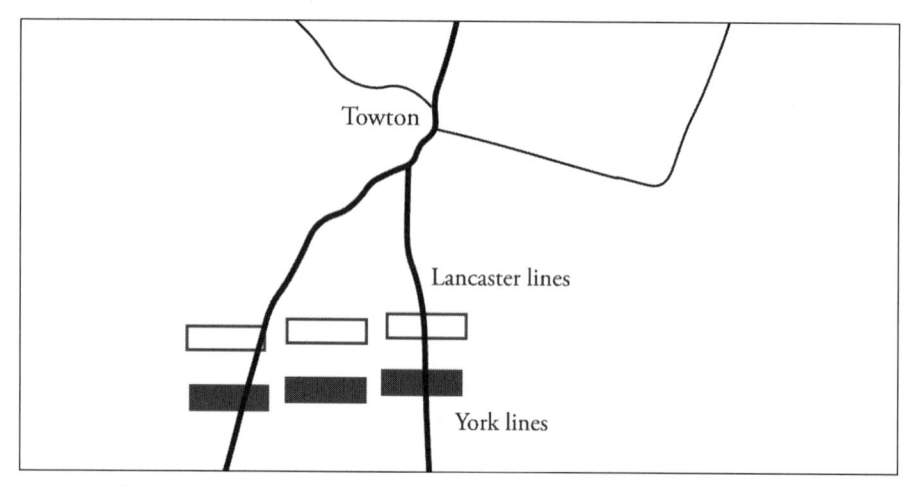

Towton, battle's closing stages, from a logical analysis by the author.

the case, it is clear from all accounts that eventually the Lancastrians did break. There was likely a decision made on the Yorkist side to form a pursuit force, although this had a dangerous effect. Those Yorkists who broke off from fighting and made for their horses to pursue their fleeing opponents could have looked to be retreating themselves, and may also have weakened their own line.

Nevertheless, there must have come a time when so many Lancastrians decided to go that the word the battle was lost would have percolated along the line. There must have also been a moment when the Yorkist commanders decided to take some of their men and send them as cavalry to pursue the fleeing enemy. The remainder of the Yorkist footmen, sensing victory, would have pressed forward to take advantage of the moment. Whether this was what some term a 'wave' or a 'shiver', and whether the whole line dissolved or it happened piece by piece, is not known.

It is safe to presume the Yorkists' horses would have been made ready, although a squadron could have been already formed up. It is not known whether a pursuit unit of horsemen were waiting, or whether the men-at-arms would have had to go to the horses and mount up, exchanging poleaxes for lances, and ensuring they had secondary weapons, either a mace or a sword. They probably would have taken shields as a matter of custom, but there was little danger of needing them to fight any Lancaster horsemen. Any Lancaster cavalry would have seen what was happening and been preparing to use their own mounts to flee. Making a counter-charge with their own lances was highly unlikely, as they would see that the Yorkists had the organisation and weight of numbers to overpower them. The only thought for any horsed Lancastrian would have been a speedy escape.

Most Lancastrians however, were going to have to make their escape on foot. Having been fighting that way, they could not make a safe move towards their rear to recover their own horses. As well as potentially meeting resistance from their own side, such a move would have taken time – to find their horse, saddle it, mount and move off. Men would instead have begun to walk away from the battle, often in ones and twos, hoping to escape notice both from their own side and the Yorkists still engaged. More and more would have begun deserting the battle, probably accelerating to a run as fear and panic gripped those on the losing side.

We can expect that some of the Lancastrian left would have begun to flee not towards the boxed-in corner, anticipating the crowding and disaster that awaited them, and instead would have looked for the northern track which heads for the road which then would have existed, as it still does now, as the west to east highway heading for York. They also had a slight downhill slope to assist them, with the road providing easier going than the muddy fields through which thousands of their comrades had tramped uphill into battle a few hours earlier.

The effectiveness of pursuit

The state of the ground in the aftermath of the battle was not conducive for horse pursuit. Icy, snowy conditions are particularly hazardous to a horse, and one carrying a heavily armoured and armed rider would have had great difficulty keeping its footing.

Effective pursuit in a medieval rout meant proceeding at a faster speed than a hurrying – albeit walking – footman. It also meant being able to deliver combat blows from the saddle with a mace or sword, or riding down the fleeing soldier using a lance. All of these factors required effective control of the horse. In bad weather, the possibility of a horse slipping in its canter increased, as did the lack of steadiness as a striking platform for the rider and his ability to accelerate as per normal.

The pursuing Yorkists were faced with what by all accounts was a particularly trying day weather-wise. Based on personal experience as a cross-country rider in cold and wet conditions, and having had fencing experience with sabre and epee, the author can predicted that the weather would have reduced the mounted man's effectiveness by between 50 and 70 per cent.

However, it would have been just as difficult for Lancastrian troops fleeing from Towton to get very far. First, the ground was wet and slippery, making running and even walking more difficult than usual, with a high risk of falling for both the pursued and the pursuers. The steel shoes worn by those in full armour did not make for good traction.

The fleeing men would also be exhausted from the battle itself. They had been fighting, by all accounts, for several hours, even with the system of constant rotation through the front line. Their arms would have been aching from the constant holding and swinging of their weapons. Their legs would have been exhausted too, trembling with the exertion of activity and holding up the weight of their armour.

Still, they would have been given some extra energy for their flight, with fear producing the body's 'fight or flight' reaction:

> Patterns of nerve cell firing and chemical release cause our body to undergo a series of very dramatic changes. Our respiratory rate increases. Blood is shunted away from our digestive tract and directed into our muscles and limbs, which require extra energy and fuel for running and fighting. Our pupils dilate. Our awareness intensifies. Our sight sharpens. Our impulses quicken. Our perception of pain diminishes. Our immune system mobilizes with increased activation. We become prepared – physically and psychologically – for fight or flight. We scan and search our environment, 'looking for the enemy'.[16]

Without going too deeply into this physiological response, it would be interesting to see if a person in a combat situation was further charged with physical abilities. But one would hardly expect the defeated soldier to just sit and wait for death. Many would have been on a losing side before, and would have automatically tried to preserve life and limb.

Fleeing soldiers would be given better performance by the body's circulation of the hormone epinephrine, usually known as adrenaline:

> Performance, and particularly that involving strength and endurance, can appreciably improve with appropriate motivation even in the form of stress such as fear. Also, some forms of stress, such as fear, anxiety, or sudden appearance or unexpected appearance of a stimulus (startle response), typically induce circulation of an increased amount of adrenaline which can enhance performance requiring strength or endurance.[17]

However, this does not mean a soldier would be 'super-charged' for long periods. Indeed, it may cause injury if someone is in such a stressful situation for long periods.[18]

The rout re-thought

There are two reasons connected with the end of the battle for a rethinking that the number slain at Towton was less than usually stated: the ability of those fleeing to defend themselves, and the inability of the pursuers to inflict death.

There has been an assumption by many historians and commentators that the fleeing of the Lancastrian soldiers – what was commonly called a rout – would have been when most of the fatalities were inflicted. For example, the *Croyland Chronicle* said:

> For their ranks now being broken and scattered in flight, the king's army eagerly pursued them, and cutting down the fugitives with their swords, just like so many sheep for the slaughter, made immense havoc amongst them for a distance of 10 miles as far as the city of York.[19]

Andrew Boardman says the Lancastrians were pursued 'relentlessly by Yorkist horsemen'. Tudor chronicler Edward Hall does not describe men being killed by their pursuers, but rather by drowning as they plunged into streams and rivers in their haste to escape.[20]

Christopher Gravett suggests that 'Norfolk's division were no doubt already mounted' and began the pursuit. He has the Lancastrians trying to find ways across rivers barring their way, and being cut down as they did so. The Yorkist archers, he says, 'May have well gone up to the bank to pick off enemy soldiers.' Gravett adds: 'All along the way between Towton and Tadcaster was a scene of slaughter as Yorkists harried the enemy, taking advantage of the easy targets presented by running foes.'[21]

Goodwin reports 'thousands of slipping and sliding brothers-in-arms' drowning, but also says that 'the chase did not stop at Tadcaster, it continued into the night and on another 10 miles to York itself'.[22] So there are several assumptions made that the Lancastrians suffered their losses on the run. This assumption, however, is overstated. Admittedly, any soldiers trying to cross the flooded rivers would have been most disadvantaged, and probably perished as described. But this was not necessarily the case for the soldiers on any roads.

Firstly, any soldiers moving into this stage of battle – that is, any of the defeated side not dead or wounded to the point of incapacity – would have been under little illusion as to what would happen next. The Wars of the Roses, as has been pointed out, were marked by little quarter on the battlefield, and revenge killing post-battle.

Secondly, the fleeing soldiers would have known what the shape of their pursuit would have looked like. They may have seen in the distance the Yorkist horse gathered at the rear of the enemy lines. They would certainly have known of their own use of horsemen in attacking fleeting soldiers. However, the majority of the Lancastrians were armed with excellent defensive weapons against horse attack: the bill and the bow.

Indeed, it was at this point that the 'heavy tanks' of the Lancastrians – the plated men – were at a disadvantage. Armed with poleaxes, they were superbly equipped to smash the ranks of other infantry, even to inflict damage upon similarly plated opposition soldiers. But the poleaxe, although it could inflict a killing injury upon a horse if its user swung hard at the right time, was not an easy weapon to use to trip a horse or hook its rider from the saddle.

The fleeing plated man was also very heavily armoured, which would have made him slow. He could not easily defend against a couched lance charge from a horse's rider, so he may well have taken off some of his pieces of plate. This would have been a common reaction by defeated

Lancastrians in defending themselves, as it allowed them to move faster and aided manoeuvrability, with which it might have been possible to evade an aggressive horseman. It has been suggested that most protective harness – for example the helmet and jack – would have been flung off as troops fled, and this accounts for the frequency of head wounds found in the Towton mass grave, the head being the natural target for mounted troops.[23] While agreeing with this latter point, as remarked earlier, it is still suggested here that the Towton mass grave personnel were the victims of executions, not battle casualties.

But why must it have been the case that a soldier would have deprived himself of all his armament? A sword does not weigh much – 2–3 kilograms perhaps for most – and is a most effective means of defence: it does not need reloading, and in the hands of a trained man it can be used to defend against an attacking horseman. Some men armed with bows and bills amongst the retreating soldiers might also have retained their weapons to use. Of course, others would have panicked and flung down everything, making off as fast as they could.

The defence of the bowmen in retreat

The Lancastrian bowmen's usefulness as the battle line broke was still negated. They were not usable as a force of archers to turn the battle around. If they observed the Yorkists who were mounting up to become cavalry, their targets were too far away to be hit effectively by arrow fire. It would have also required a Lancastrian commander to be quick-witted and decisive enough to call off bowmen acting as skirmishers and order them to take up their bows. However, there is no reason to presume the bowmen's weapons would have been removed from the battlefield. They were probably gathered ready nearby in large numbers, together with quivers, bags of spare strings and other paraphernalia such as food and drink especially placed by an experienced commander, for easy access while the archers were acting as light infantry.

As the Lancastrian bowmen saw the fight was lost, they would have begun to drift away from the battlefield. Here they were in danger from their own side. Medieval armies, some have said, used 'prickers' – a sort of military police detachment placed along the rear of the lines to deter deserters and 'prick' troops on to go forward. (The re-enactors whom the author interviewed knew of such a concept.) If the Lancastrian bowmen were seen to be deserting, they thus stood a chance of being attacked by their compatriots. But at this point in the battle, all the Lancastrians' reserves would have been committed, and there were unlikely to be many men who were not busy desperately fighting.

Given the archers were in household groups, forming an organised withdrawal might have been a possibility. Hanson cites this in the days of the Greek phalanx: 'True, initially to step backward away from the enemy, re-form the ranks, turn around 180 degrees, and establish a credible rear guard was not easy, but it offered the best chance for saving both reputation and lives.'[24] He goes on to cite several successful withdrawals.

So bowmen leaving the field would have taken up their bows from nearby, and in their household groups started to leave. There is no reason to think the same household's billmen would not have been with them: the infantry understood what protection those great bows could be. The bowmen were trained to shoot against cavalry, and in the main they would have realised how dangerous they could still be to approaching horsemen. There is no reason to think they would have been out of arrows, as after the initial arrow storm – as has been shown – they were effectively excluded from the battle as bowmen. This likely meant they had plenty of the 24 or 48 shafts they had started with, perhaps more than half.

Small groups of bowmen and billmen, if they kept their heads, would have been largely invulnerable to pursuing cavalry. The threat of facing even half a dozen bowmen with arrows nocked to the string would have been enough for a small group of horsemen to sheer off and look for an easier target. The ground around Towton is either flat or gently sloping, and there would have been little chance of cavalry surprising archers before they could have an arrow on the string. The bowmen and any other fighters would have kept up their hurried escape, making ground towards safer havens.

The Yorkist infantry would have found it almost impossible to catch up. Their formed ranks would have been slower than hurrying small groups of routed Lancastrians. The closer they came to the fleeing bowmen and billmen, the more they would have been the target for the enemy to turn, nock and loose a volley.

The defence of the billmen in retreat

The billmen had less hopes of survival than did the bowmen. By trade they were less experienced, mostly farm labourers taken into the service of their local lord or knight. Nevertheless, the long shaft and hooked blade with which they were armed was designed to drag a mounted man from the saddle, and the blade itself possessed considerable penetrating and percussive power when swung by a trained man and impacting at full speed. Groups of billmen without the protection of bowmen consequently still stood a chance of survival in the rout.

Nevertheless, a fully plated rider, armed with a lance, shield and secondary weapon such a sword or mace, was a specialised warrior. He was trained from early youth to ride against the targets his commander ordered him to attack. He practised his skills against targets, but also in real life. Hunting animals had 'tested the cutting power of warriors' strikes, and also accustomed a fighter to seeing the effect of his strikes on living flesh'.[25] Being unleashed now against fleeing Lancastrian foot-soldiers was something he was trained for. He could alter his tactics and weapon handling to cope with fleeing, charging or stationery forces. Lance-wielding riders would change their grip from having their lance held with the knuckles down to having them uppermost if using it in a melee involving infantry. Once the initial charge was done, then this change to how the lance was handled was a usual practise. (Examples of this variation of using the lance may be seen in the Bayeux Tapestry.)

Good cavalry well-handled would charge through infantry, and this is where the billmen stood only a small chance. If the cavalry unit re-formed and charged again, then once more billmen would be lanced, bowled over or struck from above with an edged or percussive weapon. Helmets, if they were still being worn, could offer some protection against swords and maces.

Nevertheless, if the billmen held their nerve and kept together, then they had a much better chance than when simply ridden down. In such scenarios, men look to their companions, the men they have drunk with, fought with and endured much with. There is every reason to presume they would have stuck together, rather than scatter and divide.

Yet there would still have been much bloodshed. Any Lancastrian turning his back on his own line was vulnerable to attack from behind. His weapon was now in the wrong position to defend himself. It would have been difficult to walk or run, turn his head constantly to see what was behind him, and face any enemy who arrived in the immediate proximity. As the Yorkist cavalry began to arrive on the scene, he was vulnerable to their lances, maces and swords. But if he kept in a group, if he kept his head, and especially if he was a bowman or accompanied by a group of them, then he had a chance of survival.

However, the bodies of men said to have been struck down in the rout from Towton have not been found. They would have more likely been buried by the side of the road rather than in a central grave area. The modern road has been widened considerably, evolving from coping with single or a pair of horses to being a tarmacked carriageway, suitable for two cars to pass going in opposite directions. In keeping with 21st-century traffic conditions, the road has drainage ditches on either side to prevent water washing across it and making driving dangerous. The road to York, along which some commentators would have the Lancastrians fleeing, has been even more changed, now being a multi-lane highway. There was no stream of reports of the finding of human remains on any of these roads as they were modernised through the 20th century. Nor have there been many bodies found buried in the surrounding farmland. The fields around Towton are farmed, and have been for hundreds of years. Bodies appearing regularly in shallow graves would have been remarked upon and been part of the history of the area, yet there are no such reports.

The corpses could have been gathered by cart. Gathering thousands of bodies post-battle for mass graves would have required horsed transport, preferably horses drawing carts. Taking up such transport would have been difficult but possible: rather than gathering them from nearby farms, the Lancastrian baggage train carts could have been used, although their drivers may well have fled. Utilising the Yorkists' own baggage train drivers for this could have been a possibility. Loot from the Lancastrian train would first need to be confiscated and loaded – something not to be ignored, with pay an important consideration for the victorious army. It is just about feasible to postulate that this process of using the wagons to organise the dead could have been carried out over several days. However, there are no records of it, and even if the bodies were gathered, where were they put? This will be discussed in more detail in the next chapter.

There are indeed accounts of heavy casualties in the battle. Bishop Neville, writing only weeks later on 7 April, noted: 'Quite lately one might still see the bodies of these unfortunate men lying unburied, over a space nearly six miles in length and three or four furlongs broad.'[26] But how many were there? Were they one body every 3 metres, or one every 10 or 20? There is no verifiable count at all.

Another oddity about the battle fatalities is the lack of wounded. Generally speaking, throughout military history, the number of wounded compared to those who died is four to one: four injured for every death. There are variations to this, particularly in the case of massacres or of armies who simply won't give up – the latter persistent attitude was typical of the Japanese in World War II, where 97 per cent of their army personnel often died in encounters where they were defeated. For a long time, the Japanese soldier had been conditioned to think of his life as not his own; it was the country's, exemplified by the Emperor. There was a complete rejection of the concepts of not doing one's utmost, even to the end. The idea of surrender, let alone of being captured, was not part of the system. Japan's 1941 Field Service Code, issued by General Tojo, explained it bluntly and firmly: 'Do not live in shame as a prisoner. Die, and leave no ignominious crime behind you.'[27]

But the Japanese are unusual. Almost five millennia of battles are known of, from the battle of Banquan in 2500 BC through the first fight recorded in detail – the battle of Megiddo, around 1500 BC – and in general, casualties have been around four wounded to one dead. However, Polydore Vergil strangely records of Towton: 'And the number of captives and wounded, of whom some were cured and others died, was about 10,000.'[28] As a few sentences previously he had stated that 'About 20,000 men died on both sides', this is disproportionate: one would usually expect 80,000 wounded. One explanation could be the savagery of fighting in the Wars of the Roses, but in general, even though battles were more bloody than the norm, executions afterwards were confined to the leaders. There are no accounts of thousands of the common billmen and bowmen being massacred after such battles, let alone the despatching of thousands of wounded. The killing of wounded prisoners, who were largely Englishmen just like those on the victorious side, would have been abhorrent to the common soldier.

These are various reasons why the numbers of dead at Towton must be in dispute. No one has excavated the verges of the roads that led from Towton, which are still largely in the same place they were then. Neither has anyone made a scientific search for the thousands of dead who supposedly died in the fight. There are no mass graves on the battlefield, nor thousands of individual graves. There must therefore be considerable doubt as to how many actually were killed in the rout.

As the losers, there must have been a large number of Lancaster soldiers who were wounded, trapped, outrun or simply within range of vengeful victors. Towton, many say, was distinguished by the deaths of many thousands of Lancastrians. But it was not always the case that the average bowman and man-at-arms was targeted. Instead, the Wars of the Roses was characterised by the deaths of many of the nobility and the sparing of the common soldiery. Revenge for past executions was a hallmark of these wars. Andrew Boardman quite rightly has said: 'During the most intense periods of the Wars of the Roses, factional opposition rendered the codes of chivalry, and the merciful aspects of quarter, almost obsolete on the English battlefield.'[29]

Some of the more accurate historical records of the Wars of the Roses attest to the two most usual habits at the finale of battles. First, the common soldiers were spared, but the knights and nobles were specifically targeted. Second, the immediate aftermath of the battle saw executions of the leading members of the losing side.

Philippe de Commines confirms the ordering of this routine: 'Spare the common soldiers and kill the lords.'[30] Proclamations made by commanders before battle that only the commoners were to be spared were an incitement for soldiers to swarm around the distinctively armed and apparelled nobles, and perhaps gain rewards for killing them.[31]

Knusel and Boylston point out that ransoming was the norm in the Hundred Years' War, which preceded the Wars of the Roses, but the practise was not followed in the later conflict. They catalogue the execution of leaders on the losing side following most Wars of the Roses battles: 42 Lancastrian knights were slain after Towton, for example.[32] But it may have been the case, as they point out, that reprisals were also the norm for those of lesser rank: 'Despite pronouncements against the execution of common soldiery, and contrary to the canon of chivalric ideals, many experienced the same fate as the noblemen whom they served.' This depiction is preferred by some historians, for example Hugh Bicheno, who argues there was 'no mercy shown even to the humble conscripts who made up the vast majority of armies'.[33]

Goodman suggests, quoting Commines, that at the battle of Barnet, 'The slaughter was exceedingly heavy' because King Edward did not adhere to his custom of ordering that the commons should be saved and the nobles killed. Rather, he bore animosity towards the people for a favour they had done the Earl of Warwick. Goodman proposes that the same was the policy at Tewkesbury.[34]

This could have been the case at Towton too, but why so? Both of the Yorkist and Lancastrian armies had been gathered by the Commissioners of Array and their immediate lords and leaders. Why would there be an unusual animosity now?

Boardman goes on analyse the nobles, and indeed proves conclusively enough that they died in quantity. But he does not explain why the vast bulk of the dead must have included the common soldiery. It is very likely that the numbers of combat personnel at Towton were vastly inflated, a subject to which this investigation now turns.

CHAPTER 10

The Myth of Fatalities in Medieval Battle

How many died?

A hypothesis of medieval battle has been established by this investigation: that it was fought by its infantry in lines, the front line being relieved by the second, which was relieved by a third, and so on. This was because of the reality of physical combat: no man could fight in armour with edged and percussive weapons for long due to his own limitations, even at peak fitness.

But what is the truth about medieval combat deaths? This study will still use the battle of Towton as an example, but this time as one where truth replaces the propaganda of enormous fatality counts. For what is elsewhere recorded for Towton cannot be true; and it is likely that all medieval combat deaths are vastly exaggerated. In furthering this discussion, it is acknowledged that the Towton conclusion reached here largely follows the work of experts in the archaeological field – in particular Sutherland, Curry and Foard – but the author combines this with the tactical analysis carried out above and a deconstruction of the composition of medieval armies.

The earliest claims of a large number of Towton dead seem to be from a letter sent nine days after the battle by George Neville, then Chancellor of England. He wrote that 28,000 men died. This figure is in accord with a letter sent by Edward IV to his mother.[1] A newsletter dated 4 April 1461 also reported a widely circulated figure of 28,000 casualties in the battle, which Charles Ross and other historians believe was exaggerated.

The number was taken from the heralds' estimate – notably an estimate, not a count – of the dead. It appeared in letters from King Edward and the Bishop of Salisbury, Richard Beauchamp.

Modern sources repeat figures around this without question:

- Adrian Waite: 'Richard Beauchamp, Bishop of Salisbury added that: "The Heralds counted [sic] 28,000 slain, a number unheard of in our realm ... without counting those wounded and drowned."'[2]
- Katy Emery: 'Over 28,000 men lost their lives in this single battle. For being such a major battle in English history, there is little known about the day itself and the men who fought.'[3]
- The Exiles, a company of medieval martial artists: 'During the battle and ensuing rout of the Lancastrians, an estimated 22,000 to 28,000 men lost their lives.'[4]
- *The Yorkshire Post*: 'Exact losses are a matter of continuing debate, but there are estimates of up to 30,000 casualties.'[5]
- Andrew Boardman: 'between 20,000 and 28,000 dead.'[6]

What graves are known of?

If questioning these figures, one must ask whether there are that many mortal remains to be found. As has been shown in the previous chapter, they have not been found. Nor has any examination of the rout of the battle taken place. This is not unusual: vast grave sites have not been discovered from any medieval British battles. According to some historians, the bodies of the 10,000 men generally thought to have died at the battle of Hastings have not been located.[7] Nor have the supposed 80,000 who died at an AD 60 battle between British and Roman forces been found – this rather doubtful action is referred to in a few pages.

There was generally a medieval convention that the fallen, who were usually Christians, would be buried by some sort of common consent. Anne Curry notes that the French were allowed by the English victors to return to the Agincourt battlefield after the action for this purpose,[8] and Anthony Goodman discusses the ritual in English practice in the Wars of the Roses. But this was no organised affair with set patterns.

Back of Towton Hall, where a medieval gravepit was discovered and disinterred in 1996. (Author photo)

Most soldiers were paid for only the days up to and including the battle. Afterwards, they just wanted to get home. There is consequently no evidence of hundreds of soldiers being retained after the battle to be used on burial duty.

There is some suggestion the Towton battlefield was cleaned up afterwards, but that still does not explain where the bodies are. The chronicler Leland, writing many decades later, mentions 'five great pits, half a mile away in Saxton fields' where bodies were buried.[9] They have not been located, despite all of the village's surrounding area being farmed. There are only a few mass burial sites at Towton. One is at Towton Hall, and another is on the battlefield itself, the latter site appearing to have been imperfectly cleared hundreds of years ago. Yet the two together do not even account for 100 individuals.

In July 1996, preparations for a new garage block at Towton Hall uncovered human bones. Twenty-three sets of remains were counted by

Lord Dacre's grave at Saxton Church, with the marker (right) where bones dug up behind Towton Hall were reburied in the late 1990s. (Author photo)

the construction company. These skeletal remains were reburied at Saxton churchyard beside Lord Dacre.[10] The following month, a mass burial pit was discovered near the battlefield. The remains were excavated by osteoarchaeologists and archaeologists from the Archaeological Sciences department at the University of Bradford and members of the West Yorkshire Archaeology Service. The mass grave included 43 individuals within a 6m × 2m × 50cm space.[11] Four individual skeletons, the remains of soldiers, were then found in 2005 underneath Towton Hall.[12]

An excavation of a grave pit was carried out in 1816, likely in the area of Chapel Hill, approximately 100m east of Towton Hall, and recovered a few items of human remains.[13] In 1993, an excavation was made of two mounds south-east of Castle Hill Wood, but no human remains or artifacts were uncovered. These sites were also the wrong shape for mass graves, being circular and probably prehistoric barrows.[14]

In February 2004, York Osteoarchaeology Ltd was commissioned by the Towton Battlefield Society, and reported the following:

> On the battlefield itself, a sample evaluation of a large pit revealed over three hundred human bone fragments. It is thought that the pit is a mass grave, which was cleared in 1483 following the orders of a grant by Richard III. The skeletons were re-interred in Saxton churchyard. The remaining bones were all small and may have been discarded or missed by the grave diggers. They represented individuals aged between fifteen to mature adulthood and included two cranial weapon injuries.
>
> Where sex could be established, all individuals were male. Osteological and palaeopathological results largely corresponded with those established for the skeletons from the 1996 mass grave. Differences in physical expressions between individuals excavated at Towton Hall and the battlefield suggest that the two burial sites may represent different social groups of combatants.[15]

Studies have been carried out at Towton using the landscape in order to understand how the battle was fought. In order to do this, an archaeological team from the University of Bradford used existing historical data from the North Yorkshire County Council Sites and Monuments Record, as well as maps and aerial photography. In addition to this, they conducted their own surveys through field walking and metal detector searches. They were thus able to locate the boundaries of the battlefield and clarify where supposed burials were located.[16]

Research by the Richard III Society has shown that a chapel with a cemetery was established after Towton, perhaps on the site of a previous place of worship. A papal bull was issued in 1467 intending to renovate the older building, and in 1472 there was a chaplain assigned to it. Later references also show three burial pits were established on the battlefield. After Bosworth, progress was difficult – likely due to the new Lancastrian/Tudor monarchy of Henry VII not wanting to be associated with the site of a Yorkist victory – and it appears that eventually the building was demolished and its materials used elsewhere, perhaps in construction at Towton Hall.[17]

But nothing seems to have been done at Towton to the extent it has at Bosworth, for example by Foard and Curry, who examined on a very wide scale the topography and archaeology of the battlefield, together with what primary sources could be found.[18,19] The best work at Towton seems to have been done by Tim Sutherland, but it has not been able to find vast grave sites. Indeed, Sutherland is on record as saying the numbers of deaths in the battle must be only around 10 per cent of previous estimates:

> Current estimates, based upon the geophysical survey anomalies of the dimensions of the pits, suggest that this would be a few thousand (Sutherland 2006) and not tens of thousands as previously believed, although this would obviously need to be confirmed by excavation. This hypothesis would lead to a stark conclusion; that the number of deaths from the battle of Towton might have been grossly exaggerated.[20]

However, even this smaller number of graves have not yet been found. Indeed, the dispersal of arrowheads found on the battlefield so far indicate a small force, although admittedly an archaeological survey of the entire *possible* battlefield has not been done.[21]

Burial by the side of the road for those fleeing at the end of the battle could have been the fate for many rather than recovery to a central grave area. As pointed out previously, the road, or track – it was not one of the Roman-constructed roads – of those days has now been widened considerably, with drainage ditches on either side. There has been no steady stream of reports over the last century reporting the finding of human remains on either side of the highway as it was modernised.

It was snowing on the day of the battle – the ground that evening and the next day would have been frozen and not allowed easy burial. However, Boardman quotes the *Croyland Chronicle* as saying that a thaw set in, enabling bodies to be found under heaps of snow and graves to be dug.[22]

There is another factor militating against the accepted Towton casualty figure. That is the sheer amount of space needed. Burying one body would need a grave approximately 180cm long, 50cm wide and 20cm deep merely to get the body underground. Ten bodies, buried side by side, would necessitate a 5m width; 100 bodies would need 50m.

It could of course be argued that bodies might not be buried in such a fashion. Maybe two were buried at a time, one on top of the other. This would go against the Christian attitudes of those filling the graves.

Then again, practicality may have overcome tradition: battlefield grave pits were often used, and mass burial is a feature of plague burials. This can therefore be allowed for the sake of analysis, which permits the investigator to be generous with the amount of space needed: not so much of the battlefield area is taken up this way, with 200 bodies needing a pit 2m × 50m (or 4m × 25m), taking the same amount of land as 100 bodies in the traditionally accepted formula. Why stop there, it might be argued; why not stack bodies three deep? The problem there is that Towton is basically a shallow layer of earth over a rock base. This author interviewed the farmer who has operated the farm which lies over the battlefield area since 1983.[23] He confirmed there is no more than 3ft of soil before the average dig hits rock. The medieval soldiers were not miners; they were not equipped with quarrying equipment such as picks and crowbars, merely being part-time fighters who would by now be anxious to leave their duties.

Detail of the soil at Towton. Despite centuries of farming since the battle, few graves have been found, and the soil becomes rock around a metre down. (Author photo)

Scaling up the figures, for every 1,000 burials there could be expected to be five 2m × 50m grave pits, so for the 25,000 that have been said to have fallen at Towton, there would need to be 125 such pits.

That this practice was carried out can be shown from other battles. Following the English victory at Agincourt, for example, 'the abbot of Ruisseauville and the bailli of Aire had a twenty-five foot square measured out in which they had three ditches, as deep as two men, dug, into which were put, according to the count made, 5,800 men'.[24]

While somewhat macabre in imagining, this makes the point against so many mass burials at Towton well enough. If that many people died, where are they buried? Why have bodies from the supposed rout not been found along the roads leading away from the battlefield? Why have bodies not been found in the farming processes constantly carried out in the Towton and Saxton region over the centuries? As can be seen from modern aerial photographs, the entire area is farmed, and tilling of the soil would reveal mass graves. If the graves were deeper then suggested here, where is the excavated rock?

How many soldiers participated in medieval battles?

It must be the case that the Towton figures overall are highly exaggerated. The number of soldiers who fought at the battle of Towton is extremely difficult to estimate, but this must be attempted before trying to arrive at a casualty count.

England's wars were not always fought between Englishmen, whatever that definition was. The country had been invaded by the Normans, from Normandy in what is now part of modern France, in 1066. Thereafter the Welsh clung obstinately to their language and customs and the Cornish were just as dour and localised, while the men of Devon had their own dialect, just as incomprehensible as the other two. But several hundred years later, these had been melded into a sort of hybrid Englishman. Mercenaries and foreign troops were used in the Wars of the Roses, but in general this was a series of battles fought using the retainers and men forced into battle by the levy systems.

England's population was around two million during the Wars of the Roses, of whom around 750,000 were possible fighting men.[25] Between 30 and 45 per cent of the general populace had died in the Black Death of 1348–50, although in some villages, 80–90 per cent of the population died. A death-rate of 30 per cent is massive, higher than the total British losses in World War I. One historian summed it up: 'The Black Death raged in London until spring 1350, and is generally assumed to have killed between one third and one half of the populace.'[26] Nor was 1350 the end of it. Plague reoccurred in 1361–64, 1368, 1371, 1373–75, 1390 and 1405, and continued into the fifteenth century.[27]

By the 1370s, the population of England had thus been halved, and by the time of Towton it was still not recovering.[28] This would have had an effect on the number of fighting men available: it meant there were substantially fewer men available to work in the fields and carry out the heavy farming labour necessary to survive, and therefore fewer still available to fight. Considerations also had to be made when withdrawing men: if an entire village's male population had been conscripted, there would be no-one available to get the harvest in and carry out all the other duties necessary to supply food for the village.

Britain's population was not large anyway. The Black Death had decreased it to 2.1 million in the early 15th century. Even by 1545, towards the end of Henry VIII's reign, it stood at only 3.2 million, according to one source.[29] Another analysis confirms a population of 2.1 million during the Wars of the Roses, with 'about 500,000 men of fighting age'.[30]

By 1461, the population could have been no more than 2.5 million. Out of that, if an equal ratio of males and females is presumed, there were 1.25 million men. The average life expectancy for a male child born in the nation between 1276 and 1300 was 31.3 years.[31] It can be presumed therefore that half of the male population was 15 years old or less – not of a fighting age. There were thus probably only 750,000 men, scattered across the entire length and breadth of the country, who were possible soldiers. Given the extremely slow communications of the time – letters were carried by cart, in general, and there were no newspapers – it would have been very difficult to speedily muster a large armed force.

Gathering so many men would have meant a massive effort over several weeks. To get to a destination, soldiers walked. Horses were the province of rich men and their men-at-arms, and wagons were not used for carrying people but for hauling freight, and they moved more slowly than a good walker. While a horsed soldier could travel some 15–19 miles a day, a soldier on foot, carrying his equipment, could manage only around 12–15 miles.[32]

Gordon Corrigan suggests that it was 'normal for British soldiers in the Great War to cover 20 miles in a day, but also points out they wore boots.[33] Modern troops do have a distinct advantage in footwear over their medieval counterpart, who wore individually made shoes without the heavy nailed soles of the 19th and 20th centuries, or in more recent times Kevlar. Consequently, medieval soldiers could walk lesser distances.

In 2017, the United States Rangers, a 'commando' unit of the US Army, underwent a walking test which required a 16-mile hike, while carrying a 65lb pack, to be completed in five hours and 20 minutes.[34] This was a test component, and therefore meant the soldiers concerned were exerting themselves, which is not something an armed force would do except in urgent need. Any soldiers completing such distances would not be in great condition afterwards, and they would not have stopped to eat in that time, meaning they would be exhausted upon arrival and in no shape for combat. Records for forced marches are widespread, but they are all relative to the equipment carried, the quality of roads to be traversed and the weather.

In general, a rate of three 3 miles an hour could be sustained by medieval troops on foot. However, this rate could not be kept up for days on end. The rate of 'best march' was really only for a day or two, maybe three at the most. More than that would see soldiers falling out of the ranks, and a gradual depletion of the force. Their limit, then, would be some 12–15 miles per day. It would be likely less: although these were hardy peasants, the levied forces were not all trained soldiers, nor were they used to walking such distances day after day.

A major implication in obtaining a large army to fight at Towton would have been the immense distances to be covered on foot. The following table presents some possibilities with gathering armed forces from the regional centres of 1377:[35]

Centre	Population	Males of fighting age	Distance from Towton (miles)	Time in hours of marching	Days of marching at eight hours a day[36]
London	23,314	5,828	203	51	6
York	7,248	1,812	12	3	.5
Bristol	6,345	1,586	210	53	6.5
Coventry	4,817	1,204	122	31	3.8
Norwich	3,952	988	167	42	5.2
Lincoln	3,569	892	67	17	4
Salisbury	3,226	806	245	61	8
King's Lynn	3,217	804	126	32	4
Colchester	2,955	738	199	50	6
Boston	2,871	717	99	25	3
Total possible levies in 1377		15,375			

A hundred years later, it can be assumed that towns had grown in population substantially if London is any guide. So perhaps a total possible levy of 25,000 was possible in 1461.

One factor that needs to be taken into account is that the available force must be split in half, as the two sides at Towton seemed roughly equal according to the sources. This point is supported by the fact that if they didn't have a reasonable possibility of success, neither Yorkists nor Lancastrians would have stayed to fight; they would have sought a better time and place.

The times in the table to gather the levies show that it would have been possible for them to do so. For instance, Lord Fauconberg left London on 11 March with 10,000 men, and was followed two days later by King

Edward and his retinue.[37] Fauconberg could have been an advance guard, or perhaps the main body. Boardman estimates Fauconberg, Edward and Warwick to have had 20,000 men with them, and the Duke of Norfolk another 5,000.[38]

Although it is unlikely the gathering would have been able to keep up a steady daily rate – given the weather, victualling and the need for a Sabbath and its mandatory service – the two forces could still have gathered. That is of course if the two commanders knew where they wanted to go, and proceeded in straight lines. However, the political recordings of the day – far more reliable than military accounts – indicate that this did not happen. Indeed, there were skirmishes and minor clashes in the days prior to Towton.

What this analysis does show us is the low numbers of fighting men available from the towns. The 10 centres shown in the table were the largest English populations. Even if the men possible from a geographic concentration were surveyed rather than numbers available, there is still no chance of the large numbers recorded being gathered. It has been noted in a previous chapter that when Edward IV 'asked for 20,000 archers to be raised in 1453 [for his European campaigns], he was forced to drop his request to 13,000 archers, and even this number proved too high for the stock of skilled English longbowmen'.[39] Note that this was the English king, recruiting for a campaign which promised adventure in a foreign land, the chance to attack the French and gain loot – a much more attractive prospect than killing fellow countrymen. If the king could not raise 13,000 bowmen for such a campaign, then can it seriously be contemplated that tens of thousands could be raised for Towton? The professional men-at-arms have to be added to these numbers, but even so, with a levy of 12,500 available to either side, it must be doubted whether each army could have grown to much more than 16,000 each.

In summary, for a huge pair of armies to gather at Towton was unlikely. The average size of an army for the Wars of the Roses was usually around 10,000 a side, as will be seen, although those numbers too were likely overstated. Another two factors count against the huge armies stated in the sources: the problem of supply and over-reporting, especially of fatalities, which were a constant issue in the medieval world. It is worthwhile employing Inherent Military Probability to analyse the supply issue, coupled with the author's own military experience, part of which involved half a year of service in an army of 43,000 in the Middle East.

The problem of supply

It is an obvious fact that medieval armies must be fed, yet this is rarely mentioned in accounts of battles. Not only must men be fed, they must be watered too. Their horses must also be maintained. A working horse cannot offer much if it is merely turned out to graze on whatever grass is available near a camp. A usual provision is oats or chaff, while hay is an alternative if the grazing is poor. Such provisions must be carried in the carts of the supply train, along with some of the soldiers' food: spices, provisions carried in jars or bottles, bread, fruit and vegetables.

Meat was a high-energy food, but in the days before refrigeration or the use of tins there was limited ability to keep it fresh. Far more preferable was the acquisition of fresh meat, either from local hunting and fishing or the slaughter of animals carried along with the army: cattle, pigs and poultry. But this system could last only so long as the provisions lasted. Food could also be purchased locally, and accounts sometimes relate how officials of an army were sent ahead to negotiate such deals. There was also the possibility of the plundering of foodstuffs, but this had the disadvantage of angering the local population, most of whom were capable of defending their goods from lightly armed soldiers using bills and bows.

Like an army's horses, soldiers too needed high-energy food – and lots of it – if they were to fight effectively. The provision of such food is staggering in its quantities. If, for example, a soldier might survive well on half a loaf of bread and half a chicken a day, the implication for an army of 10,000 was 5,000 loaves and 5,000 chickens per day. The slaughter of one bullock was much more feasible. One study argues that a cow can feed 4,500 men with one small burger each – an impressive total. (The study cited below argues for the very small burger an outlet such as McDonalds sells, not the bigger product such as the quarter-pounder. If that was required for the marching soldier, the cow could only supply about 1,000 such burgers.)[40] But that is only one meal. To feed an army of 10,000 three such meals a day would mean around 42 cattle a week would need to be processed. And of course man cannot live on meat alone: bread was a necessity, as were some vegetables and/or fruit.

Water was also a problem. It would be required in tremendous amounts, but the water of the time was only available from streams and rivers, and was easily contaminated. The horses, and other animals such as those destined to be food, travelling in the supply train, would need watering, and they would contaminate the water with their faeces. Wine and beer keeps better than water, and the 'small beer' of the time was drunk by almost everyone: a beer not necessarily alcoholic, and consumed in large quantities. But again, the means of making or obtaining such liquids was a problem for armies.

Such a supply problem was of course not just for the day of the battle, but the weeks preceding it and the days following before an army dispersed. Men returning home would expect to have been paid, from which they could purchase food. Again, the provision of such pay was a significant aspect of marshalling an army.

The supply train did not supply just food and drink. It contained a myriad of equipment and the means of solving the multitude of problems the soldiers encountered in their day-to-day existence. There were armourers to repair the weapons and armour, fletchers to make arrows, bowyers to produce and repair bows, sadlers for the bridles and saddles of the horsemen, farriers for shoeing horses, blacksmiths to make those shoes and repair metal items such as weapons, servants for the knights and noblemen, butchers to slaughter and prepare meat, cooks of varying abilities, clerks to keep paperwork (including the soldiers' pay), men to attend to animal husbandry and still more besides: cartwrights, coopers (barrelmakers), tentmakers, priests and mere 'hangers-on', including women, children, opportunists, prostitutes, labourers and thieves. Martin van Creveld, in his book *Supplying*

War, points out that a 17th-century army might be followed by a 'tail' around 150 per cent of its own size.[41] All the official members of this logistical tail had to be fed and housed too. The army would not supply those not on its books, but such people still had an impact on the local food and drink available by their very presence: they would demand food from their friends, scrounge what they could and generally have an impact.

Adding to these numbers and their inherent problems was the fact that armies of the Wars of the Roses were often met by a force of commensurate size, thereby doubling the impact on supplies. For the battle of Towton, the nearest centre of any size with the possibility of sustaining either of the two forces was York, with a population of less than 10,000. The suggestion that such a small town – but reckoned a big one for its day – being able to supply two forces numbering over 50,000 for a week or two is preposterous.[42] It is therefore far more likely the two forces at Towton were small armies, of a size similar to the other battles between Lancastrians and Yorkists, each numbering in the low thousands. It is indeed illogical to suppose that huge armies could be mustered at any time during the Wars of the Roses.

Over-reporting numbers in battles

Medieval battle numbers might be a study in difficulty, but in most medieval and ancient fights there seems to be little reliable evidence of total casualties caused.

Author Dando-Collins in *The Armies of Rome* can be used as an example. He suggests around 80,000 British soldiers and civilians were killed in action in an AD 60 battle between the forces of the warrior queen Boudicca and the Romans, somewhere north of London. This may have taken place near a village now called Mancetter, on the border of Warwickshire and Leicestershire. (The clash is sometimes referred to as the Battle of Watling Street.) Seven other sites have been suggested for the battle, but nothing definitive in terms of archaeological evidence has been found.[43]

Nevertheless, the two sides met and fought. The Britons were eventually involved in a crush due to the constraints of the chosen ground and were heavily defeated, not helped by their indiscipline and chariot tactics.

The massive casualty figures of the Britons sound most dubious, especially as only about 400 Romans are given as killed. Dando-Collins also suggests, quoting the Roman historian Dio, that the Britons had '230,000 fighting men'.[44] This must be seriously questioned: the population of Britain in AD 1000 was estimated at only two million, and must have been much less in Boudicca's time. Even given that number, to say that about half of all males of fighting age must have been in the action begs disbelief. How would they have known to be there; how would they have travelled there; what would they have lived on, especially given the analysis of supply given above; and where are the bodies of the slain? Dando-Collins also says the battle was never given a name, only later becoming known as the battle of Watling Street, yet a combat action which killed so many would have become a household word, especially as it involved one-in-three males in the population at the time.[45,46]

Are such exaggerations utilised because the victors want to show how fierce they are, and how important the battle was? Is it because the defeated want to exaggerate the scale of their loss, to show how fiercely they fought and how heavy was their sacrifice? Boardman believes so, writing: 'Chroniclers often increased the length of battle to enhance their stories, or for propaganda purposes.' He also suggests, as have others, that Towton is linked with the battle of Ferrybridge, fought the previous day,[47] while Sutherland links clashes at both Ferrybridge and Dintingdale.[48] Is such over-reporting simply the fog of war? The author noticed in a Baghdad enemy attack he was involved in, which produced chaos all around, that the number killed in action was only three, with about 20 wounded. Yet at the time, he would have believed 20 killed and 60 wounded.

The battle of Towton is usually reported as having involved around 75,000 men, with 28,000 fatalities. George Goodwin, who wrote a book on Towton to coincide with the battle's 550th anniversary in 2011, reckoned as many as 75,000 men, perhaps 10 per cent of the country's fighting-age population, took the field that day.[49] Other reports agree: 'An estimated 50,000 to 80,000 soldiers participated in the conflict';[50] 'Up to 60,000 men … history records, [and] 28,000 lay dead or dying.'[51]

This is an enormous army, given the normal numbers participating in British battles in both international and civil wars of the times. Then again, wild reporting was par for the course: John Keegan notes that the French numbers at Agincourt have been 'variously counted between 10,000 and **200,000** [author's emphasis]' – a 2,000 per cent discrepancy.[52]

However, Goodman notes that there were plenty of incentives not to fight on either side in the Wars of the Roses, including the devastating firepower of the bowmen, the possibility of not being allowed quarter and the risks posed if your side was routed.[53] Boardman comments: 'Especially in the crucial years of 1469–70, [the authorities] had great difficulties when calling upon their tenantry to comply.'[54] Soldiers were recruited through indenture, the Commissioners of Array, the mustering of local militias and the gathering of mercenaries.[55] Towton, according to Boardman, 'drained the country of its best fighting men'.[56]

Michael D. Miller, in his enormous body of research published on his website, suggests:

> A total Lancastrian strength of 19,000, whilst that of the Yorkists was 14,000, or 33,000 in all who were present at the start of the battle. Allowance has to be made for the Duke of Norfolk's division, perhaps 2,000 strong, which arrived late. This finds a grand total of 35,000 men who took part in the battle.[57]

These must be looked on as maximum, or extreme, figures; they still mean one in every 100 of the total population, and this high figure invites doubts of its own. In fact, as a look through the table overleaf shows, the suggested forces at Towton are so far out of the ordinary that they stand out peculiarly in the Wars of the Roses.

Combatant counts in the battles of the Wars of the Roses[58,59]

Date	Name	House of York strength	House of Lancaster strength	Victor	Duration of battle (hours)	House of York fatalities	House of Lancaster fatalities	Percentage[60] of total force killed in action
22 May 1455	First St Albans, Hertfordshire	3,000[61] 'not over 3,000 men'[62]	2,500[63]	York	3[64]	Overall casualties about 300[65] 100 men in total[66]	'Not more than 120 persons in all perished, possibly as few as sixty: of forty-eight bodies buried by the abbot only twenty-five were those of unknown common soldiers, the others were lords, knights, squires, and officers of the king's household'[67]	Highest estimate = 5% Lowest estimate = 2%
23 Sep 1459	Blore Heath, near Market Drayton, Shropshire	5,000[68]	10,000[69]	York	4[70]	Yorkist casualties minimal[71]	Lancastrian leader Audley slain; with him fell the flower of the Cheshire knights, Sir Hugh Venables, Sir Thomas Dutton, Sir Richard Molineux and many more. Lancastrian casualties estimated at 2,000	Estimate = 14%
12 Oct 1459	Ludford Bridge, Shropshire	Unknown		Lanc	n/a[72]	None[73]		

(Continued)

Date	Name	House of York strength	House of Lancaster strength	Victor	Duration of battle (hours)	House of York fatalities	House of Lancaster fatalities	Percentage[60] of total force killed in action
10 Jul 1460	Northampton	20,000[74]	10,000[75]	York	30 mins[76]	300 men in total[77]	'Less than 300 men perished, including a few who were drowned as they tried to ford the Nen. But among the list of slain were nearly all the Lancastrian leaders. Warwick's orders had been carried out; the rank and file were allowed to escape, but the victors gave no quarter to knights and nobles. Buckingham, Beaumont, Egremont, Shrewsbury, and Sir William Lucy, were all slaughtered close to the king's tent, as they strove by a last rally to gain him time to flee.'[78]	Estimate = 1%
30 Dec 1460	Wakefield	8,000[79] 5–12,000[80] 5,000[81]	18,000[82] 15–22,000[83] 15,000[84]	Lanc	30 mins[85]	Between 700 and 2,500[86]		Lowest estimate = 3% Highest estimate = 7%
2 Feb 1461	Mortimer's Cross, Herefordshire	11,000[87] between 2,000 and 3,000 men[88] 51,000[89]	8,000[90] 8,000[91]	York		3,000[92]		Lowest estimate = 5% Highest estimate = 33%

(Continued)

Date	Name	House of York strength	House of Lancaster strength	Victor	Duration of battle (hours)	House of York fatalities	House of Lancaster fatalities	Percentage[60] of total force killed in action
17 Feb 1461	Second St Albans, Bernards Heath, St Albans, Hertfordshire	10,000[93] 25,000[94]	14,000 25,000	Lanc	Several hours	Yorkists 4,000[95] A most dubious set of figures. St Albans was basically a series of house-to-house fights within a walled town. World War II conflicts in similar circumstances produced casualties in the hundreds, not thousands, and such fights utilised much more powerful weapons such as automatic firearms and grenades.	Lancastrians 2,000	25% using the first of the two army numbers indicated: 10,000 and 14,000
28 Mar 1461	Ferrybridge, Yorkshire	Unknown	Unknown	York				
29 Mar 1461	Towton, west of York	36,000[96] 20–25,000[97,98]	40,000[99] 30,000[100] 20–25,000[101]	York		Possibly losing 8,000[102] c.10,000[103] 20–28,000 for both sides[104]	20,000[105] c.20,000[106]	53% of the total force
25 Apr 1464	Hedgeley Moor, Northumberland	5,000[107]	5,000[108]	York		Unknown		
15 May 1464	Hexham, Northumberland	5,000[109]	5,000[110]	York		Unknown		

(Continued)

Date	Name	House of York strength	House of Lancaster strength	Victor	Duration of battle (hours)	House of York fatalities	House of Lancaster fatalities	Percentage[60] of total force killed in action
24 Jul 1469	Edgecote Moor, Northamptonshire	5–6,000;[111]	Unknown	York		Uncertain but possibly high[112]	Uncertain but possibly high[113]	
12 Mar 1470	Losecote Field, Rutland	Unknown	Unknown	Lanc				
14 Apr 1471	Barnet, near London	10,000[114] 10,000–12,000[115]	15,000[116] 15,000[117]	York	4[118]	'Casualties at Barnet reflected the evenness of the battle. Wesel thought 1500 fell on both sides. Commynes gave the same figure for the Yorkists, more among the defeated Lancastrians. These neutral estimates fall between John Paston's 1,000 "of both parties" and Warkworth's 4,000.'[119]		Lowest estimate = 4% Middle estimate = 6% Highest estimate = 15%[120]
4 May 1471	Tewkesbury, Gloucestershire	5,000[121] 6,000[122]	7,000[123]	York	4[124]	500?[125] c. 2,000[126]		Lowest estimate = 19% Highest estimate = 20%
22 Aug 1485	Bosworth, near Market Bosworth, Leicestershire	10,000[127]	5,000[128]	Lanc	2[129]	Possibly 1,000 royal[130] 100 rebel[131]		Estimate = 7%
16 Jun 1487	Stoke Field, Nottinghamshire	c. 8,000[132]	c. 15,000[133]	Lanc	2½[134]	Royal: possibly just 100; Rebel: up to 4,000[135]		Estimate = 18%

The percentage said to be slain at Towton — around half of the combatants — is well above the norm for a one-day battle. Dr Williams has suggested to the author that with the exception of the Japanese in World War II, there are no battles where one side loses half its men if it has a way to escape; morale always breaks before that and the soldiers flee.[136]

If there is no escape for a defeated force, such as in the battles of Cannae or Isandlwana, then half or more of an army can be wiped out. The battle of Cannae was fought on 2 August 216 BC, in south-eastern Italy, between the forces of Rome and Carthage during the Second Punic War. The eight Roman legions were caught in a valley and annihilated. At Isandlwana, a between British and Zulu forces on 22 January 1879, the Zulus encircled their opponents and only a handful of British troops escaped. However, this sort of battle is extremely rare in history. At Towton, there were plenty of ways out for the defeated side. Nowhere in the Lancastrian rear was there a wall of enemy or an uncrossable obstacle. A look at the table opposite is instructive.

A comparison of Towton with other one-day battles

Name	Date	Combatant numbers	Total Casualties	Total KIA	Weaponry	% of the total KIA
Towton	29 Mar 1461	York 20–25,000[137,138] versus Lancaster 20–25,000[139]		20–28,000 for both sides[140]	• Arrows • Edged • Percussive	Lowest 40% to highest 56%
Culloden[141] – British government forces put down a rebellion led by 'Bonnie Prince Charlie'	16 April 1746	Jacobites 5,250 versus British 7,800 Total: 13,050		1,500 Jacobites 50 British Total = 1,550	• Muskets • Infantry with swords • Cavalry with swords	12.6%
Waterloo – Final battle of the Napoleonic Wars, resulting in Napoleon's defeat by British and Prussian forces[142]	18 Jun 1815	French 72,000 versus British 67,000 and Prussians 53,000 Total: 192,000	25,000 French 22,000 Allied	4,000 French 3,500 British 1,200 Prussians[143] Total = 8,700	• Single-shot muzzleloader muskets/rifles • Muzzleloading artillery • Cavalry with spears and sabres	4.5%
Battle of the Alma[144] – Crimean War, Russia versus Britain, France and Turkey	20 Sep 1854	Russian 33,000 + 3,400 cavalry + 116 guns versus British 26,000 + 60 guns French & Turks 37,000 + 68 guns Total = 99,400	Russian 5,511 British 2,000 French 1,243	Russians 1,810 British 362 French 1,243 Total = 3,415	• Single-shot muzzleloaders • Muzzleloading artillery • Cavalry with spears and sabres[145]	3.4%
1st **Battle of the Somme**[146,147] – First day of massive six-month battle fought between Germany and the Allies in World War I	1 Jul 1916	French 5 divisions British Empire 13 divisions versus German[148] 16 divisions = a total of 34 @ 15,000 = 510,000		British Empire 19,240 French 1,590 German 11,000 Total = 31,830	• Quick-firing rifles • Automatic crew-served weapons • Mortars • Breechloading artillery	6.3%

The Somme is most instructive for the argument that medieval battles were not that efficient as killing machines. The Somme is often given as a one-day battle – 1 July 1916 – with 60,000 casualties. In fact it lasted for months, and the eventual casualties were in the hundreds of thousands. On that first day, though, there were over 20,000 dead on the Allied side.

These grim totals were brought about by several factors:

- An enormous battlefront of around 23 miles.
- A steady supply of victims hurrying to the killing zone.
- The efficient processing of soldiers into the combat areas, using protected trench networks and mechanised transport to bring them to the rear of the trench system.
- Quick-firing weapons.
- Heavy artillery of enormous destructive power.
- Aircraft bombing and strafing.
- No protective armour for the victims.

If a modern war with all of these factors results in the deaths of just 6.3 per cent of combatants, then surely it is impossible for a medieval army with comparatively primitive percussive and club weapons and short-range missiles to inflict a much greater amount of killing percentage-wise. Towton was also said to have lasted only some three hours, not the entire day as did the Somme's initial engagement. Note the other fatality rates above: 12.6 per cent for Culloden, 4.5 per cent for Waterloo and 3.4 per cent for the Alma. All of these battles involved firearms and explosives, which are more efficient killing devices then the muscle-powered weapons utilised at Towton.

The previously mentioned arrangement of medieval battles should also be noted. Only the front line engaged in combat, although this sometimes spilled into the ranks behind, given the surge back and forth as one side prevailed. Sometimes this became a disastrous 'feed' of casualties against the victorious side's weapons, as at Agincourt, but often – especially given the inevitable tendency to place the platemen forward – it must have simply led to an ebb and flow, without too much in the way of fatalities.

It is worthwhile quoting Richard Gabriel's words when discussing Greek phalanx combat:

> It is commonly assumed that battles involving this type of close combat were horrifically bloody; in fact, they were rarely so. Only the first two ranks could actually engage in any kind of dangerous behavior toward one another, and in most battles one side usually gave way within minutes of the initial clash so that the rear ranks rarely encountered any actual fighting. The real purpose of the massed formation behind the front ranks was to enforce both a physical and moral pressure on the cutting edge of the battle formation to prevent panic. Modern studies have also shown that the press of the ranks, the large shield, sufficient armor, and the use of the spear for overhand thrusting actually made it very difficult to land a killing blow.[149]

For all of the reasons highlighted above, not only the numbers of soldiers engaged in the battle of Towton must be suspect, but the fatality count too. There are no mass burial pits, nor areas where farming or roadworks have turned up multiple bodies. This is not surprising, for with the military technology of the time, the claimed number of deaths simply could not have been caused.

If the figures for Towton are suspect – and they must be – then it is likely that other medieval battles are also exaggerated. To arrive at actual numbers would take much more research and calculation than was available for this study, but it can nevertheless be concluded that both the numbers present and the fatalities incurred in medieval battles are vastly overstated.

Conclusion

A New Theory of Medieval Battle

This work suggests several new possibilities regarding medieval military combat. First, that medieval heavy infantry soldiers in plate armour only fought for a short amount of time – around 14 minutes – before needing to rest. To maintain a front line, they constantly changed its members so they could continue fighting. The cyclical movement of men through the front line was a solution, but only a temporary one. Depending on how many lines a section of the front had, soldiers still had to move forward for more fighting after a short interval. It has been shown that rather than two sides merely coming into contact and flailing at each other until one side won, a system of constantly replacing those swinging their weapons with fresher men was essential. Fatigue was a considerable factor in lessening performance, even though battles probably did not last very long. There may even have been intervals where both sides periodically broke off combat through exhaustion.

The complicated rhythm of replacing the front line is a previously misunderstood facet of medieval combat. Accounts from writers at the time did not include it, probably because the authors had not witnessed it, were not soldiers and were often employed merely to tell of the overall result. The soldiers of the time – largely illiterate – had little interest in describing the mechanics of battle. Any paid scribes had little need or incentive to do more than paint in positive terms the knight or lord who employed them.

This is not to say the medieval battle was an orderly affair of rigid lines moved with iron discipline, as was the case with the British Army in the

Napoleonic Wars. Soldiers served under the literal banner of a local lord, usually marked by his device on their clothes, and their battlefield tactics would have varied from company to company. It was probably not the case that all companies fought alike: there would have been preferences for what tactics were best, just as there were variations in armour and weapons. There would have been inexperienced commanders who blundered and whose men lost badly as a result, just as there would have been highly experienced captains who were experts in how to win in battle.

The armies of the time were likely composed of professional men-at-arms in plate, levied billmen wearing much lighter armour – carrying bills or spears, mauls, swords and daggers – and levied bowmen, in helmet and jacks – with the occasional professional master bowman – who also acted as light infantry. Their arrangement in battle varied from the company next to them according to expertise, training, equipment and morale. Nevertheless, companies could not have maintained a front line unless they fought in replenished rows.

Secondly, despite savage fighting and horrific injuries inflicted by ferociously wielded weapons such as poleaxes, this work suggests that medieval combat was not very efficient. Even at its ultimate of close-quarter infantry hand-to-hand combat, medieval soldiers were not very good at despatching each other. The extreme personal violence of such combat is both impressive and horrifying, and perhaps this has blinded many to the reality of the situation: medieval technology in the shape of armour and fairly inefficient weapons – especially compared to the firearm – both protected its users and caused violent death. But by comparison with the age of the firearm and the artillery piece, medieval combat likely did not cause a lot of deaths.

Only the front line of a medieval infantry battle was in position to give and receive fatal wounds. The bowmen's usefulness was largely militated for fear of hitting their own. Where both sides employed bowmen, it cannot realistically be envisaged that they closed to inflict fire on the enemy's rear ranks, dut to the accuracy of the weapon and the danger of opposing fire.

Medieval armour was a lessening factor in terms of receiving wounds or being killed. Even the best battlefield weapon – the poleaxe – was deterred by good plate. It is unlikely the factor seen in most wars across history, of around one in 10 combatants dying, was exceeded. It might also be noted that if death on a large scale was the result of such battles, it would have been highly unlikely that soldiers could have been compelled to march to the battlefield.

Much of the time, battlefield injuries were not fatal: a piercing wound or a percussive blow did not always result in death. It is also likely that medieval battle saw no more than the usual ratio of wounded to killed – perhaps four or five wounded for every death – for the psychological reason that if half or more of the combatants who were injured died, then very few people would have fought in the first place. These soldiers therefore thought they would survive, not die.

The weaponry used by both sides was inefficient when matched against similar weapons. The protective equipment of armour used by both sides was, conversely, quite efficient. Once bowmen had encouraged the heavy infantry to close, the fighting that took place was unlikely to have killed enormous numbers of people, simply because of factors such as the protection offered by plate armour, the inefficiency of billmen's weapons and the fact that all combatants got very tired very quickly.

The likelihood that medieval battle used small forces (which then incurred low fatality counts) is backed up by the difficulties of supply. The two sides of the Wars of the Roses had little ability to gather a force and supply and keep it going for more than a few weeks. Even then, they needed to keep moving to avoid exhausting the ability of the local countryside to sustain the supply train they brought along.

A third new theory about medieval battles is that they were difficult to organise and very hard to sustain, but short and sharp when they did occur. There is little evidence for the vastness of scale such as that reported at Towton. Rather than believe such a battle of scale happened, an examination of the battlefield itself and the lack of mass burial sites show the supposed death toll must be a case of over-eager reportage rather than reality.

Over-reporting is likely to have been the case in regard to the size of the armies involved and the fatalities incurred. There was plenty of incentive for those telling the tales to do this: if they won, it made their victory more magnificent; if they lost, it gave good reason why they did so. Similarly, overstating the numbers of dead made the battle seem a significant one, and both sides wanted to think they had been in a decisive battle rather than a minor affair.

Fourthly, this study has seen that the rout as part of a medieval battle needs rethinking. Fleeing soldiers were the ultimate realists: they saw that now was perhaps their time to die, and like any human, they had a very strong will to survive. In their hands they carried excellent defence mechanisms: edged, percussive, staff and missile weapons. While some may have flung down their spears, bows and swords to lighten their load as they fled, many would not have. It cannot be said that they would all have panicked: these were men who had just been in the middle of a melee, and to whom carrying weapons was normal.

Furthermore, if the defeated soldiers held together in a band, they increased their chance of survival. Perhaps the best at this were the bowmen, being masters of a distance missile weapon. While they had shafts and bows, they still had life. Concentrated fire from a group would have made mounted pursuers avoid them, particularly as a group was much more dangerous than an individual: it could not be overcome when a single bowman was exhausted or had run out of shafts.

The reality of the rout, given such rethinking, is that it may well account for far fewer fatalities than have been reported in medieval battles. Coupled with exaggeration of numbers of combatants, this may in turn explain the absence of mass graves on so many medieval battlefields: the masses of dead were never there to begin with.

Given all of the above, it is likely that medieval battles have been much misunderstood. Although Towton was more deadly than others battles of the Wars of the Roses, as it was likely bigger, the casualties in these other actions would also have been exaggerated. It has been shown that the Towton battlefield presents little or no evidence of massive slaughter, and that logical analysis suggests casualties were no worse percentage-wise than any other battle.

Modern retellings – particularly in film, but also in books – are content to show a general melee carried on across a vast battle frontage, and suggest that is the complete battle. But because they have never put on armour or swung an edged weapon, these storytellers ignore the physical constraints of such equipment. Furthermore, modern films are an emotional experience, so viewers need to see faces, meaning fighting without helmets, in defiance of reality, is the norm. Movie directors, to provide a cleverly told story in a matter of a few hours, rarely highlight the practicality – and indeed boredom – of armed forces: supplying them, moving them and getting them to the battlefront. To the moviemakers, and to an audience expecting drama, such matters are both tiresome and a waste of film time. Documentary makers are faced with just as big a challenge: how to tell a story quickly and capably enough to take an audience uneducated in military matters with them. There are thus few documentaries that include all of this military minutiae.

This work has sought to show how medieval battles were likely fought tactically, and has encompassed a new telling of old tales. It is doubtless, though, not a final report – merely the beginnings of a new understanding.

APPENDIX I

Accounts of the Battle of Towton

Polydore Vergil[1]

But things turned out otherwise than Henry imagined, since instead of two heads there remained one, and him by far the most powerful, who could not be put down. For Edward was the darling of the Londoners, favoured by the common folk, on everybody's lips, in everybody's mouths. He enjoyed the support of all men of both high and low degree. All men praised him to the skies for his liberality, mercy, integrity, and fortitude. And so with marvellous enthusiasm men of all ages and conditions came flocking and swore their homage to him.

Induced by these things to hope for victory, Edward readied his forces as best he could so that he could join battle with his enemies and could someday set the seal on all his efforts and victories. And so, defended by these forces, he marched for York, and came within about eleven miles of it. There halted at a hamlet named Towton. When Henry learned that his enemies were at hand he did not immediately leave his camp, for this was Palm Sunday, sacred to the Lord, and he thought he should pray rather than fight, so as to be more prosperous in battle on the following day. But his soldiers, being habitually impatient of delay, brought it about that on the dawn of that very day, after consuming many words in urging each man to fight boldly for himself, he gave the signal for battle. His adversaries were not behindhand in doing the same.

The fight was begun by the archers, but soon they used up their arrows and they came to the hand-to-hand fighting, with so much slaughter that the bodies of the dead served to impede those in the fight. And so they fought for more than ten hours, with the victory still hanging in the balance, when Henry saw that that the enemy forces were growing and his own men were falling back a little. So once more he urged them to fight harder, then in the company of a few horsemen he retired from that place a little, waiting to see the outcome of the fight when, behold, suddenly his soldiers fled the field. Seeing this, he too took to his heels.

About 20,000 men died on both sides. Among these were Henry, the third Earl of Northumbria, Andrew Trollope, and a number of other noblemen. And the number of captives and wounded, of whom some were cured and others died, was about 10,000. This fight weakened England marvellously, for those who died were adequate to wage a foreign war, both in their number and in their strength.

To take advantage of this victory Edward sent ahead some lightly armed horsemen to arrest Henry and the queen in mid-flight. But they rode continually through the night, so that, not breaking their journey that night or the following day, on the second day they came to Scotland safe and sound, and immediately miserably sent to King James, asking in the name of their old kinship that they be received in his kingdom and protected by his resources in the midst of such a calamity. Because of the king's young age, their realm was under the government of several nobles, particularly James Kennedy Archbishop of St. Andrews, as I have shown. Afterwards he consoled him, and urged him to bear the outcome of the late war with equanimity, and he treated him most kindly, liberally, and honourably the whole time he was in Scotland. Henry, obliged by this kindness, that he might likewise bind to himself a king on whose help he at present greatly depended and relied, or to diminish his adversaries' wealth, gave him Berwick to keep forever.

Latin Original

Sed secus atque Henricus rebatur evenit, quando pro duobus capitibus unum longe valentissimum extitit quod deprimi non potuit. Erat enim Edouardus in desiderio Londinensium, in grata cum plebe, in ore, in sermone omnium habebat cum humilium tum amplissimorum hominum studia, a cunctis propter liberalitatem, clementiam, integritatem, fortitudinem generatim in coelum laudibus ferebatur. Quapropter miro omnium aetatum et ordinum studio mortalium concursus ad eum fiebat, ut alii sua ad bellandum nomina darent, alii ex parte civitatum operam et opes pollicitarentur ac in eius verba iurarent. Quibus rebus Edouardus in spem victoriae adductus, quam maxime poterat copiis parabat ut, commisso cum hostibus praelio, unus denique dies omnes labores ac victorias confirmaret. Itaque, his munitus copiis, Eboracum contendit, accedit proper millia passuum xj, ac ibi ad viculum nomine Touton considet. Henricus ubi cognovit hostes adesse non statim de castris exivit, quod dies Palmarum, quem vocant, domino sacer instaret, quo potuis orandum quam pugnandum sibi statuerat, ut postridie eius diei felicius praelio serviret. Sed miles, more suo nequicquam patiens morae, effecit ut eo ipso die prima luce, postquam multis verbis hortatus est ut pro se quisque fortiter pugnaret, signum praeliandi dederit. Adversarii nihilo secius idem fecerunt. A sagittariis pugna incipitur, sed brevi, consumptis sagittis, res cominus geritur tanta caede ut cadavera sola pugnantibus impedimento essent. Ita amplius horas decem erat dimicatum, dubia adhuc victoria, cum rex Henricus vidit hostium copias augeri et suos paulatim pedem referre, quos rursus hortatus cum acrius instare coegisset, ipse cum paucis equitibus paulum ex eo loco progressus eventum pugnae expectabat, cum ecce, subito eius milites in fugam se conferunt. Quo viso, in pedes se quoque dedit. Desiderata sunt ex utraque parte circiter viginta millia hominum. In iis fuit Henricus tertius comes Northumbriae et Andreas Trolopius compluresque alii principes. Numerus vero captivorum aut convulneratorum, quorum partim curati, alii mortui sunt, omnino fuit millia decem. Ea pugna mirabilem in modum debilitavit republicae Anglicae vires, quando ii qui caesi sunt et numero et robore ad quaevis externa bella gerenda satis fuissent. Edouardus, ut bene victoria uteretur, postquam suos parum a tanto labore refecit, aliquot equites levis armaturae misit qui in fuga Henricum aut reginam comprehenderent. Sed illi tota ea nocte continenter ierunt, ita ut nullam partem noctis aut diei insequentis itinere intermisso in fines Scotorum die secundo incolumes pervenerint, qui statim misere ad Iacobum regem, ut pro veteri necessitudine regno reciperentur atque eius opibus in tanta calamitate tegerentur. Erant in procuratione regni propter regis aetatem complures principes, et in primis Iacobus Chennethus divi Andreae archiepiscopus, uti supra ostendimus. Horum consilio monitus puer Iacobus, postquam audivit qui missi fuerant, tantum abfuit ut Henrici preces vel fortunam despexerit ut etiam confestim illi obviam factus sit atque in regiam duxerit, quem postea plurimum consolatus ut parato aequoque animo ferret quod proximus belli eventus tulisset, multo humanissime accepit tractavitque liberalissime pariter atque honorificentissime toto tempore quo in Scotia fuit. Hac humanitate devinctus, Henricus, ut regem cuius auxilio in praesentia maximopere nitebatur et confidebat, quopiam beneficio sibi obligaret, sive ut adversariorum opes minueret, Bervicum oppidum ei tradidit in perpetuum habendum. Fama tamen tenet Henricum ea miseria coopertum non sponte id fecisse, sed invitum, quo sibi in terra Scotia esse tutum liceret. Verum quoquo modo res transacta sit, satis constat Iacobum, recepto oppido, promisisse se Henrico suum officium pro sua parte praestaturum, id quod haud segniter postea fecit. His actis, Margarita cum Edouardo filio in Gallias ad Rhenatum patrem Andegavensium ducem se contulit, exercitum illic ope patris paratura. Henricus autem in Scotia cum aliquot principibus suae factionis, qui eum secuti sunt, morari statuit dum per amicos adiutus rursum arma caperet, ut brevi fore sperabat, et sibi ac rebus suis consulere liceret. Haec de Henrico Sexti regis varia fortuna hactenus, qui regnavit annos xxxviij. Veruntamen cum ille post decimum annum quam pulsus fuerat regnum denuo recuperasset, commodum in proximo libro reliqua de eius pariter vita atque morte persequemur.

Edward Hall

Extract from text of 'Hall's chronicle: containing the history of England, during the reign of Henry the Fourth, and the succeeding monarchs, to the end of the reign of Henry the Eighth, in which are particularly described the manners and customs of those periods. Carefully collated with the editions of 1548 and 1550.'[2]

THE lusty kyng Edward, perceiuyng the courage of his trusty frtkl the erle of Warwycke, made proclamacion that all men, whiche were alrayde to fighie, shoulde incontinent de-parte, and to all me that tarried the battell, he promised great rewat des with this addicion, that if any souldiour, which volutariely would abide, and in, or before the conflict flye, or turue his backe, that then he that could kill him should haue a great remuneracio and double wages. After thys proclamacio ended the lord Fawconbridge, syr Water Ulont, Robert Home with the forward, passed the ryuer at Castelford. iii. myles from Ferebridge, entending to haue enuironed and enclosed I he lord Clyfford and his copany, but they beyng therof aduertised, departed in great haste toward kyng Henries army, but they mete with some that Thecon they loked not for, and were attrappod or they were ware. For the lord Clifforde, either biidge. Ffor heat or payne, putting of his gorget, sodainly w an arrowe (as some say) without an hedde, was striken into the throte, and incontinent rendered hys spirite, and the erle of Westmerlandes brother and all hi company almost were there slayn, at a place called Dintingdale, not farr fr5 Towton. This ende had he, which slew the yong erle of Rutland, kneling on his knees: whose yong sonne Thomas Clifford was brought vp \V a sheppcrd, in poore habile, & dissimuled behauior euer in feare, to publish his lignage or degre, till kyng Henry the. vii. obteyned the croune, and gat the diadeine: by whome he was restored to his name and possessions. When this conflict was ended at Ferebridge, the lord Fawcdbridge, bauyng the foreward, because the duke of Northfolk was fallen sycke, valeaiitly vpon Palm sunday in the twylight, set furth his army, and came to Saxton, where he might apparantly perceyue the hoste of his aduersaries, which were accompted. Ix. M. men, and therof aduertised kyng Edward, whose whole army, they that knew it, and payed the wages, aflirme to persons, which incotinet with y erle of Warwycke set forward leuyng the rereward vndery^ gouernace of syr Ihon Wenlocke, and syr Ihon Dynham and other.

And first of all he made proclamacion, that no prisoner should be take, nor one enernie saued. So the same day about, ix. of the clocke, which was the. xxix. day of Marche, beyng The conflict Palmsundaye, both the hostes approched in a playn felde, betwene Towton and Saxto. When eche parte perceyued other, they made a great shoute, and at thesarnc instante time, their fell a small snyt or snow, which by violence of the wyn was driuen into the faces of them, which were of kyng Heries parte, so that their sight was somwhat blemished and minished.

The lord Fawconbridge, which led the forward of kyng Edwardes battaill (as before is rehersed) being a man of great polecie, and of much experience in marciall feates, caused euery archer vnder his standard, to shot one flyght (which before he caused them to prouide) and then made them to stad still. The northre me, feling the shoot, but by reason of jr snow, not wel vewing y distance betwene them and their enemies, like hardy men shot their schiefe arrowes as fast as they might, but al their shot was lost, & their labor vayn for they came not nere the Southerne, by. xl. taylors yerdes. Whe their shot was almost spent, the lord Fauconbridge marched forwarde with his archers, which not onely shot their awne whole sheues, but also gathered the arrowes of their enemies, and Jet a great parte of them flye agaynst their awne masters, and another part thei let stand on y groud which sore noyed the legges of the owners, when the battayle ioyned. The erle of Northumberlad, and Andrew Trolopc, whiche were chefetayns of kyng Hf-ries vawgard, seynge their shot not to preuayle, hasted forward to ioine with their enemies: you may besure the other part northing retarded, but valeaontly fought with their enemies. This battayl was sore foughte, for hope of life was set on side on euery parte and takynge of prisoners was proclaymed as a f great offence, by reason wherof euery man determined, either to conquere or to dye in the felde. This deadly battayle and bloudy conflicte, continued, x. houres in doubtfull victorie. The one parte, some time flowyng, and sometime ebbyng, but inconclusio, kyng Edward so coragiously comforted his me, refreshyng the wery, and helping the wounded, that the other part was discomfited and ouercome, and Jyke me amased, fledde toward Tadcaster bridge to saue the selfes: but in the meane way there is a litle broke called Cocke, not very broade, but of a great deapnes, in the whiche, what for hast of escapyng, and what for feare of folowers, a great number were drent and drowned, in so much that the common people there affirme, that men alyue passed the ryuer vpon dead carcasis, and that the great ryuer of Wharfe, which is the great sewer of y broke, & of all the water comyng from Towton, was colored with bloude. The chace continued all night, and the most parte of the next day, and euer y' Northren men, when they saw or perceiued any aduauntage, returned again and fought with their enemies, to the great losse of both partes.

APPENDIX 2

Percussive Weapons of the Leeds Armouries Database

Item description	Leeds Armoury item number	Period	Length – mm	Length – inches	Handle width – mm	Head length excluding langets – mm	Head length excluding langets – inches	Handle width – inches	Head width – mm	Head width – inches	Head depth – mm	Head depth – inches	Spike length – mm	Weight – kilograms	Weight – pounds	Notes
Mace	VIII.123	1475–1500	510		40				70.5							
Mace	VII-1643	1500–1530														
Mace	XXVIC.58	1700–1799	775											1.5		Indian
Mace	XXVIC.82	1300–1399	400											1.17		Chinese
Mace	XXVIC.35	1771–1799	700						80					1.16		Turkish
Mace	XXVIC.57	1700–1799	328											0.224		
Mace	XXVIC.79	1700–1799	885						120					1.35		Indian
Mace	VIII.13	1500–1599	521												3.50	
Mace	VIII.8	1500–1599	597	23.5											3.10	
Mace	XXVIC.68	1700–1799	719											1.675		Indian
Mace	XXVIC.4	1700–1799	842											1.675		Indian
Mace	VII.1642	1500–1530	1892											2.55	11.90	
Mace	XXVIC.37	1771–1799	612											1.15		Indian

(Continued)

Item description	Leeds Armoury item number	Period	Length – mm	Length – inches	Handle width – mm	Head length excluding langets – mm	Head length excluding langets – inches	Handle width – inches	Head width – mm	Head width – inches	Head depth – mm	Head depth – inches	Spike length – mm	Weight – kilograms	Weight – pounds	Notes
Pollaxe	VII.1509	1480–1520	1840						142		115					English
Pollaxe	VII.1827	1400–1599	1959			327								2.08		Europe
Pollaxe	VII.1578	1450–1499	1485			173	6.8		165	1.5				2.02		
Pollaxe	VII.875	1400–1499	1850	73		215			180				210	2.67	5.13.5	Europe
Pollaxe	VII.1670	1450–1500	1410			215								1.835		
Pollaxe	VII.1669	1450–1500				205										
Pollaxe	VII.1542	1490–1510	1778	70		205								2.92	6.70	England
			Average poleaxe length in mm 1720.333333			Average head excluding langets 225								Average poleaxe weight - kg 2.305	Average poleaxe weight - lb	
Test model						250			160							

APPENDIX 3

Re-enactor Analysis

Re-enactor name	Age	Weight of armour (lb)	Weapon	Weight of weapon (lbs)	Continuous fighting ability until first rest	Continuous fighting ability until 10 min rest	Continuous fighting ability in a 6–10 hour battle	Line of battle frontage necessary (feet)
Steve Arnold	52	18	Lucern hammer	6	5	30	20	4
Ewen Cameron	42	30	Bill	8	4	20	30	2
Andreas Dracocardos	39	60	Spear	2	20	60	40	2
Matthew Greatrex	26	90	Arming sword	3	30	120	35	3
Anthony Green	37	42	Bill	2	20	45	40	2
Neil Griffiths	25	70	Spear	8	10	60	30	2
Robert Johnson	35	84	Poleaxe	20	8	50	30	5
Mike Loveless	33	52	Poleaxe	4	15	45	30	8
Liam Lowther	28	100	Glaive	10	10	30	20	2
Jonathan Preston	48	98	Lucern hammer	12	10	30	25	2
Some names are non-de-plumes								
Averages	36.5	64.4		7.5	13.2	49	30	3.2

APPENDIX 3: RE-ENACTOR ANALYSIS • 205

Armour-clad men-at-arms able to be killed in an hour?	Brigandine and sallet-clad fighters able to be killed in an hour?	Effect of cold (to freezing) conditions on yourself in combat?	Attacks against plate by your weapon – %	Fight in ranks?	Fight in ranks?	Ability to change ranks in a fight?	Majority of fatalities beginning; through fight or after?	Difficulty of advancing evenly in rank?
1	10	Slow a bit	5	Yes	3	Yes	After	Possible
10	20	Nil	10	Yes	3	Yes	After	Easy
2	20	Nil	0	Yes	3	Yes	After	Easy with good sergeant
2.5	25	Nil	5	Yes	2.5	Yes	After	Yes
0	5	Nil	0	Yes	3	Yes	After	Yes
10	30	Nil	10	Yes	3	Yes but hard	After	Difficult
2	5	Nil	10	Yes	5	Yes	After	Easy
1	10	Nil	5	Yes	3	Yes	After	Yes
2	15	Nil	30	Yes	3	Yes	After	Easy
2.5	12	Nil	10	Yes	3	Yes	After	Easy
3.3	15.2	Nil	8.5	Yes	3.15	Yes	After	Yes

Endnotes

1. The Wars of the Roses

1. Milner, N. P. (trans. and Introduction writer). *Vegetius: Epitome of Military Science.* Liverpool: Liverpool University Press, 1993.
2. *Encyclopedia Brittanica*. 'Vegetius, Roman Military Author'. https://www.britannica.com/biography/Vegetius. (accessed June 2015). Quoted verbatim.
3. Hooper, Nicholas and Bennett, Matthew. *The Cambridge Illustrated Atlas of Warfare: the Middle Ages*. London: Cambridge University Press 1996. (p. 168)
4. Mortimer, Ian. *The Time Traveller's Guide to Medieval England: A Handbook for Visitors to the Fourteenth Century*. London: The Bodley Head Ltd, 2008. (pp. 122, 130)
5. Roser, Max. 'Homicides'. *OurWorldInData.org*. https://ourworldindata.org/homicides/, 2017. (accessed June 2017).
6. Milner, N. P. (trans. and Introduction writer). *Vegetius: Epitome of Military Science.* Liverpool: Liverpool University Press, 1993. (p. 49)

2. The Genesis of Infantry Combat

1. Young, Richard W. 'Evolution of the human hand: the role of throwing and clubbing'. *Journal of Anatomy*. January 2003. https://www.ncbi.nlm.nih.gov/pmc/articles/PMC1571064/. (accessed January 2018).
2. Koch, Christof. 'Does Brain Size Matter?' *Scientific American*. 1 January 2016. https://www.scientificamerican.com/article/does-brain-size-matter1/. (accessed June 2019).
3. D'Amato, Raffaele and Sumner, Graham. *Arms and Armour of the Imperial Roman Soldier*. Barnsley: Frontline Books, 2009.
4. *Victori. The Roman Military*. Hollis, Benjamin. 'Formations of the Legion'. https://romanmilitary.net/strategy/legform/. (accessed June 2017).

3. The Black Hole of Knowledge Regarding Medieval Combat

1. Gray, Sir Thomas. *Scalacronica, 1272–1363*. (Trans. Andy King). Woodbridge, Suffolk: Surtees Society, 2005.

2   The full account in both English and Latin can be seen in Appendix 1.
3   See Appendix 1.
4   Turner, Sharon. *The History of England During the Middle Ages: Comprizing the reigns of Henry VI., Edward IV., Edward V., Richard III. and Henry VII.* (Book II). United Kingdom: Longman, Hurst, Rees, Orme and Brown, 1823. (pp: 298–99)
5   Roser, Max and Ortiz-Ospina, Esteban. 'Literacy'. *OurWorldInData.org.* (2016). https://ourworldindata.org/literacy/. (accessed October 2015).
6   Fordham University. *Medieval London.* 'Stained Glass Window'. https://medievallondon.ace.fordham.edu/exhibits/show/medieval-london-objects/stainedglasswindow. (accessed March 2019).
7   *Touch of Tapestry.* 'History of Tapestries from Medieval to Modern Times'. https://touchoftapestry.com/History-of-Tapestries-7.html. (accessed March 2019).
8   Musset, Lucien. *The Bayeux Tapestry.* Boydell Press, 2005.
9   See for example *Enyclopedia Brittanica.* 'World War I'. https://www.britannica.com/event/World-War-I. (accessed July 2015).
10 Readers are recommended to John Terraine's *The Smoke and the Fire.* London: Sidgwick and Jackson, 1980; and Gordon Corrigan's *Mud, Blood and Poppycock.* United Kingdom: Cassell Military Paperbacks, 2007.
11 For an excellent analysis of this, see Terraine, John. *The Smoke and the Fire.* London: Sidgwick and Jackson, 1980.
12 Matthews, Professor Jill Julius. 'Leisure time, 1913'. Australian National University, 27 August 2013. 'Between 1892 to 1923, Sydney's population including suburbs grew from about 383,000 to 900,000; that is, expanded almost two and a half times. During that same 30-year period the number of magazines published in the city, in Sydney itself, increased fivefold from around 50 to over 250. This number excludes newspapers, newsletters and annual publications.' http://www.nma.gov.au/audio/transcripts/1913/NMA_1913_Matthews_leisure_20130827.html. (accessed August 2014).
13 Matthews, Professor Jill Julius. 'Leisure time, 1913'. Australian National University, 27 August 2013.
14 Mortimer, Ian. *The Time Traveller's Guide to Medieval England: A Handbook for Visitors to the Fourteenth Century.* London: The Bodley Head Ltd, 2008. (pp: 66–67)
15 Macaulay, Thomas Babington. *The History of England from the Accession of James II.* Vol. I Ch. 5. London: Longman, Brown, Green, and Longmans, 1854. Letter to John Croker on 8 August 1815.
16 Fiorato, V. et. al. *Blood Red Roses: the Archaeology of a Mass Grave from the Battle of Towton AD 1461.* Oxford: Oxbow Books, 2000. (p. 27)
17 *Life in Tudor Times.* 'Act of Attainder'. http://www.tudorplace.com.ar/Documents/act_attainder.htm. (accessed February 2016).
18 Zuvich, Andrea. 'How Chivalry in the Middle Ages Inspired Victorian England'. (24 November 2003). http://www.andreazuvich.com/history/how-chivalry-in-the-middle-ages-inspired-victorian-england/. (accessed November 2016).

19 Turnbull, Stephen. *The Book of the Medieval Knight*. London: Arms and Armour Press, 1995. See 'The Tenets of Chivalry' from p. 47.
20 McGlynn, Sean. 'The Myths of Medieval Warfare'. *History Today* Vol. 44. (1994). http://deremilitari.org/2013/06/the-myths-of-medieval-warfare/.
21 Some brasses of Joan of Arc have been said to have been struck.
22 Burne (1886–1959) was a British Army officer of artillery who served in World War I, where he earned a DSO, and in World War II. From 1938–57 he was the Military Editor for the *Chambers Encyclopedia*. He is generally regarded as an expert on the history of land warfare.
23 Bullein, William. *A Dialogue Against the Fever Pestilence*. Early English Text Society, Extra Series. London: N. Trubner & Co., 1988. (p. 59)
24 Contamine, P. *War in the Middle Ages*. Oxford: Basil Blackwell, 1984. (pp. 116–20, 130–35)
25 Bennett, Matthew, Bradbury, Jim, De Vries, Kelly, Dickie, Iain and Jestice, Phyllis G. *Fighting Techniques of the Medieval World, AD 500 – AD 1500: equipment, combat skills and tactics*. Staplehurst: Spellmount, 2005.
26 Hanson, Victor Davis. *The Western Way of War*. Oxford: Oxford University Press, 1989. (p. 49)
27 *Ibid*. (p. 60)
28 Boardman, Andrew. *The Medieval Soldier in the Wars of the Roses*. Stroud: Sutton, 1998. (p. 148)
29 Strickland, Matthew and Hardy, Robert. *The Great Warbow*. Gloucestershire: Haynes Publishing, 2005. (p. 379)
30 *Ibid*. (p. 379)
31 Rimer, Graeme. 'Weapons'. In Fiorato, Boylston and Knusel (eds). *Blood Red Roses: The Archaeology of a Mass Grave From the Battle of Towton AD 1461*. Oxford: Oxbow Books, 2000. (p. 126)
32 Goodman, A. *The Wars of the Roses: the soldier's experience*. Stroud: Tempus, 2005. (p. 85)
33 Boardman, Andrew. *The Medieval Soldier in the Wars of the Roses*. Stroud: Sutton, 1998. (p. 75)
34 The Exiles – Company of Medieval Martial Artists. 'The Bloody Cost of Medieval Warfare'. University of Bradford, courtesy of Anthea Boylston. http://www.the-exiles.org/Article%20Towton.htm. (accessed June 2015).

4. Misunderstanding Medieval Tactics, Armour and Weapons Through Modern Books and Movies

1 Gibson, Mel (Dir.). *Braveheart*. Icon Productions, The Ladd Company, 1995.
2 Scott, Walter. *Ivanhoe: A Romance*. http://www.gutenberg.org/files/82/82-0.txt. 2008.
3 Martin, George R. R. *A Dance with Dragons. Part 2: After the Feast*. London: Harper Voyager, 2016. (p. 449)

4   Stromberg, Robert (Dir.). *Maleficent*. Walt Disney Pictures, Roth Films, 2014.
5   Jackson, Peter (Dir.). *Lord of the Rings: The Fellowship of the Ring*. New Line Cinema, 2012.
6   Branagh, Kenneth (Dir.). *Henry V*. BBC Films, 1989. See YouTube: https://www.youtube.com/watch?v=JLbMPqEykr4. (accessed October 2016).
7   Mortimer, Ian. *1415: Henry V's Year of Glory*. London: Bodley Head, 2009.
8   Benioff, David, and Weiss, D. B. *Game of Thrones*. 'The Battle Between Jon & Ramsay's Forces'. https://www.youtube.com/watch?v=ToOIvD5mlow. (accessed June 2016).
9   Scott, Ridley (Dir.). *Kingdom of Heaven*. Scott Free Productions, 2005.
10 Boorman, John (Dir.). *Excalibur*. Orion Pictures, 1991.

5. Armour in the Medieval Period

1   In the book area the influential works of Oakeshott, Capwell, Hewitt and Woosnam-Savage are recommended, with full details to be found in the Bibliography in this work.
2   Grose, Francis. *A Treatise on Ancient Armour and Weapons*. London: S. Hooper, 1708. (See Bibliography for further information.) (pp. 13–14)
3   Welch, Ronald. *Knight Crusader*. London: Oxford University Press, 1954. (p. 52)
4   Capwell, Tobias. *Arms and Armour of the Medieval Joust*. Leeds: Royal Armouries Museum, 2018. (p. 21)
5   Grose, Francis. *A Treatise on Ancient Armour and Weapons*. London: S. Hooper, 1708. The plate illustrations follow from p. 118.
6   See for examples Oakeshott, Ewart. *Records of the Medieval Sword*. Woodbridge: The Boydell Press, 1991.
7   Grose, Francis. *A Treatise on Ancient Armour and Weapons*. London: S. Hooper, 1708. (p. 22)
8   *FACT Open House 2012 – Poleaxe in Armour*. https://www.youtube.com/watch?v=vZWkDhh9Zsg.
9   Watts, Karen (Senior Curator for Armour and Art). 'Henry VIII's foot combat armour'. Leeds Armouries. https://royalarmouries.org/stories/object-of-the-month/object-of-the-month-for-april-henry-viiis-foot-combat-armour/. (accessed June 2018).
10 Capwell, Tobias. *Arms and Armour of the Medieval Joust*. Leeds: Royal Armouries Museum, 2018. (p. 64)
11 Hanson, Victor Davis. *The Western Way of War*. Oxford: Oxford University Press, 1989. (p. 60)
12 Boardman, Andrew. *The Medieval Soldier in the Wars of the Roses*. Stroud: Sutton, 1998. (p. 122)
13 *Ibid*. (p. 122)
14 *Ibid*. (pp. 140–41)

15 Armstrong, C. A. J. (ed.), Mancini, Dominic. *The Usurpation of Richard III.* 1969. (pp. 98–99)
16 Boardman, Andrew. *The Medieval Soldier in the Wars of the Roses.* Stroud: Sutton, 1998. (p. 125)
17 Tattersall, Kate. 'Dragoons, hussars, and lancers: the glorious British cavalry of the mid 1800s'. (30 April 2015). http://www.katetattersall.com/hussars-dragoons-the-glorious-british-cavalry-of-the-mid-1800s/. (accessed June 2015).
18 See for analysis of the French cavalry system *Napoleon, His Army and Enemies.* 'French Cavalry During the Napoleonic Wars'. http://www.napolun.com/mirror/web2.airmail.net/napoleon/cavalry_Napoleon.html. (accessed July 2015).
19 Enfilade: Noun: a volley of gunfire directed along a line from end to end – 'they were mown down by an enfilade of artillery'. Verb: direct a volley of gunfire along the length of (a target) – 'a sweeping crossfire enfiladed our riflemen'. (*Oxford Dictionary*).
20 Boardman, Andrew. *The Medieval Soldier in the Wars of the Roses.* Stroud: Sutton, 1998. (p. 120)
21 Hanson, Victor Davis. *The Western Way of War.* Oxford: Oxford University Press, 1989. (p. 49)

6. The Longbow's Place in Medieval Battle

1 Strickland, Matthew and Hardy, Robert. *The Great Warbow.* Gloucestershire: Haynes Publishing, 2005. (p. 143)
2 *Ibid.* (p. 152)
3 De Vries, Kelly. *Medieval Military Technology.* Canada: University of Toronto Press, 2010. (p.39)
4 Singman, Jeffrey L. *The Middle Ages: Everyday Life in Medieval Europe.* New York: Stirling, 2013. (p. 141)
5 Mortimer, John J., Jr. *Tactics, Strategy, and Battlefield Formation during the Hundred Years War: The Role of the Longbow in the 'Infantry Revolution'.* Master of Arts Thesis. Indiana University of Pennsylvania, August 2013. See p. 78. http://citeseerx.ist.psu.edu/viewdoc/download?doi=10.1.1.843.3571&rep=rep1&type=pdf.
6 Strickland, Matthew and Hardy, Robert. *The Great Warbow.* Gloucestershire: Haynes Publishing, 2005. (p. 378)
7 Hardy, Robert. Author and expert in the longbow. Interview with the author, July 2016.
8 Oman, Charles. *A History of the Art of War in the Middle Ages.* Vol. II. London: Methuen and Co. Ltd, 1924. (pp. 405–06)
9 Hardy, Robert. Author and expert in the longbow. Interview with the author, July 2016.
10 Mortimer, John J., Jr. *Tactics, Strategy, and Battlefield Formation during the Hundred Years War: The Role of the Longbow in the 'Infantry Revolution'.* Master of Arts Thesis.

Indiana University of Pennsylvania, August 2013. http://citeseerx.ist.psu.edu/viewdoc/download?doi=10.1.1.843.3571&rep=rep1&type=pdf.

11   Mortimer, John J., Jr. *Tactics, Strategy, and Battlefield Formation during the Hundred Years War: The Role of the Longbow in the 'Infantry Revolution'*. Master of Arts Thesis. Indiana University of Pennsylvania, August 2013. (p. 49) http://citeseerx.ist.psu.edu/viewdoc/download?doi=10.1.1.843.3571&rep=rep1&type=pdf.
12   De Vries, Kelly. *Infantry Warfare in the Early Fourteenth-century: Discipline, Tactics, and Technology*. United Kingdom: Boydell Brewer Ltd, 2000. (p. 4)
13   Boardman, A. *Towton: the Bloodiest Battle*. Stroud: The History Press, 2009. (p. 154)
14   Ibid. (p. 170)
15   Strickland, Matthew and Hardy, Robert. *The Great Warbow*. Gloucestershire: Haynes Publishing, 2005. (p. 374)
16   Boardman, A. *Towton: the Bloodiest Battle*. Stroud: The History Press, 2009. (p. 113)
17   Strickland, Matthew and Hardy, Robert. *The Great Warbow*. Gloucestershire: Haynes Publishing, 2005. (p. 204)
18   Ibid. (p. 298)
19   Hardy, Robert. Author and expert in the longbow. Interview with the author, July 2016.
20   Waite, Adrian. *Medieval Pole Weapons 1287–1513*. Bristol: Stuart Press, 2001. (p. 15)
21   Boardman, Andrew. *The Medieval Soldier in the Wars of the Roses*. Stroud: Sutton, 1998. (p. 111)
22   Hardy, Robert. *Longbow*. Somerset: Patrick Stephens, 2002. (pp. 68, 81)
23   Hardy, Robert. Author and expert in the longbow. Interview with the author, July 2016.
24   Hardy, Robert. *Longbow*. Somerset: Patrick Stephens, 2002. (p. 73) Quotation used with permission in interview with the author.
25   Goodman, A. *The Wars of the Roses: the soldier's experience*. Stroud: Tempus, 2005. (p. 139)
26   Strickland, Matthew and Hardy, Robert. *The Great Warbow*. Gloucestershire: Haynes Publishing, 2005. (p. 375)
27   Novak, Shannon A. 'Battle-Related Trauma' in Fiorato, Boylston and Knusel (eds). *Blood Red Roses: The Archaeology of a Mass Grave From the Battle of Towton AD 1461*. Oxford: Oxbow Books, 2000. (p. 99)
28   See figure 6.22 on page 273: Sutherland, Tim. 'The Bloody Battle of Towton, England', in Carver, Martin and Klapste, Jan (eds). *The Archaeology of Medieval Europe, Vol. 2: Twelfth to Sixteenth Centuries*. Lancaster, Aarhus University Press, 2011.
29   Scholagladiatoria. *English longbows vs medieval plate armour – Battlefield Detectives documentary review*. https://www.youtube.com/watch?v=HMvz-z1SPLQ&t=925s.
30   Mortimer, John J., Jr. *Tactics, Strategy, and Battlefield Formation during the Hundred Years War: The Role of the Longbow in the 'Infantry Revolution'*. Master of Arts Thesis.

Indiana University of Pennsylvania, August 2013. (p. 31) http://citeseerx.ist.psu. edu/viewdoc/download?doi=10.1.1.843.3571&rep=rep1&type=pdf.
31   *Ibid.* (p. 22)
32   Jones, Peter. 'Some Technical Considerations' in Hardy, Robert. *Longbow.* Somerset: Patrick Stephens, 2002. (pp. 235–37)
33   Barker, Juliet. *Agincourt.* New York: Hachette Book Group, 2006. (p. 316)
34   Mortimer, John J., Jr. *Tactics, Strategy, and Battlefield Formation during the Hundred Years War: The Role of the Longbow in the 'Infantry Revolution'.* Master of Arts Thesis. Indiana University of Pennsylvania, August 2013. (p. 66) http://citeseerx.ist.psu. edu/viewdoc/download?doi=10.1.1.843.3571&rep=rep1&type=pdf.
35   Strickland, Matthew and Hardy, Robert. *The Great Warbow.* Gloucestershire: Haynes Publishing, 2005. (p. 211)

7. The Fight of the Poleaxe Soldier

1   Snook, George A. MD. 'The Halberd and Other Polearms of the Late Medieval Period'. Americansocietyofarmscollectors.org. http://americansocietyofarmscollectors. org/wp-content/uploads/2015/05/Halberd-and-other-polearms-of-the-late-medieval-period-B079_Snook.pdf (79/13).
2   Personal inspection by the author, November 2013.
3   Grose, Francis. *A Treatise on Ancient Armour and Weapons.* London: S. Hooper, 1708. See from p. 52.
4   Bennett, Matthew, Bradbury, Jim, De Vries, Kelly, Dickie, Iain and Jetsice, Phyllis G. 'The Role of the Infantry'. *Fighting Techniques of the Medieval World, AD 500 – AD 1500: equipment, combat skills and tactics.* Staplehurst: Spellmount, 2005.
5   *Ibid.* (p. 36)
6   Goranov, Alexi. 'The Medieval Poleaxe'. https://myarmoury.com/feature_spot_poleaxe.html. (accessed June 2016).
7   Docherty, Frank. 'A Brief History of the Quarterstaff'. *Journal of Western Martial Art.* May 2001. http://ejmas.com/jwma/articles/2001/jwmaart_docherty_0501. htm. (accessed June 2014).
8   Discussions with Ric Fallu, 2019.
9   Yallop, Henry. Assistant Curator – European Edged Weapons. Leeds Armouries. Emails to the author, October 2016.
10 Watts, Karen. Senior Curator for Armour and Art. 'Henry VIII's foot combat armour'. Leeds Armouries. https://royalarmouries.org/stories/object-of-the-month/object-of-the-month-for-april-henry-viiis-foot-combat-armour/.
11 *FACT Open House 2013 – Armoured Combat.* https://www.youtube.com/watch?v=0SpTNTldthI.
12 The Exiles – Company of Medieval Martial Artists. 'The Bloody Cost of Medieval Warfare'. University of Bradford, courtesy of Anthea Boylston. http://www.the-exiles.org/Article%20Towton.htm. (accessed June 2015).

13 Boardman, A. *Towton: the Bloodiest Battle*. Stroud: The History Press, 2009. (p. 121)
14 Novak, Shannon A. 'Battle-Related Trauma'. Fiorato, Boylston and Knusel (eds). *Blood Red Roses: The Archaeology of a Mass Grave From the Battle of Towton AD 1461*. Oxford: Oxbow Books, 2000. (p. 101)
15 Waldman, John. *Hafted Weapons in Medieval and Renaissance Europe*. Netherlands: Brill, 2005. (p. 159)
16 Oakeshott, Ewart. *Records of the Medieval Sword*. Woodbridge: The Boydell Press, 1991. See for example p. 175.
17 Novak, Shannon A. 'Battle-Related Trauma'. Fiorato, Boylston and Knusel (eds). *Blood Red Roses: The Archaeology of a Mass Grave From the Battle of Towton AD 1461*. Oxford: Oxbow Books, 2000. (p. 99). 'Perimortem' is defined (p. 91) as an injury that occurs 'at or near the time of death'.
18 *FACT Open House 2012 – Poleaxe in Armour*. 3'30". https://www.youtube.com/watch?v=vZWkDhh9Zsg.

8. How Were Medieval Battles Actually Fought?

1 Battle of Tewkesbury Re-Enactors Series (BTRS). Series of 10 interviews with re-enactors carried out by the author on 9 July 2016 at the Tewkesbury Medieval Festival.
2 Lewis, Tom. 'On medieval jousting in modern times'. *The Journal of the Arms Collectors' Association of the Northern Territory*. March 2019.
3 Oman, Charles. *A History of the Art of War in the Middle Ages*. Vol. II. London: Methuen and Co. Ltd, 1924. (p. 379)
4 Battle of Tewkesbury Re-Enactors Series (BTRS). Series of 10 interviews with re-enactors carried out by the author on 9 July 2016 at the Tewkesbury Medieval Festival.
5 Mortimer, Ian. *The Time Traveller's Guide to Medieval England: A Handbook for Visitors to the Fourteenth Century*. London: The Bodley Head Ltd, 2008. (pp. 173–74)
6 Waller, John. 'Archery'. Fiorato, Boylston and Knusel (eds). *Blood Red Roses: The Archaeology of a Mass Grave From the Battle of Towton AD 1461*. Oxford: Oxbow Books, 2000. (p. 135)
7 Hanson, Victor Davis. *The Western Way of War*. Oxford: Oxford University Press, 1989. (p. 72)
8 Dando-Collins, Stephen. *Legions of Rome*. New York: St Martin's Press, 2010. (See pp. 38, 68–69). Arrian was a governor of Cappadocia, a region of what is now Turkey, in the reign of the Emperor Hadrian.
9 Milner, N. P. (trans. and Introduction writer). *Vegetius: Epitome of Military Science*. Liverpool: Liverpool University Press, 1993. (pp. 38–39)
10 See Gleason, Bruce P. 'Cavalry and Court Trumpeters and Kettledrummers from the Renaissance to the Nineteenth Century'. *Galpin Society Journal* LXII (2009). https://springfieldarsenal.files.wordpress.com/2011/05/gleasongsj622009.pdf. (accessed

October 2016). Amongst other items of interest in this well-researched piece are suggestions that commands were decided before battles rather than adhering to a usual system, that kettledrummers had a place in many battle arrays and that musicians were employed as such in peacetime as well by well-off households.

11 Milner, N. P. (trans. and Introduction writer). *Vegetius: Epitome of Military Science*. Liverpool: Liverpool University Press, 1993. (pp. 70–71)
12 Foard, Glenn and Curry, Anne. *Bosworth 1485: A Battlefield Rediscovered*. Oxford: Oxbow Books, 2013. (p. 55)
13 LeShan, Lawrence L. *The psychology of war: comprehending its mystique and its madness*. Chicago: Noble Press, 1992. (pp. 84–85)
14 Webster, Daniel Kenyon. *Parachute Infantry*. Baton Rouge LA: Louisiana State University Press, 1994. (p. XV)
15 Barrett, John. *We Were There*. New South Wales: Allen and Unwin, 1995. (p. 189)
16 Ambrose, Stephen E. *Band of Brothers: E Company, 506th Regiment, 101st Airborne: from Normandy to Hitler's Eagle's Nest*. New York: Simon & Schuster, 1992. (p. 20)
17 *Ibid*. (pp. 227–28)
18 Graves, Robert. *Goodbye to All That*. London: Penguin, 1960. (p. 225)
19 Sledge, E. B. *With the old breed, at Peleliu and Okinawa*. Novato, Calif: Presidio Press, 1981. (p. 267)
20 Moore, Harold G. and Galloway, Joseph L.. *We were soldiers once and young: Ia Drang: the battle that changed the war in Vietnam*. New York: Random House, 1992. (p. 191)
21 Sajer, Guy. *The Forgotten Soldier*. London: Weidenfeld and Nicolson, 1971. (p. 113)
22 Ambrose, Stephen E. *Band of Brothers: E Company, 506th Regiment, 101st Airborne: from Normandy to Hitler's Eagle's Nest*. New York: Simon & Schuster, 1992. (p. 173)
23 Caputo, Philip. *A Rumor of War*. New York: Holt, Rinehart and Winston, 1977. (p. 247)
24 Coppard, George. *With a machine gun to Cambrai: the tale of a young Tommy in Kitchener's army 1914–1918*. London: H.M.S.O., 1969. (p. 107)
25 Baker, Clive and Knight, Greg. *Milne Bay 1942*. New South Wales: Baker-Knight Publications, 1991. (p. 271)
26 Phibbs, Brendan. *The Other Side of Time: A Combat Surgeon in World War II*. Boston: Little, Brown, 1987. (p. 128)
27 *Henry V*. Dir. Kenneth Branagh. BBC Films. 1989.
28 Scoble, A. R. (ed.). *The memoirs of Philip de Commines, Lord of Argenton*. 1911. Vol. 1. (p. 21) https://archive.org/details/memoirsofphilipd01comm. (accessed Jan 2017).
29 *Luminarium: Encyclopedia Project*. 'Speech to the Troops at Tilbury'. http://www.luminarium.org/renlit/tilbury.htm. (accessed July 2016).
30 Phibbs, Brendan. *The Other Side of Time: A Combat Surgeon in World War II*. Boston: Little, Brown, 1987. (p. 213)
31 Hart, Peter. *To the last round: the South Notts Hussars, 1939–1942*. Barnsley, England: Pen & Sword Books, 1996. (p. 163)
32 Hastings, Max. *Armageddon: The Battle for Germany 1944–1945*. New York: Macmillan, 2004. (p. 56)

33 Ambrose, Stephen E. *Band of Brothers: E Company, 506th Regiment, 101st Airborne: from Normandy to Hitler's Eagle's Nest*. New York: Simon & Schuster, 1992. (pp. 94–102)
34 *Ibid.* (p.155)
35 Young, Peter. *Storm from the Sea*. Great Britain: Wren's Park Publishing, 2002. (p. 216)
36 Astor, Gerald. *Operation Iceberg: the Invasion and Conquest of Okinawa in World War II*. New York: Donald I. Fine, 1995. (p. 407)
37 Phillips, C. E. Lucas. *The Greatest Raid of All*. London: Readers Book Club, 1958. (p. 212)
38 Fitz-Gibbon, Spencer. *Not Mentioned in Despatches*. Cambridge: The Lutterworth Press, 1995. Fitz-Gibbon spends considerable time on the different accounts of Colonel Jones' death.
39 Lukowiak, Ken. *A Soldier's Song*. London: Secker and Warburg, 1993. (p. 53)
40 McKee, Alexander. *Caen: Anvil of victory*. London: Souvenir Press, 1964. (p. 324)
41 Caputo, Philip. *A Rumor of War*. New York: Holt, Rinehart and Winston, 1977. (p. 122)
42 *Ibid.* (pp. 267–68)
43 Oman, Charles. *A History of the Art of War in the Middle Ages*. Vol. II. London: Methuen and Co. Ltd, 1924. (p. 379)
44 See McGlynn, Sean. 'The Myths of Medieval Warfare'. *History Today*. Vol. 44 (1994). http://deremilitari.org/2013/06/the-myths-of-medieval-warfare/.
45 Milner, N. P. (trans. and Introduction writer). *Vegetius: Epitome of Military Science*. Liverpool: Liverpool University Press, 1993. (p. 44)
46 Keegan, John. *The Face of Battle*. London: Pimlico, 1991. (p. 89)
47 Mortimer, Ian. *The Time Traveller's Guide to Medieval England: A Handbook for Visitors to the Fourteenth Century*. London: The Bodley Head Ltd, 2008. (p. 39)
48 Boardman, Andrew. *The Medieval Soldier in the Wars of the Roses*. Stroud: Sutton, 1998. (p. 151)
49 The Bridport Muster Roll lists 23 pavises and 27 bucklers, the much smaller shields worn on one arm, for the 201 soldiers detailed on the muster. However, the Bridport Roll was for a force destined for cross-Channel or local defence warfare. Richardson, Thom. 'Armour'. Fiorato, Boylston and Knusel (eds). *Blood Red Roses: The Archaeology of a Mass Grave From the Battle of Towton AD 1461*. Oxford: Oxbow Books, 2000. (p. 143)
50 Oman, Charles. *A History of the Art of War in the Middle Ages*. Vol. II. London: Methuen and Co. Ltd, 1924. (p. 379)
51 Hardy, Robert. *Longbow*. Somerset: Patrick Stephens, 2002. (pp. 68, 81)
52 Oman, Charles. *A History of the Art of War in the Middle Ages*. Vol. II. London: Methuen and Co. Ltd, 1924. (p. 409)
53 Boardman, Andrew. *The Medieval Soldier in the Wars of the Roses*. Stroud: Sutton, 1998. (p. 45)

54 *Ibid.* (p. 82)
55 Scoble, A. R. (ed.). *The Memoirs of Philip de Commines, Lord of Argenton.* 1911. Vol. 1. (p. 24) https://archive.org/details/memoirsofphilipd01comm. (accessed Jan 2017).
56 Milner, N. P. (trans. and Introduction writer). *Vegetius: Epitome of Military Science.* Liverpool: Liverpool University Press, 1993. (p. 47)
57 Keegan, John. *The Face of Battle.* London: Pimlico, 1991. (p. 89)
58 Boardman, Andrew. *The Medieval Soldier in the Wars of the Roses.* Stroud: Sutton, 1998. (p. 148)
59 Dando-Collins, Stephen. *Legions of Rome.* New York: St Martin's Press, 2010. (pp. 50–52)
60 Frontinus, Sextus Julius. *Stratagems* III. 'On the Disposition of Troops for Battle'. Paragraphs 10–11. Book II. http://penelope.uchicago.edu/Thayer/E/Roman/Texts/Frontinus/Strategemata/2*.html#3.
61 Brady, Lt. Col. S. G. *The Military Affairs of Ancient Rome and Roman Art of War in Caesar's Time.* The Military Service Publishing Company, 1947. http://www.digitalattic.org/home/war/romanarmy/. (accessed Nov 2016).
62 Sabin, Philip. 'The Roman Face of Battle'. *Journal of Roman Studies.* Vol. 90 (2000). (p. 5)
63 Gabriel, Richard A. *Soldiers' Lives through History – The Ancient World.* Westport CT: Greenwood Press, 2007. (pp. 115–16)
64 Waite, Adrian. *Medieval Pole Weapons 1287–1513.* Bristol: Stuart Press, 2001. (p. 15)
65 Battle of Tewkesbury Re-Enactors Series (BTRS). Series of 10 interviews with re-enactors carried out by the author on 9 July 2016 at the Tewkesbury Medieval Festival.
66 Milner, N. P. (trans. and Introduction writer). *Vegetius: Epitome of Military Science.* Liverpool: Liverpool University Press, 1993. (p. 48)
67 Curry, Anne. *Agincourt – a New History.* Gloucestershire: The History Press, 2010. (p. 255)
68 Boardman, A. *Towton: the Bloodiest Battle.* Stroud: The History Press, 2009. (p. 112)
69 Keegan, John. *The Face of Battle.* London: Pimlico, 1991. (p. 101)
70 Welch, Ronald. *Sun of York.* Oxford: Oxford University Press, 1970.
71 Barker, Juliet. *Agincourt.* New York: Hachette Book Group, 2006. (p. 318)
72 Battle of Tewkesbury Re-Enactors Series (BTRS). Series of 10 interviews with re-enactors carried out by the author on 9 July 2016 at the Tewkesbury Medieval Festival.
73 Griggs, Mary Beth. *Popular Mechanics.* 21 July 2011. 'Medieval Knights on a Treadmill put Historical Myths to the Test'. http://www.popularmechanics.com/culture/a6749/medieval-knights-on-a-treadmill-put-historical-myths-to-the-test/. (accessed January 2017).
74 Mitchelson, Tom. 'Bludgeoned, hacked and poleaxed! My skull-shattering stab at medieval fighting, the world's most violent hobby'. *The Daily Mail.* 22 August 2013. http://www.dailymail.co.uk/news/article-2399431/The-worlds-violent-hobby-My-skull-shattering-stab-medieval-fighting.html#ixzz4X7SLeE3l.

75 Hanson, Victor Davis. *The Western Way of War*. Oxford: Oxford University Press, 1989. (pp. 56, 191)
76 Gabriel, Richard A. *Soldiers' Lives through History – The Ancient World*. Westport CT: Greenwood Press, 2007. (p. 229)
77 Miller, Michael D. *Wars of the Roses*. An Analysis of the causes of the Wars and the course which they took. http://www.warsoftheroses.co.uk/contact.htm. (accessed June 2017).
78 Welch, Ronald. *Sun of York*. Oxford: Oxford University Press, 1970. (pp. 58–59)
79 Griggs, Mary Beth. *Popular Mechanics*. 21 July 2011. 'Medieval Knights on a Treadmill put Historical Myths to the Test'. http://www.popularmechanics.com/culture/a6749/medieval-knights-on-a-treadmill-put-historical-myths-to-the-test/. (accessed January 2017).
80 Boardman, Andrew. *The Medieval Soldier in the Wars of the Roses*. Stroud: Sutton, 1998. (p. 176)
81 Battle of Tewkesbury Re-Enactors Series (BTRS). Series of 10n interviews with re-enactors carried out by the author on 9 July 2016 at the Tewkesbury Medieval Festival.
82 *Ibid*.
83 Milner, N. P. (trans. and Introduction writer.) *Vegetius: Epitome of Military Science*. Liverpool: Liverpool University Press, 1993. (p. 48)
84 Boardman, A. *Towton: the Bloodiest Battle*. Stroud: The History Press, 2009. (p. 120)
85 Milner, N. P. (trans. and Introduction writer.) *Vegetius: Epitome of Military Science*. Liverpool: Liverpool University Press, 1993. (p. 24)
86 Battle of Tewkesbury Re-Enactors Series (BTRS). Series of 10 interviews with re-enactors carried out by the author on 9 July 2016 at the Tewkesbury Medieval Festival.
87 Wilson, Fred. 'Battle Rhythm in emergency management'. *The Australian Journal of Emergency Management*. https://ajem.infoservices.com.au/items/AJEM-25-04-09#sthash.ipsr0hHL.dpuf. (accessed October 2016).
88 See again *FACT Open House 2012 – Poleaxe in Armour*. 3'30". https://www.youtube.com/watch?v=vZWkDhh9Zsg.
89 Often ascribed to General Von Moltke, Prussian Chief of Staff under Bismarck during the Franco-Prussian War of the 19th century.
90 Gabriel, Richard A. *Soldiers' Lives through History – The Ancient World*. Westport CT: Greenwood Press, 2007. (pp. 253–54)
91 Hardy, Robert. *Longbow*. Somerset: Patrick Stephens, 2002. (p. 86)
92 Goodman, A. *The Wars of the Roses: the soldier's experience*. Stroud: Tempus, 2005. (p. 140)

9. Towton as an Example of Medieval Battle

1 Sutherland, Tim. 'Killing Time: Challenging the Common Perceptions of Three Medieval Conflicts – Ferrybridge, Dintingdale and Towton – The Largest Battle

on British Soil'. Undated article. http://www.towton.org.uk/wp-content/uploads/killing-time_tim_sutherland.pdf.
2 'English Heritage Battlefield Report: Towton 1461'. English Heritage (1995). (pp. 4–5) https://content.historicengland.org.uk/content/docs/battlefields/towton.pdf. (accessed June 2016).
3 *Ibid.*
4 Foard, Glenn and Curry, Anne. *Bosworth 1485: A Battlefield Rediscovered*. Oxford: Oxbow Books, 2013. (p. 54)
5 *Towton Battlefield Society*. http://www.towton.org.uk/re-enactors/ (June 2015). A useful analysis of artillery at the time, and the presence of some 3cm ammunition at Towton, can be found on pp. 201–04 of Starkey's *Fatal Colours*.
6 Fiorato, Boylston and Knusel (eds). *Blood Red Roses: The Archaeology of a Mass Grave From the Battle of Towton AD 1461*. Oxford: Oxbow Books, 2000. (p. 25)
7 *Luminarium: Encyclopedia Project. Wars of the Roses*. 'Humphrey Stafford, Earl of Devon (1439–1469)'. http://www.luminarium.org/encyclopedia/humphreystafforddevon.htm. (accessed June 2015).
8 Scoble, A. R. (ed.) *The memoirs of Philip de Commines, Lord of Argenton*. 1911. Vol. 1. (p. 21) https://archive.org/details/memoirsofphilipd01comm. (accessed Jan 2017).
9 Keegan, John. *The Face of Battle*. London: Pimlico, 1991. (p. 113)
10 Gravett, Christopher. *Towton 1461 – England's Bloodiest Battle. Campaign 120*. Oxford: Osprey Publishing, 2003.
11 Boardman, A. *Towton: the Bloodiest Battle*. Stroud: The History Press, 2009. (p. 173)
12 Fiorato, Boylston and Knusel (eds). *Blood Red Roses: The Archaeology of a Mass Grave From the Battle of Towton AD 1461*. Oxford: Oxbow Books, 2000. (p. 15) See Ellis, H. (ed.). *Three Books of Polydore Vergil's English History*. Camden Society, 1844.
13 *Time and Date.com*. https://www.timeanddate.com/sun/uk/oxford. (accessed April 2016).
14 Both Hall and Vergil's accounts may be read in Appendix 1.
15 'English Heritage Battlefield Report: Towton 1461'. English Heritage (1995). (pp. 4–5) https://content.historicengland.org.uk/content/docs/battlefields/towton.pdf Accessed June 2016.
16 Dr Neill MD. 'What is the "fight or flight response?"'. Undated article. http://www.thebodysoulconnection.com/EducationCenter/fight.html. (accessed June 2016).
17 Buckalew, Louis W. 'Soldier Performance as a Function of Stress and Load: A Review'. Virginia: US Army Research Institute for the Behavioral and Social Sciences, 1990. http://oai.dtic.mil/oai/oai?verb=getRecord&metadataPrefix=html&identifier=ADA221530 (p. 18). (ccessed June 2016).
18 *Ibid.*
19 The *Croyland Chronicle*, quoted in Andrew Boardman's 'The Historical Background to the Battle...'. Fiorato, Boylston and Knusel (eds). *Blood red roses: the archaeology of a mass grave from the battle of Towton AD 1461*. Oxford: Oxbow Books, 2000. (p. 23)

20 Boardman, Andrew. *Towton: the Bloodiest Battle*, quoting H. Ellis (ed.). *Edward Hall's Chronicle* (1809), p. 256. (p. 139)
21 Gravett, Christopher. *Towton 1461 – England's Bloodiest Battle. Campaign 120*. Oxford: Osprey Publishing, 2003. (pp. 72–73)
22 Goodwin, George. *Fatal colours: the battle of Towton, 1461*. London: Weidenfeld and Nicolson. 2011. (pp. 223, 226)
23 Richardson, Thom. 'Armour'. Fiorato, Boylston and Knusel (eds). *Blood Red Roses: The Archaeology of a Mass Grave From the Battle of Towton AD 1461*. Oxford: Oxbow Books, 2000. (p. 147)
24 Hanson, Victor Davis. *The Western Way of War*. Oxford: Oxford University Press, 1989. (p. 178)
25 Gassmann, Jack and Certaminis, Artes. 'Thoughts on the Role of Cavalry in Medieval Warfare'. *Acta Periodica Duellatorum*. Undated article. (pp. 149–77). https://static1.squarespace.com/static/57f6449959cc68cbbd3df1c2/t/5849294f2994ca9650c2c607/1481189716627/APD2%282014%29_Gassman.pdf. (accessed June 2016).
26 Strickland, Matthew and Hardy, Robert. *The Great Warbow*. Gloucestershire: Haynes Publishing, 2005. (p. 376) quoting Calendar of State Papers, Venice, 1, 100, 102, 103 and cf. 106, 108; Paston Letters, III, 268.
27 Powers, D. BBC History. *World Wars: Japan: No Surrender in World War Two*. bbc.co.uk. (2019) http://www.bbc.co.uk/history/worldwars/wwtwo/japan_no_surrender_01.shtml. (accessed May 2019).
28 *The Philological Museum*. 'Polydore Vergil, Anglica Historia' (1555 version). http://www.philological.bham.ac.uk/polverg/23eng.html. (accessed May 2016).
29 Boardman, Andrew. *The Medieval Soldier in the Wars of the Roses*. Stroud: Sutton, 1998. (p. 54)
30 Boardman, A. *Towton: the Bloodiest Battle*. Stroud: The History Press, 2009. (p. 135)
31 Goodman, A. *The Wars of the Roses: the soldier's experience*. Stroud: Tempus, 2005. (p. 177)
32 Knusel, Christopher and Boylston, Anthea. 'How has the Towton project contributed to our knowledge of medieval warfare?'. Fiorato, Boylston and Knusel (eds). *Blood Red Roses: The Archaeology of a Mass Grave From the Battle of Towton AD 1461*. Oxford: Oxbow Books. (2000). (pp. 182–83)
33 Bicheno, Hugh. *Blood Royal. The Wars of the Roses: 1462–1485*. New York: Pegasus Books, 2017. (p. 43)
34 Goodman, A. *The Wars of the Roses: the soldier's experience*. Stroud: Tempus, 2005. (pp. 183–84). Commynes, Philippe de. *Memoirs, the Reign of Louis XI 1461–83*. Trans. and ed.: M. Jones. Harmondsworth, 1972.

10. The Myth of Fatalities in Medieval Battle

1 *The Economist*. 'The battle of Towton. Nasty, brutish and not that short'. (16 Dec 2010). http://www.economist.com/node/17722650.

2   Waite, Adrian. *Medieval Pole Weapons 1287–1513*. Bristol: Stuart Press, 2001. (p. 11)
3   Meyers Emery, Katy. 'The War of the Roses: Towton Massacre'. (13 March 2011) https://bonesdontlie.wordpress.com/2011/03/13/the-war-of-the-roses-towton-massacre/.
4   The Exiles – Company of Medieval Martial Artists. 'The Bloody Cost of Medieval Warfare'. http://www.the-exiles.org/Article%20Towton.htm.
5   *Yorkshire Post*. (16 March 2010). 'Secrets buried with the dead after Britain's bloodiest battle'. http://www.yorkshirepost.co.uk/news/analysis/secrets-buried-with-the-dead-after-britain-s-bloodiest-battle-1-2567631#ixzz3yRpdiTms. http://www.yorkshirepost.co.uk/news/analysis/secrets-buried-with-the-dead-after-britain-s-bloodiest-battle-1-2567631#ixzz3yRpScbNV. Note: 'Casualties' is used, but it would seem from the article that they mean 'fatalities', not casualties in the usual sense of being both dead and wounded.
6   Boardman, Andrew. *The Medieval Soldier in the Wars of the Roses*. Stroud: Sutton, 1998. (p. 18)
7   The *Telegraph*. 'Are bodies of 10,000 lost warriors from Battle of Hastings buried in this field?'. http://www.telegraph.co.uk/news/earth/environment/archaeology/9632922/25 Oct 2012. Are-bodies-of-10000-lost-warriors-from-Battle-of-Hastings-buried-in-this-field.html. (accessed October 2015).
8   See Curry, Anne. *Agincourt – a New History*. Gloucestershire: The History Press, 2010. (pp. 273–75); and Goodman, A. *The Wars of the Roses: the soldier's experience*. Stroud: Tempus, 2005. (p. 212)
9   Goodman, A. *The Wars of the Roses: the soldier's experience*. Stroud: Tempus, 2005. (p. 204). Leland, John. *Travels in Tudor England*. Ed. Chandler, J. Stroud. 1993.
10 Fiorato, V. et. al. *Blood Red Roses: The Archaeology of a Mass Grave From the Battle of Towton AD 1461*. Oxford: Oxbow Books, 2000. (p. 2)
11 Meyers Emery, Katy. 'The War of the Roses: Towton Massacre'. (13 March 2011). https://bonesdontlie.wordpress.com/2011/03/13/the-war-of-the-roses-towton-massacre/.
12 Sutherland, Tim. 'Unknown Soldiers: The Discovery of War Graves from the Battle of Towton AD1461'. University of Bradford. (1–2 December 2006). http://www.archprospection.org/sites/archprospection.org/files/artefacts-anomalies/Sutherland_Text.pdf.
13 Fiorato, Boylston and Knusel (eds). *Blood Red Roses: The Archaeology of a Mass Grave From the Battle of Towton AD 1461*. Oxford: Oxbow Books, 2000. (p. 33)
14 Ibid. (pp. 33,163)
15 York Osteoarchaeology Ltd. *Osteological Analysis Towton Hall & Towton Battlefield, Towton North Yorkshire*. Report No. 0504. (June 2004). http://www.towton.org.uk/wp-content/uploads/osteological_analysis_towton_hall_and_towton_battlefield.pdf. (p. III)
16 Meyers Emery, Katy. 'The War Of The Roses: Towton Massacre'. (13 March 2011). https://bonesdontlie.wordpress.com/2011/03/13/the-war-of-the-roses-towton-massacre/.
17 Boardman, A. *Towton: The bloodiest battle*. Stroud: The History Press, 2009. (pp. 162–69).

18 Foard, Glenn, and Vurry, Anne. *Bosworth 1485: A Battlefield Rediscovered*. Oxford: Oxbow Books, 2013. See Archaeology Data Service. 'The Bosworth Battlefield Project. The Battlefields Trust' (2013) http://archaeologydataservice.ac.uk/archives/view/bosworth_hlf_2011/overview.cfm for an overview of findings.
19 Also see Curry, Anne and Foard, Glenn. 'Where are the dead of medieval battles? A preliminary survey'. *Journal of Conflict Archaeology* (2016). 11:2-3, 61-77, DOI: 10.1080/15740773.2017.1324675. Curry and Foard cite Sutherland: 'Sutherland's conclusion is that the numbers of dead have been much exaggerated by chroniclers, perhaps by as much as tenfold.'
20 Sutherland, Tim. 'Killing Time: Challenging the Common Perceptions of Three Medieval Conflicts – Ferrybridge, Dintingdale and Towton – The Largest Battle on British Soil'. (Undated article). http://www.towton.org.uk/wp-content/uploads/killing-time_tim_sutherland.pdf. (accessed January 2017).
21 Sutherland, Tim. 'The Bloody Battle of Towton, England'. Carver, Martin and Klapste, Jan (eds). *The Archaeology of Medieval Europe, Vol. 2: Twelfth to Sixteenth Centuries*. Lancaster, Aarhus University Press, 2011.
22 Boardman, A. *Towton: The bloodiest battle*. Stroud: The History Press, 2009. (p. 144)
23 Personal communication, 2016.
24 Curry, Anne. *The Battle of Agincourt. Sources and Interpretations*. Woodbridge: Boydell Press, 2000. (pp. 242, 258). Curry notes in 'Where are the dead of medieval battles? A preliminary survey' that the grave has not been discovered.
25 Boardman, Andrew. *The Medieval Soldier in the Wars of the Roses*. Stroud: Sutton, 1998. (p. 67)
26 Ibeji, Dr Mike. 'Black Death'. BBC History. (2011). http://www.bbc.co.uk/history/british/middle_ages/black_01.shtml. (accessed June 2015).
27 *Ibid.*
28 *Ibid.*
29 Spengler, Joseph J. Reviewing Josiah Cox Russell's *British Medieval Population*. *The Journal of Economic History*, vol. 11, no. 1 (1951). (pp. 71–73). www.jstor.org/stable/2113862.
30 Fiorato, V. et. al. *Blood Red Roses: The Archaeology of a Mass Grave from the Battle of Towton AD 1461*. Oxford: Oxbow Books. (2007). (p. 25)
31 BBC. 'Health: A millennium of health improvement'. http://news.bbc.co.uk/2/hi/health/241864.stm. (27 Dec 1998). (accessed Jun 2017).
32 Mortimer, Ian. *The Time Traveller's Guide to Medieval England: A Handbook for Visitors to the Fourteenth Century*. London: The Bodley Head Ltd, 2008. (pp. 126–33 gives a useful analysis of mileage rates for horsed riders.)
33 Corrigan, Gordon. *Mud, Blood and Poppycock*. London: Cassell, 2004. (p. 78)
34 Military.com. 'Army Ranger PFT'. http://www.military.com/military-fitness/army-special-operations/army-ranger-pft. (accessed June 2017).
35 Hoskins, W. G. *Local History in England*. London & New York: Longman, 1984.
36 Distances/times have been rounded up from .5.

37 Boardman, Andrew. *The Medieval Soldier in the Wars of the Roses*. Stroud: Sutton, 1998. (p. 104)
38 Boardman, A. *Towton: The bloodiest battle*. Stroud: The History Press, 2009. (p. 102)
39 De Vries, Kelly. *Medieval Military Technology*. Canada: University of Toronto Press, 2010. (p.39)
40 Mercola. 'How Many Burgers Can You Make from One Cow?'. https://articles.mercola.com/sites/articles/archive/2015/11/14/cafo-beef-hamburger.aspx. (14 November 2015). (accessed June 2017).
41 Van Creveld, Martin. *Supplying War*. Cambridge: Cambridge University Press, 2005. (p. 6)
42 Hoskins, W. G. *Local History in England*. London & New York: Longman, 1984.
43 Hughes, Margaret. 'The site of Boudica's last battle'. (29 June 2013). https://www.academia.edu/12774243/On_Boudicas_trail_possible_sites_for_Boudicas_last_battle?auto=download. (accessed Jan 2017).
44 Dando-Collins, Stephen. *Legions of Rome*. New York: St Martin's Press, 2010. (p. 310)
45 BBC History. 'British Population Animation'. http://www.bbc.co.uk/history/interactive/animations/population/index_embed.shtml. This source suggests 1.5 million people in the population; therefore it is estimated there would have been 750,000 males.
46 Hughes, Margaret. 'Boudica's Last Battle: the Mancetter candidacy'. (Undated article.) https://www.academia.edu/12813670/Boudicas_Last_Battle_the_Mancetter_candidacy?auto=download. (accessed Jan 2017).
47 Boardman, Andrew. *The Medieval Soldier in the Wars of the Roses*. Stroud: Sutton, 1998. (p. 120)
48 Sutherland, Tim. 'Killing Time: Challenging the Common Perceptions of Three Medieval Conflicts – Ferrybridge, Dintingdale and Towton – The Largest Battle on British Soil'. (Undated article.) http://www.towton.org.uk/wp-content/uploads/killing-time_tim_sutherland.pdf. (accessed Jan 2017).
49 *The Economist*. 'The battle of Towton. Nasty, brutish and not that short'. (16 Dec 2010.) http://www.economist.com/node/17722650.
50 *Yorkshire Post*. 'Secrets buried with the dead after Britain's bloodiest battle'. (16 March 2010.) http://www.yorkshirepost.co.uk/news/analysis/secrets-buried-with-the-dead-after-britain-s-bloodiest-battle-1-2567631#ixzz3yRpdiTms. (accessed July 2017).
51 Timeline. *The Battle of Towton, Britain's Bloodiest Battle*. https://www.youtube.com/watch?v=jvvhtIx2DRc&t=986s.
52 Keegan, John. *The Face of Battle*. London: Pimlico, 1991. (p. 88)
53 Goodman, A. *The Wars of the Roses: The soldier's experience*. Stroud: Tempus, 2005. (p. 184). Commynes, Philippe de. *Memoirs, the Reign of Louis XI 1461–83*. Trans. and ed.: M. Jones. Harmondsworth, 1972.

54 Boardman, Andrew. *The Medieval Soldier in the Wars of the Roses.* Stroud: Sutton, 1998. (p. 77)
55 *Ibid.* (p. 61)
56 *Ibid.* (p. 69)
57 Miller, Michael D. *Wars of the Roses.* An analysis of the causes of the Wars and the course which they took. http://www.warsoftheroses.co.uk/contact.htm. (accessed June 2017).
58 *Wars of the Roses.* http://www.warsoftheroses.com/battles.cfm.
59 The Richard III Society. http://www.richardiii.net/9_1_1_wotr_battles.php.
60 Percentage is calculated using rounding to go up from => .6 to the next whole number; down from .4. The .5 of a per cent has been left halfway.
61 *Wars of the Roses.* http://www.warsoftheroses.com/battles.cfm.
62 *Luminarium: Encyclopedia Project.* 'Wars of the Roses'. http://www.luminarium.org/encyclopedia/. (accessed July 2016).
63 *Wars of the Roses.* http://www.warsoftheroses.com/battles.cfm.
64 *Wars of the Roses.* http://www.warsoftheroses.com/stalbans1.cfm.
65 *Wars of the Roses.* http://www.warsoftheroses.com/battles.cfm.
66 The Richard III Society. http://www.richardiii.net/9_1_1_wotr_battles.php.
67 *Luminarium: Encyclopedia Project.* 'Wars of the Roses'. http://www.luminarium.org/encyclopedia/. (accessed July 2016).
68 *Wars of the Roses.* http://www.warsoftheroses.com/battles.cfm.
69 *Ibid.*
70 UK Battlefields Resource Centre. http://www.battlefieldstrust.com/resource-centre/warsoftheroses/battleview.asp?BattleFieldId=6.
71 The Richard III Society. http://www.richardiii.net/9_1_1_wotr_battles.php.
72 *Wars of the Roses.* http://www.warsoftheroses.com/ludfordbridge.cfm.
73 The Richard III Society. http://www.richardiii.net/9_1_1_wotr_battles.php.
74 *Wars of the Roses.* http://www.warsoftheroses.com/battles.cfm.
75 *Ibid.*
76 UK Battlefields Resource Centre. http://www.battlefieldstrust.com/resource-centre/warsoftheroses/battleview.asp?BattleFieldId=33.
77 The Richard III Society. http://www.richardiii.net/9_1_1_wotr_battles.php.
78 *Luminarium: Encyclopedia Project.* 'Wars of the Roses'. http://www.luminarium.org/encyclopedia/. (accessed July 2016).
79 *Wars of the Roses.* http://www.warsoftheroses.com/battles.cfm.
80 The Richard III Society. http://www.richardiii.net/9_1_1_wotr_battles.php.
81 Boardman, A. *Towton: The bloodiest battle.* Stroud: The History Press, 2009. (p. 25)
82 *Wars of the Roses.* http://www.warsoftheroses.com/battles.cfm.
83 The Richard III Society. http://www.richardiii.net/9_1_1_wotr_battles.php.
84 Boardman, A. *Towton: The bloodiest battle.* Stroud: The History Press, 2009. (p. 25)
85 Boardman, Andrew. *The Medieval Soldier in the Wars of the Roses.* Stroud: Sutton, 1998. (p. 176)

86 The Richard III Society. http://www.richardiii.net/9_1_1_wotr_battles.php.
87 *Wars of the Roses.* http://www.warsoftheroses.com/battles.cfm.
88 The Richard III Society. http://www.richardiii.net/9_1_1_wotr_battles.php.
89 Boardman, A. *Towton: The bloodiest battle.* Stroud: The History Press, 2009. (p. 33). Boardman is quoting William Worcester, and calls this number 'a gross exaggeration'.
90 *Wars of the Roses.* http://www.warsoftheroses.com/battles.cfm.
91 Boardman, A. *Towton: The bloodiest battle.* Stroud: The History Press, 2009. (p. 33)
92 *Ibid.* (p. 36). A quote from 'Gregory's Chronicle' in *The Historical Collections of a Citizen of London.* J. Gairdner (ed.) 1876.
93 Castelow, Ellen. *Historic UK.* 'The Second Battle of St Albans'. https://www.historic-uk.com/HistoryMagazine/DestinationsUK/The-Second-Battle-of-St-Albans/.
94 *Wars of the Roses.* http://www.warsoftheroses.com/battles.cfm.
95 Castelow, Ellen. *Historic UK.* 'The Second Battle of St Albans'. https://www.historic-uk.com/HistoryMagazine/DestinationsUK/The-Second-Battle-of-St-Albans/.
96 *Wars of the Roses.* http://www.warsoftheroses.com/battles.cfm.
97 *Ibid.*
98 Boardman, A. *Towton: The bloodiest battle.* Stroud: The History Press, 2009. (p. 175)
99 *Wars of the Roses.* http://www.warsoftheroses.com/battles.cfm.
100 The Richard III Society. http://www.richardiii.net/9_1_1_wotr_battles.php.
101 Boardman, A. *Towton: The bloodiest battle.* Stroud: The History Press, 2009. (p. 175)
102 The Richard III Society. http://www.richardiii.net/9_1_1_wotr_battles.php.
103 UK Battlefields Resource Centre. http://www.battlefieldstrust.com/resource-centre/warsoftheroses/battleview.asp?BattleFieldId=46.
104 Boardman, Andrew. *The Medieval Soldier in the Wars of the Roses.* Stroud: Sutton, 1998. (p. 18)
105 The Richard III Society. http://www.richardiii.net/9_1_1_wotr_battles.php.
106 http://www.battlefieldstrust.com/resource-centre/warsoftheroses/battleview.asp?BattleFieldId=46.
107 *Wars of the Roses.* http://www.warsoftheroses.com/battles.cfm.
108 *Ibid.*
109 *Ibid.*
110 *Ibid.*
111 UK Battlefields Resource Centre. http://www.battlefieldstrust.com/resource-centre/warsoftheroses/battleview.asp?BattleFieldId=13.
112 *Ibid.*
113 *Ibid.*
114 *Wars of the Roses.* http://www.warsoftheroses.com/battles.cfm.
115 UK Battlefields Resource Centre. http://www.battlefieldstrust.com/resource-centre/warsoftheroses/battleview.asp?BattleFieldId=5.
116 *Wars of the Roses.* http://www.warsoftheroses.com/battles.cfm.
117 http://www.battlefieldstrust.com/resource-centre/warsoftheroses/battleview.asp?BattleFieldId=5.

118 *Ibid.*
119 Brooks, Richard. *Cassell's Battlefields of Britain & Ireland.* London: Weidenfeld & Nicholson 2005. http://www.battlefieldstrust.com/resource-centre/warsoftheroses/battleview.asp?BattleFieldId=5.
120 Strength figures as 26,000 for all three calculations.
121 *Wars of the Roses.* http://www.warsoftheroses.com/battles.cfm.
122 Boardman, Andrew. *The Medieval Soldier in the Wars of the Roses.* Stroud: Sutton, 1998. (p. 82)
123 *Wars of the Roses.* http://www.warsoftheroses.com/battles.cfm.
124 UK Battlefields Resource Centre. http://www.battlefieldstrust.com/resource-centre/warsoftheroses/battleview.asp?BattleFieldId=45.
125 *Ibid.*
126 *Ibid.*
127 *Wars of the Roses.* http://www.warsoftheroses.com/battles.cfm.
128 *Ibid.*
129 UK Battlefields Resource Centre. http://www.battlefieldstrust.com/resource-centre/warsoftheroses/battleview.asp?BattleFieldId=8.
130 *Ibid.*
131 *Ibid.*
132 UK Battlefields Resource Centre. http://www.battlefieldstrust.com/resource-centre/warsoftheroses/battleview.asp?BattleFieldId=42.
133 *Ibid.*
134 *Ibid.*
135 *Ibid.*
136 Email to the author, 30 August 2017.
137 *Wars of the Roses.* http://www.warsoftheroses.com/battles.cfm.
138 Boardman, A. *Towton: The bloodiest battle.* Stroud: The History Press, 2009. (p. 175)
139 *Ibid.*
140 Boardman, Andrew. *The Medieval Soldier in the Wars of the Roses.* Stroud: Sutton, 1998. (p. 18)
141 Historic Scotland. 'The Inventory of Historic Battlefields – Battle of Culloden'. http://data.historic-scotland.gov.uk/data/docs/battlefields/culloden_full.pdf. (accessed June 2016).
142 Dupuy, R. Ernest and Dupuy, Trevor N. *The Collins Encyclopaedia of Military History.* (4th ed.) The Netherlands: BCA, 2007. (p. 840). Elizabeth Longford's *Wellington* gives 'close to 15,000' men lost to the British; the French 25,000 dead and wounded, and the Prussians 'over 7,000' without distinguishing between fatalities and injuries. (p. 483)
143 Barbero, Alessandro. *The Battle: A New History of Waterloo.* London: Atlantic Books, 2005. The French fatality figure for this battle is most elusive. The figure used here is from '24,000 to 26,000 casualties, including 6,000 to 7,000 captured'. Less the captured, and presuming 18,000 casualties, a figure of 4,000 is approximated, using the formula of four wounded for every one dead.

144 History of War. 'Battle of the Alma, 20 September 1854'. http://www.historyofwar.org/articles/battles_alma.html. The French figure here is given as 'Casualties' and not dead and wounded.
145 Nearly 40 years of improvements had been made with firearms and artillery since Waterloo, with varied introductions of rifled weapons being the biggest change.
146 Imperial War Museums. 'What Happened During The Battle Of The Somme?' http://www.iwm.org.uk/history/what-happened-during-the-battle-of-the-somme.
147 Sheffield, G. *The Somme*. London: Cassell, 2003. (pp: 41-69).
148 First World War.com. 'The Battle of the Somme, 1916'. http://www.firstworldwar.com/battles/somme.htm.
149 Gabriel, Richard A. *Soldiers' Lives through History – The Ancient World*. Westport CT: Greenwood Press, 2007. (p. 229)

Appendix 1

1 *The Philological Museum*. 'Polydore Vergil, Anglica Historia' (1555 version). http://www.philological.bham.ac.uk/polverg/23eng.html. (accessed May 2016).
2 Hall, Edward. *The Union of the Two Noble and Illustre Families of Lancastre and Yorke*. https://archive.org/stream/hallschronicleco00halluoft/hallschronicleco00halluoft_djvu.txt.

Bibliography

Books, Articles, Essays

Ambrose, Stephen E. *Band of Brothers: E Company, 506th Regiment, 101st Airborne: from Normandy to Hitler's Eagle's Nest*. New York: Simon & Schuster, 1992.
Archaeology Data Service. 'The Bosworth Battlefield Project. The Battlefields Trust'. 2013. http://archaeologydataservice.ac.uk/archives/view/bosworth_hlf_2011/overview.cfm
Astor, Gerald. *Operation Iceberg: the Invasion and Conquest of Okinawa in World War II*. New York: Donald I. Fine, 1995.
Baker, Clive and Knight, Greg. *Milne Bay 1942*. NSW: Baker-Knight Publications, 1991.
Barbero, Alessandro. *The Battle: A New History of Waterloo*. London: Atlantic Books, 2005.
Barker, Juliet. *Agincourt*. New York: Hachette Book Group, 2006.
Barrett, John. *We Were There*. New South Wales: Allen and Unwin, 1995.
BBC. 'Health: A millennium of health improvement'. http://news.bbc.co.uk/2/hi/health/241864.stm 27 Dec 1998. Accessed Jun 2017.
Bennett, Matthew, Bradbury, Jim, De Vries, Kelly, Dickie, Iain and Jestice, Phyllis G. *Fighting Techniques of the Medieval World, AD 500 – AD 1500: equipment, combat skills and tactics*. Staplehurst: Spellmount, 2005.
Bicheno, Hugh. *Blood Royal. The Wars of the Roses: 1462–1485*. New York: Pegasus Books, 2017.
Boardman, Andrew. *The Medieval Soldier in the Wars of the Roses*. Stroud: Sutton, 1998.
Boardman, A. *Towton: the Bloodiest Battle*. Stroud: The History Press, 2009.
Boardman, A. *The first battle of St. Albans, 1455*. Stroud: Tempus, 2006.
Brady, Lt. Col. S. G. *The Military Affairs of Ancient Rome and Roman Art of War in Caesar's Time*. The Military Service Publishing Company, 1947. http://www.digitalattic.org/home/war/romanarmy/
Bullein, William. *A Dialogue Against the Fever Pestilence*. Early English Text Society, Extra Series. London: N. Trubner & Co., 1988.
Cahill, Michael. 'The Battle of Towton 1461, a multi-disciplinary discussion based on diverse scholarly analyses of this Medieval battle site'. *Academia*.
Caputo, Philip. *A Rumor of War*. New York: Holt, Rinehart and Winston, 1977.

Capwell, Tobias. *The Real Fighting Stuff: Arms and Armour at Glasgow Museums.* Glasgow: Glasgow Museums Publishing, 2007.
Capwell, Tobias. *Arms and Armour of the English Knight 1400–1450.* UK: Thomas Del Mar Ltd, 2015.
Capwell, Tobias. *Arms and Armour of the Medieval Joust.* Leeds: Royal Armouries Museum, 2018.
Capwell, Dr Tobias. *The World Encyclopedia of Knives, Daggers and Bayonets.* UK: Anness Publishing, 2011.
Capwell, Tobias, Edge, David and Warren, Jeremy. *Masterpieces of European Arms and Armour in the Wallace Collection.* UK: The Wallace Collection, 2011.
Castelow, Ellen. *Historic UK.* 'The Second Battle of St Albans'. https://www.historic-uk.com/HistoryMagazine/DestinationsUK/The-Second-Battle-of-St-Albans/
Commines, Philippe de. *Memoirs, the Reign of Louis XI 1461–83.* Trans. and ed. by M. Jones. Harmondsworth: 1972.
Contamine, P. *War in the Middle Ages.* Oxford: Basil Blackwell, 1984.
Coppard, George. *With a machine gun to Cambrai: the tale of a young Tommy in Kitchener's army 1914–1918.* London: H.M.S.O., 1969.
Corrigan, Gordon. *Mud, Blood and Poppycock.* London: Cassell, 2004.
Curry, Anne. *The Battle of Agincourt. Sources and Interpretations.* Woodbridge, Suffolk: Boydell Press, 2000.
Curry, Anne. *Agincourt – a New History.* Gloucestershire: The History Press, 2010.
Curry, Anne and Foard, Glenn. 'Where are the dead of medieval battles? A preliminary survey'. *Journal of Conflict Archaeology* (2016). 11:2-3, 61-77, DOI: 10.1080/15740773.2017.1324675.
D'Amato, Raffaele and Sumner, Graham. *Arms and Armour of the Imperial Roman Soldier.* Barnsley: Frontline Books, 2009.
Dando-Collins, Stephen. *Legions of Rome.* New York: St Martin's Press, 2010.
Defoe, Daniel and Hamblyn, Richard (eds). *The Storm.* New York: Penguin Classics, 2005.
Department of Archaeological Sciences, University of Bradford. *Battlefield Archaeology: a Guide to the Archaeology of Conflict.* \.
De Vries, Kelly. *Infantry Warfare in the Early Fourteenth century: Discipline, Tactics, and Technology.* United Kingdom: Boydell Brewer Ltd, 2000.
De Vries, Kelly. *Medieval Military Technology.* Canada: University of Toronto Press, 2010.
DeVries, Kelly and Smith, Robert D. *Medieval Weapons – An Illustrated History of their Impact.* California: ABC-CLIO, 2007.
Docherty, Frank. 'A Brief History of the Quarterstaff'. *Journal of Western Martial Art* (May 2001). http://ejmas.com/jwma/articles/2001/jwmaart_docherty_0501.htm
Dr Neill MD. 'What is the "fight or flight response?"'. Undated article. http://www.thebodysoulconnection.com/EducationCenter/fight.html. Accessed June 2016.
Dupuy, R. Ernest and Dupuy, Trevor N. *The Collins Encyclopaedia of Military History.* (4th ed.) The Netherlands: BCA, 2007 (p. 840).

Enyclopedia Brittanica. 'Vegetius Roman Military Author'. https://www.britannica.com/biography/Vegetius

Enyclopedia Brittanica. 'World War I'. https://www.britannica.com/event/World-War-I

Fiorato, Boylston and Knusel (eds). *Blood Red Roses: The Archaeology of a Mass Grave from the Battle of Towton AD 1461*. Oxford: Oxbow Books, 2000.

Fitz-Gibbon, Spencer. *Not Mentioned in Despatches*. Cambridge: The Lutterworth Press, 1995.

Foard, Glenn and Curry, Anne. *Bosworth 1485: A Battlefield Rediscovered*. Oxford: Oxbow Books, 2013.

Fordham University. *Medieval London*. 'Stained Glass Window'. https://medievallondon.ace.fordham.edu/exhibits/show/medieval-london-objects/stainedglasswindow

Frontinus, Sextus Julius. *Stratagems III*. 'On the Disposition of Troops for Battle'. Paragraphs 10–11, Book II. http://penelope.uchicago.edu/Thayer/E/Roman/Texts/Frontinus/Strategemata/2*.html#3

Gabriel, Richard A. *Soldiers' Lives through History – The Ancient World*. Westport, CT: Greenwood Press, 2007.

Gassmann, Jack and Certaminis, Artes. 'Thoughts on the Role of Cavalry in Medieval Warfare'. *Acta Periodica Duellatorum*. (undated article) (pp. 149–77). https://static1.squarespace.com/static/57f6449959cc68cbbd3df1c2/t/5849294f2994ca9650c2c607/1481189716627/APD2%282014%29_Gassman.pdf. Accessed June 2016.

Gillingham, John. 'Richard I and the Science of War in the Middle Ages'. (undated article). http://deremilitari.org/wp-content/uploads/2013/08/gillingham2.pdf. (pp. 194–207).

Gleason, Bruce P. 'Cavalry and Court Trumpeters and Kettledrummers from the Renaissance to the Nineteenth Century'. *Galpin Society Journal* LXII (2009).

Goodman, A. *The Wars of the Roses: military activity and English society, 1452–97*. Abingdon: Routledge & Kegan Paul, 1981.

Goodman, A. *The Wars of the Roses: the soldier's experience*. Stroud: Tempus, 2005.

Goodwin, George. *Fatal colours: the battle of Towton, 1461*. London: Weidenfield and Nicolson, 2011.

Goranov, Alexi. 'The Medieval Poleaxe'. (undated article). https://myarmoury.com/feature_spot_poleaxe.html.

Graves, Robert. *Goodbye to All That*. London: Penguin, 1960.

Gravett, Christopher. *Norman Knight 950–1204 AD*. London: Osprey, 1993.

Gravett, Christopher. *Towton 1461 – England's Bloodiest Battle (Campaign 120)*. Oxford: Osprey Publishing, 2003.

Gray, Sir Thomas. *Scalacronica, 1272–1363*. Trans. by Andy King. Woodbridge, Suffolk: Surtees Society, 2005.

Griggs, Mary Beth. 'Medieval Knights on a Treadmill put Historical Myths to the Test'. *Popular Mechanics* (21 July 2011). http://www.popularmechanics.com/culture/a6749/medieval-knights-on-a-treadmill-put-historical-myths-to-the-test/. Accessed January 2017.

Grose, Francis. *A Treatise on Ancient Armour and Weapons.* London: S. Hooper, 1708. (Various sources online and in libraries contain copies; for example see https://ia600905.us.archive.org/18/items/treatiseonancien00grosrich/treatiseonancien-00grosrich.pdf.)

Hall, Edward. *The Union of the Two Noble and Illustre Families of Lancastre and Yorke.* https://archive.org/stream/hallschronicleco00halluoft/hallschronicleco00halluoft_djvu.txt.

Halsall, Guy. *Warfare and Society in the Barbarian West, 450–900.* London: Routledge, 2003.

Hanson, Victor Davis. *The Western Way of War.* Oxford: Oxford University Press, 1989.

Hanson, Victor Davis. *Hoplites: the Classical Greek Battle Experience.* London: Routledge, 1993.

Hardy, Robert. *Longbow.* Somerset: Patrick Stephens, 2002.

Hart, Peter. *To the last round: the South Notts Hussars, 1939–1942.* Barnsley, England: Pen & Sword Books, 1996.

Hastings, Max. *Armageddon: The Battle for Germany 1944–1945.* USA: Macmillan, 2004.

Hewitt, John. *Ancient Armour and Weapons in Europe from the Iron Period of the Northern Nations to the End of the Thirteenth Century* (online edition). Bente Press, 2008.

Hicks, Michael. 'Propaganda and the First Battle of St Albans, 1455'. *Nottingham Medieval Studies*, Vol. 44 (2000). http://deremilitari.org/2016/10/propaganda-and-the-first-battle-of-st-albans-1455/.

Holst, M. and Sutherland, T. 'Towton Revisited – Analysis of the Human Remains from the Battle of Towton 1461', in S. Eickhoff & F. Schopper (eds). Schlachtfeld und Massengrab: Spektren Interdisziplinärer Auswertung von Orten der Gewalt (Zossen), 2014. (pp. 97–129). (Via *Academia*).

Hooper, Nicholas and Bennett, Matthew. *The Cambridge Illustrated Atlas of Warfare: the Middle Ages.* London: Cambridge University Press, 1996.

Hosler, John D. 'Blink and You'll Miss it: Medieval Warfare in Victor Davis Hanson's Carnage and Culture'. Morgan State University. https://www.academia.edu/29367775/Blink_and_Youll_Miss_it_Medieval_Warfare_in_Victor_Davis_Hansons_Carnage_and_Culture.

Hughes, Margaret. 'Boudica's Last Battle: the Mancetter candidacy'. *Academia* (undated article). https://www.academia.edu/12813670/Boudicas_Last_Battle_the_Mancetter_candidacy?auto=download.

Hughes, Margaret. 'The site of Boudica's last battle'." *Academia* (29 June 2013). https://www.academia.edu/12774243/On_Boudicas_trail_possible_sites_for_Boudicas_last_battle?auto=download.

Jones, Peter. 'Some Technical Considerations', in Robert Hardy. *Longbow.* Somerset: Patrick Stephens, 2002.

Keegan, John. *The Face of Battle.* London: Pimlico, 1991.

Knight, David James and Hunt, Brian. *Polearms of Paulus Hector Mair.* United States: Paladin Press, 2008.

Knusel, Christopher and Boylston, Anthea. 'How has the Towton project contributed to our knowledge of medieval warfare', in Fiorato, Boylston and Knusel (eds). *Blood Red Roses: The Archaeology of a Mass Grave From the Battle of Towton AD 1461.* Oxford: Oxbow Books, 2000.

Koch, Christof. 'Does Brain Size Matter?'. *Scientific American* (1 January, 2016). https://www.scientificamerican.com/article/does-brain-size-matter1/.

LeShan, Lawrence L. *The psychology of war: comprehending its mystique and its madness.* Chicago: Noble Press, 1992.

Lewis, Dr Tom, OAM. *Lethality in Combat.* Australia: Big Sky Publishing, 2012.

Lewis, Lt. Cmder. Tom, RAN. 'One Third of their Combat Power – Developing a Quantitative Model for Intelligence Analysis of Morale in Armed Forces'. *Headmark*, No. 138 (Dec. 2010).

Lewis, Tom. 'On medieval jousting in modern times'. *The Journal of the Arms Collectors' Association of the Northern Territory* (March 2019).

Life in Tudor Times. 'Act of Attainder'. http://www.tudorplace.com.ar/Documents/act_attainder.htm.

Longford, Elizabeth. *Wellington.* New York: Harper and Evanston, 1969.

Lukowiak, Ken. *A Soldier's Song.* London: Secker and Warburg, 1993.

Luminarium: Encyclopedia Project. 'Wars of the Roses'. http://www.luminarium.org/encyclopedia/.

Luminarium: Encyclopedia Project. 'Speech to the Troops at Tilbury'. http://www.luminarium.org/renlit/tilbury.htm.

Macaulay, Thomas Babington. *The History of England from the Accession of James II.* London: Longman, Brown, Green and Longmans, 1854.

Martin, George R. R. *A Game of Thrones. The Graphic Novel. Volume 1.* New York: Bantam Books, 2014.

Martin, George R. R. *A Dance with Dragons. Part 2: After the Feast.* London: Harper Voyager, 2016.

Matthews, Professor Jill Julius. 'Leisure time, 1913'. Australian National University (27 August 2013). http://www.nma.gov.au/audio/transcripts/1913/NMA_1913_Matthews_leisure_20130827.html.

McGlynn, Sean. 'The Myths of Medieval Warfare'. *History Today*, Vol. 44 (1994). http://deremilitari.org/2013/06/the-myths-of-medieval-warfare/

McKee, Alexander. *Caen: anvil of victory.* London: Souvenir Press, 1964.

Mercola. 'How Many Burgers Can You Make from One Cow?'. https://articles.mercola.com/sites/articles/archive/2015/11/14/cafo-beef-hamburger.aspx .(14 November 2015).

Milner, N. P. (trans. and Introduction). *Vegetius: Epitome of Military Science.* Liverpool: Liverpool University Press, 1993.

Mitchell, Piers D. *Medicine in the crusades: warfare, wounds and the medieval surgeon.* Cambridge: Cambridge University Press, 2004.

Mitchelson, Tom. 'Bludgeoned, hacked and poleaxed! My skull-shattering stab at medieval fighting, the world's most violent hobby'. *The Daily Mail* (22 August 2013).

http://www.dailymail.co.uk/news/article-2399431/The-worlds-violent-hobby-My-skull-shattering-stab-medieval-fighting.html#ixzz4X7SLeE3l.

Moore, Harold G. and Galloway, Joseph L. *We were soldiers once and young: Ia Drang: the battle that changed the war in Vietnam*. New York: Random House, 1992.

Morris, J. E. 'Mounted Infantry in Mediaeval Warfare'. *Transactions of the Royal Historical Society*, 3rd Series, Vol. 8 (1914). http://web.archive.org/web/20110605011314/http://www.deremilitari.org/resources/articles/morris.htm.

Mortimer, Ian. *The Time Traveller's Guide to Medieval England: A Handbook for Visitors to the Fourteenth Century*. London: The Bodley Head Ltd, 2008.

Mortimer, John J., Jr. 'Tactics, Strategy, and Battlefield Formation during the Hundred Years' War: The Role of the Longbow in the 'Infantry Revolution''. Master of Arts Thesis, Indiana University of Pennsylvania (August 2013). http://citeseerx.ist.psu.edu/viewdoc/download?doi=10.1.1.843.3571&rep=rep1&type=pdf.

Musset, Lucien. *The Bayeux Tapestry*. Woodbridge, Suffolk: Boydell Press. 2005.

Napoleon, His Army and Enemies. 'French Cavalry During the Napoleonic Wars'. http://www.napolun.com/mirror/web2.airmail.net/napoleon/cavalry_Napoleon.html.

Neillands, Robin. *The Wars of the Roses*. UK: Weidenfeld Nicolson Illustrated, 1992.

Novak, Shannon A. 'Battle-Related Trauma', in Fiorato, Boylston and Knusel (eds). *Blood Red Roses: The Archaeology of a Mass Grave From the Battle of Towton AD 1461*. Oxford: Oxbow Books, 2000.

Oakeshott, Ewart. *Records of the Medieval Sword*. Woodbridge, Suffolk: The Boydell Press, 1991.

Oman, Charles. *A History of the Art of War in the Middle Ages*. Volume II. London: Methuen and Co. Ltd, 1924.

Osgood, Richard. *Unknown Warrior: The Archaeology of the Common Soldier*. Stroud: The History Press, 2005.

Phibbs, Brendan. *The Other Side of Time: A Combat Surgeon in World War II*. Boston: Little, Brown, 1987.

Phillips, C. E. Lucas. *The Greatest Raid of All*. London: Readers Book Club, 1958.

Richardson, Thom. 'Armour', in Fiorato, Boylston and Knusel (eds). *Blood Red Roses: The Archaeology of a Mass Grave From the Battle of Towton AD 1461*. Oxford: Oxbow Books, 2000.

Richardson, T. 'The Bridport muster roll of 1457'. *Royal Armouries Yearbook* 2 (1997).

Rimer, Graeme. 'Weapons', in Fiorato, Boylston and Knusel (eds). *Blood Red Roses: The Archaeology of a Mass Grave From the Battle of Towton AD 1461*. Oxford: Oxbow Books, 2000.

Rogers, Clifford J. 'The Military Revolutions of the Hundred Years' War'. *The Journal of Military History*, 57 (April 1993).

Rogers, Clifford J. *War Cruel and Sharp: English Strategy under Edward III, 1327–1360*. Woodbridge, Suffolk: Boydell and Brewer, 2000.

Rogers, Clifford J. 'The Offensive/Defensive in Medieval Strategy, From Crecy to Mohacs: Warfare in the Late Middle Ages (1346–1526)', Acts of the XXIInd

Colloquium of the International Commission of Military History (Vienna, 1996). Vienna: Heeresgeschichtliches Museum/Militärhistorisches Institut,1997.
Rogers, Clifford J. 'The Efficacy of the Medieval Longbow: A Reply to Kelly DeVries'. *War in History* 5, No. 2 (1998).
Roser, Max. 'Homicides'. OurWorldInData.org. https://ourworldindata.org/homicides/ (2017).
Sabin, Philip. 'The Roman Face of Battle'. *Journal of Roman Studies*, Vol. 90 (2000).
Sadler, John. *The Red Rose and the White: The Wars of the Roses, 1453–1487*. UK: Longman, 2009.
Sadler, John. *Towton*. Barnsley, UK: Pen & Sword, 2014.
Sajer, Guy. *The Forgotten Soldier*. London: Weidenfeld and Nicolson, 1971.
Scoble, A. R. (ed.). *The Memoirs of Philip de Commines, Lord of Argenton*. Vol. 1. (1911) (p. 21). https://archive.org/details/memoirsofphilipd01comm. Accessed Jan 2017.
Scott, Walter. *Ivanhoe: A Romance*. http://www.gutenberg.org/files/82/82-0.txt (2008).
Simmons, Sue (ed.). *The Military Horse*. London: Marshall Cavendish, 1984.
Singman, Jeffrey L. *The Middle Ages: Everyday Life in Medieval Europe*. New York: Stirling, 2013.
Sledge, E. B. *With the old breed, at Peleliu and Okinawa*. Novato, CA: Presidio Press, 1981.
Smail. R. C. *Crusading Warfare 1097–1193*. Cambridge: Cambridge University Press, 1956.
Snook, G. A. 'The Halberd and Other Polearms of the Late Medieval Period'. *Americansocietyofarmscollectors.org*. http://americansocietyofarmscollectors.org/wp-content/uploads/2015/05/Halberd-and-other-polearms-of-the-late-medieval-period-B079_Snook.pdf
Strickland, Matthew and Hardy, Robert. *The Great Warbow*. Gloucestershire: Haynes Publishing, 2005.
Sutherland, Tim. 'Unknown Soldiers: The Discovery of War Graves from the Battle of Towton AD1461'. University of Bradford. 1–2 December 2006. http://www.archprospection.org/sites/archprospection.org/files/artefacts-anomalies/Sutherland_Text.pdf.
Sutherland, Tim. 'The Bloody Battle of Towton, England', in Carver, Martin and Klapste, Jan (eds) *The Archaeology of Medieval Europe, Vol. 2: Twelfth to Sixteenth Centuries*. Lancaster: Aarhus University Press, 2011.
Sutherland, Tim. 'The Towton Battle – A Reinterpretation'. *Arms & Armour*, Vol. 12 (2015), Issue 2.
Sutherland, Tim. 'Killing Time: Challenging the Common Perceptions of Three Medieval Conflicts – Ferrybridge, Dintingdale and Towton – The Largest Battle on British Soil'. (undated article) http://www.towton.org.uk/wp-content/uploads/killing-time_tim_sutherland.pdf. Accessed January 2017.
Sutherland, T. and Schmidt, A. 'Towton, 1461: An Integrated Approach to Battlefield Archaeology'. *Landscapes* 4 (2) (2003). (pp. 15–25)

Talhoffer, Hans. *Medieval Combat in Colour. A Fifteenth-Century Manual of Swordfighting and Close-Quarter Combat*. (Reproduction of the 1497 manual) Barnsley: Greenhill Books, 2018.

Tattersall, Kate. 'Dragoons, hussars, and lancers: the glorious British cavalry of the mid 1800s'. http://www.katetattersall.com/hussars-dragoons-the-glorious-british-cavalry-of-the-mid-1800s/. (2015).

The Exiles – Company of Medieval Martial Artists. 'The Bloody Cost of Medieval Warfare'. University of Bradford, courtesy of Anthea Boylston. http://www.the-exiles.org/Article%20Towton.htm.

The *Economist*. 'The battle of Towton. Nasty, brutish and not that short'. (6 Dec 2010). http://www.economist.com/node/17722650.

The *Philological Museum*. 'Polydore Vergil, Anglica Historia (1555 version)'. http://www.philological.bham.ac.uk/polverg/23eng.html.

The *Telegraph*. 'Towton: England's bloodiest battle'. Edited extract from Jones, Dan. *The Hollow Crown: The Wars of the Roses and the Rise of the Tudors*. http://www.telegraph.co.uk/culture/books/booknews/11047871/Towton-Englands-bloodiest-battle.html.

The *Telegraph*. 'Are bodies of 10,000 lost warriors from Battle of Hastings buried in this field?'. (25 Oct 2012). http://www.telegraph.co.uk/news/earth/environment/archaeology/9632922/25 Oct 2012. Are-bodies-of-10000-lost-warriors-from-Battle-of-Hastings-buried-in-this-field.html.

Touch of Tapestry. 'History of Tapestries from Medieval to Modern Times'. (undated article). https://touchoftapestry.com/History-of-Tapestries-7.html.

Turnbull, Stephen. *The Book of the Medieval Knight*. London: Arms and Armour Press, 1995.

Turner, Sharon. *The History of England During the Middle Ages: Comprizing the reigns of Henry VI., Edward IV., Edward V., Richard III. and Henry VII*. (Book II). United Kingdom: Longman, Hurst, Rees, Orme and Brown, 1823.

Van Creveld, Martin. *Supplying War*. Cambridge: Cambridge University Press, 2005.

Verbruggen, J. F. *The Art of Warfare in Western Europe during the Middle Ages from the Eighth Century*. Brussels: North-Holland, 1977.

Verbruggen, J. F. and DeVries, Kelly. 'The Role of the Cavalry in Medieval Warfare'. *Journal of Medieval Military History* 3. (2005).

Waite, Adrian. *Medieval Pole Weapons 1287–1513*. Bristol: Stuart Press, 2001.

Waldman, John. *Hafted Weapons in Medieval and Renaissance Europe*. Netherlands: Brill, 2005.

Waller, John. 'Archery' in Fiorato, Boylston and Knusel (eds). *Blood Red Roses: The Archaeology of a Mass Grave From the Battle of Towton AD 1461*. Oxford: Oxbow Books, 2000.

Watts, Karen (Senior Curator for Armour and Art). 'Henry VIII's foot combat armour'. Leeds Armouries. https://royalarmouries.org/stories/object-of-the-month/object-of-the-month-for-april-henry-viiis-foot-combat-armour/.

Webster, Daniel Kenyon. *Parachute Infantry*. Baton Rouge, LA: Louisiana State University Press, 1994.
Welch, Ronald. *Knight Crusader*. London: Oxford University Press, 1954.
Welch, Ronald. *Sun of York*. Oxford: Oxford University Press, 1970.
Wilson, Fred. 'Battle Rhythm in emergency management'. *The Australian Journal of Emergency Management*. https://ajem.infoservices.com.au/items/AJEM-25-04-09#sthash.ipsr0hHL.dpuf.
Woosnam-Savage, Robert C. *Arms and Armour of Late Medieval Europe*. Leeds: Royal Armouries Museum, 2017.
York Osteoarchaeology Ltd. *Osteological Analysis Towton Hall & Towton Battlefield, Towton, North Yorkshire*. Report No. 0504. (June 2004). http://www.towton.org.uk/wp-content/uploads/osteological_analysis_towton_hall_and_towton_battlefield.pdf.
Yorkshire Post. 'Secrets buried with the dead after Britain's bloodiest battle'. (16 March 2010). http://www.yorkshirepost.co.uk/news/analysis/secrets-buried-with-the-dead-after-britain-s-bloodiest-battle-1-2567631#ixzz3yRpdiTms. (Accessed July 2017).
Young, Peter. *Storm from the Sea*. Great Britain: Wren's Park Publishing, 2002.

Interviews and correspondence

Battle of Tewkesbury Re-Enactors Series (BTRS). Series of 10 interviews with re-enactors carried out by the author on 9 July 2016 at the Tewkesbury Medieval Festival. Interviews as follows:

- Steve Arnold
- Ewen Cameron
- Andreas Dracocardos
- Matthew Greatrex
- Anthony Green
- Neil Griffiths
- Robert Johnson
- Mike Loveless
- Liam Lowther
- Jonathan Preston

Fallu, Ric. Author and underwater speargun designer and builder (2018–2020).
Farmer, Towton battlefield, name suppressed, personal communication (2016).
Foster, David. Champion axeman. Interview with the author, Hobart, Tasmania (December 2016).
Gilleghan, John, MBE. Historian and author of *A Guide to All Saints Church, Saxton*. Published by the church (undated). Interview with the author, United Kingdom (20 July 2016).

Hardy, Robert, CBE. Author, actor and longbow expert. Interview with the author, United Kingdom (20 July 2016).
Ivinson, Stuart. Librarian, Royal Armouries, Leeds. Interview with the author, United Kingdom (21 July 2016).
Palmer, Peter. Historian. Telephone discussion with the author, United Kingdom (21 July 2016).
Sutherland, Tim. Battlefield archaeologist. Emails (2020).
Williams, Dr Peter. Military historian. Interview (June 2015). Other conversations up to 2020.
Yallop, Henry. Assistant Curator – European Edged Weapons, Leeds Armouries. Emails to the author (October 2016).

Films and Podcasts

Adamson, Andrew (Dir.). *Prince Caspian*. Walt Disney Studios Motion Pictures. 2008.
Benioff, David and Weiss, D. B. (Dir.). *Game of Thrones*. HBO. 2011–2019.
Benioff, David and Weiss, D. B. *Game of Thrones*. 'The Battle Between Jon & Ramsay's Forces'. HBO. YouTube. https://www.youtube.com/watch?v=ToOIvD5mlow.
Boorman, John (Dir.). *Excalibur*. Orion Pictures. 1991.
Branagh, Kenneth (Dir.). *Henry V*. BBC Films. 1989.
Cold Steel. *English Bill*. https://www.youtube.com/watch?v=aS0jzFJArTg.
Cold Steel. *Pole Axe*. https://www.youtube.com/watch?v=DFjBZF-IlY8.
Curtis, Richard and Elton, Ben. *Blackadder Goes Forth*. BBC1. 1989.
FACT Open House 2012 – Poleaxe in Armour. https://www.youtube.com/watch?v=vZWkDhh9Zsg.
FACT Open House 2013 – Armoured Combat. https://www.youtube.com/watch?v=0SpTNTldthI.
First impression: Devil's Edge xiphos and A&A knightly pole axe. https://www.youtube.com/watch?v=rCyp8GMxnZE.
Gibson, Mel (Dir.). *Braveheart*. Icon Productions, The Ladd Company. 1995.
Historical European Martial Arts. *Back to the source*. (27 Oct 2015). https://www.youtube.com/watch?v=7DBmNVHTmNs.
Historical European Martial Arts. HEMA – Swordfish 2016 – Open Longsword FINALS. https://www.youtube.com/watch?v=VBbBI5mEvQc.
Jackson, Peter (Dir.). *Lord of the Rings: The Fellowship of the Ring*. New Line Cinema. 2012.
Mendes, Sam (Dir.). *1917*. DreamWorks Pictures. 2019.
Military History. *Medieval and Stone Age Weapons*. https://www.youtube.com/watch?v=ITFrlv0sbiU.
Michôd, David (Dir.). *The King*. Plan B Entertainment. 2019.
Ross, Dr James. 'The battle of Towton – a 550-year retrospective'. (15 July 2011). https://media.nationalarchives.gov.uk/index.php/the-battle-of-towton-a-550-year-retrospective-2/.

Royal Museum of Scotland. *Pollaxe freeplay*. M. Paul Macdonald and Mike Smith of the Macdonald Academy of Arms bout with pollaxes. (25 November, 2007). https://www.youtube.com/watch?v=PVBTRFQqKGA.

Scholagladiatoria. *English longbows vs medieval plate armour – Battlefield Detectives documentary review*. https://www.youtube.com/watch?v=HMvz-z1SPLQ&t=925s.

Scott, Ridley (Dir.). *Kingdom of Heaven*. Scott Free Productions. 2005.

Skallagrim. *Helmet tests, part 5*. https://www.youtube.com/watch?v=l47Idc7anG4.

Stromberg, Robert (Dir.) *Maleficent*. Walt Disney Pictures, Roth Films. 2014.

The Wallace Collection. *Agincourt: Myths and Misconceptions*. (14 Dec 2015). https://www.youtube.com/watch?v=5uxHYQW2Nio.

Timeline. *The Battle of Towton, Britain's Bloodiest Battle*. https://www.youtube.com/watch?v=jvvhtIx2DRc&t=986s.

University of Leeds. *Medieval Poleaxe Combat Demonstration*. 2015 International Medieval Congress. https://www.youtube.com/watch?v=LdVYW9r2G3U.

Personal visits

Battlefields: Agincourt, Crecy, Towton (2013–2018).
Bayeux, France (2013).
Leeds Armouries, UK (2013, 2016).
Los Angeles *Medieval Times* (2018).
Medieval festivals – various (1990s–present day).
Musée de la Armée, Paris (2015, 2016).
Tower of London (2013, 2016).
Vienna museums – various (2019).
Wallace Collection, London (2016).

Websites

BBC History. *British Population Animation*. http://www.bbc.co.uk/history/interactive/animations/population/index_embed.shtml.

'English Heritage Battlefield Report: Towton 1461'. English Heritage 1995. (pp. 4–5). https://content.historicengland.org.uk/content/docs/battlefields/towton.pdf. (accessed June 2016).

First World War.com, *The Battle of the Somme, 1916*. http://www.firstworldwar.com/battles/somme.htm.

Miller, Michael D. *Wars of the Roses*. An Analysis of the causes of the Wars and the course which they took. http://www.warsoftheroses.co.uk/contact.htm.

Scots Clans. '1746 – Battle Of Culloden'. http://www.scotclans.com/scotland/scottish-history/jacobite-scotland/1746-culloden/.

Towton Battlefield Society. Facebook site and website http://www.towton.org.uk.

Index

Agincourt, battle of, 49, 97, 103, 108, 116, 119, 184
Alcohol, as a factor in battle, 13, 143
Armies, sizes of in The Wars of the Roses, 178–181
Armour development, 16–17, 19–20, 41, Chapter 5, 85, 96, 188–189
Armour, for horses, 75–76
Armourer, as an innovative supplier of weapons, 56, 80, 86
Arrow supply in battle, 71–72
Arrows, type, and penetrating power, 73–74
Artillery, 30, 142, 184, 188

Banners, roles on the battlefield, 110–113, 188
Bannockburn, battle of, 24
Barnet, battle of, 109
Battlefield composition, 1–2, 21–23, 36–38, 74–78, 95–96, 107–108, 110–114, 128–130, 141
Battle rhythm, 128–129
Battles, difficulty in understanding, 28–34, 91, 120–121, 123–124, 175–177
Bayeux Tapestry, 26, 79, 155
Blackadder Goes Forth, as historical myth perpetration, 29
Bill, use and efficiency as a weapon, 42, 108, 155
Billmen in battle, 116, 118, 119, 124–126, 132, 155

Bosworth, battle of, 22, 23, 26, 33
Bowmen, use of in battle, 22, 67–71, Chapter 6, 74, 108, 112, 114–115, 131–134
Brasses, as armour illustrations, 36, 48
Breaking the line, as a battle concept and aim, 108–110
Bridport Muster Roll, 60, 216

Cavalry, including techniques, 15, 17–18, 23, 57, 61, 62, 75–76, 98
deployed against billmen, 119
deployed against bowmen, 77, 78, 119, 139, 155
Chivalry, 35–36
Church windows; providing illustrations of military aspects, 25
Combatant height, strength, endurance and fighting ability, 88–90
Communications, in battle, 99–100, 114, 117, 124, 127
Crecy, battle of, 6, 9, 27, 32, 67, 70, 71, 72, 92, 98, 142
Crossbow, 68, 72

Dagger, use of in combat, 96, 133

Edgecote, battle of, 22, 95
Edward IV, King, 135, 137, 161, 172
Endurance, as a combat factor in soldiers, 89, 120, 120–121, 124, 127–128, 150–151

England, population, 169, 172
Executions, in Wars of the Roses, 9, 95, 158–159

Falkirk, battle of, 81
Fauconberg, Lord, 114, 171
Ferrybridge, 10, 137, 139, 144, 176
Films and television, military inaccuracy of
  General references, 64
  1917, 29
  Braveheart, 45
  Game of Thrones, 46, 48, 49, 50
  Maleficent, 47
  Prince Caspian, 47
  Henry V, 47, 48, 49, 103
  Lord of the Rings, 48
  Kingdom of Heaven, 50, 51, 59
  The King, 51
  Excalibur, 51, 59

Greek fighting techniques, 13–15, 41, 65, 99, 154, 185
Ground, implications in battle, 97

Halidon Hill, battle of, 70
Hastings, battle of, 91
Helmets, battle use, 18, 49, 55–56, 61, 89, 94, 99, 121
Henry V play; inspirational speech, 103
Henry VI, King, 5–6
Henry VII, King, 22, 26, 165
Henry VIII, King, armour, 58–59
'Household' groupings, 110–111
Humans, suitability for combat, 11–12

Infantry, battle techniques, WWI, 63–65
Infantry; medieval by type battle roles, 107–113, 131–134
Inherent Military Probability, 37–38, 91, 111, 130, 173

Knights and knighthood, 34–35, 111–112

Leadership, need for aggressive, 103–107
Literacy, as a barrier to understanding medieval battles, 24–25, 30–32, 91
Longbow (see Bowmen)
Loyalty, implications for combat effectiveness, 100–102

Mace, efficiency as a weapon, 40
Man-at-Arms, character and roles, 111–112
Marching, soldiers' abilities, 170–171
Margaret of Anjou, Queen, 5, 137
Melee fight, including weapon choice, 68, 87–88, 124, 131–134, 190
Morale, as a combat factor, 100–103, 113, 118, 14
Myths, surrounding medieval battles, 34–36

Norfolk, Duke of, 146, 147, 172
Norman Invasion, 7, 26, 81, 168

Over-reporting of numbers in battles, 175–177

Pack combat, 12–13
Pavise, 113
Physical endurance in combat, 20, 120–123
Platoon attack, WWI, 63–64
Poleaxe construction, 79–81, 83–87
Poleaxe, use and efficiency as a weapon, 41, 43, Chapter 7, 81–86, 131–134
Poitiers, battle of, 9, 72, 76
Population; bearing on battle numbers, 169
Prickers (battle police), 154
Propaganda, as a barrier to understanding medieval battles, 33, 35

Quarterstaff, 81–82

Ransoming, 94–95, 159
Record storing, difficulties, 33–34
Re-enactors; limitations of in understanding combat, 90, 92–97
Re-enactors; perceptions influencing understanding of combat, 117, 120, 124, 127
Richard III, King, 22, 26, 107
Roman fighting techniques, 13–15, 99, 116–117
Rout, especially analysis of, 23, 77–78, 147, 149–158, 190

Saxton, village, 140, 163, 165, 168
Siege engines, 51
Soldiers, source of in Wars of Roses, 42–44
Somme, battle of the, comparison to Towton, 183–185
Supply, armies, 173–175
Sword, efficiency as a weapon, 40–41

Tadcaster, 139, 152
Tewkesbury, battle of, 114, 115, 159

Towton, battle of, 23, 24, 97, 114, 118, Chapter 9, 175–177, 182
graves, 86, 95, 162–168
soil depth, 107
comparison with other one-day battles, 183–185

Vegetius, and *The Epitome of Military Science*, 7, 8, 92, 111, 115, 118, 125–126
Verneul, battle of, 131
Violence, as part of society, 7

Wars of the Roses, specifics, 5–6, 9–10, 137
Waterloo, battle of, 92, 184
Watling Street, battle of, 176
Weaponry types, 39–41
Weather, implications in battle, 98–99, 144
Western Front (WWI) combat misunderstood, 29–30
Wounded, as a factor for understanding battles, 157–158

York (city), 152, 156, 171